Socialist Reasoning

Socialist Reasoning

AN INQUIRY INTO THE POLITICAL
PHILOSOPHY OF SCIENTIFIC SOCIALISM

Andrew Collier

PLUTO PRESS
London

BARNES & NOBLE BOOKS
Savage, Maryland

First published in the United Kingdom 1990 by Pluto Press
345 Archway Road, London N6 5AA

Copyright   Andrew Collier 1990

All rights reserved

British Library Cataloguing in Publication Data
Collier, Andrew, *1944*–
    Socialist reasoning.
    1. Marxism
    I. Title
    335.4

   ISBN 0–7453–0364–1

First published in the United States of America in 1990 by
Barnes & Noble Books
8705 Bollman Place
Savage, Maryland 20763

Library of Congress Cataloguing in Publication Data

Available from the publisher

ALL RIGHTS RESERVED
No part of this publication may be reproduced or transmitted, in any form
or by any means, without the written permission of the publishers.

Typesetting: Ponting–Green Publishing Services, London
Printed in Great Britain by Billing and Sons Ltd, Worcester

Contents

Acknowledgements	vii
Foreword	ix
Introduction	xiii

Part 1: Political Ideas

1 Ideals and Contradictions	3
The Two Styles of Political Thought	3
Contradictions and Ideals	10
Against Utopian Residues	15
Politics without Teleology	19
Appendices: A. Cows' Tails and Capitalists	24
B. Trotsky on Means and Ends	28
Notes	31
2 Liberties without Liberalism	33
Liberties and Liberty	34
Liberty to Do What Does Not Harm Others	37
The Minimal State	45
Positive and Negative Liberty	51
Individualisms and Collectivisms	58
Conclusion	65
Appendices: A. Equalities	67
B. Fellowship	70
C. Epitaph on Contractualism	71
Notes	72
3 Liberation and Instauration	74
The Two Goals and Their Connections	74
Powerlessness over Social Forces; Gatheredness/ Dispersedness	79
Socialism or Barbarism; the Augmentation of Dispersed Powers	89
Gatheredness and Democracy	93
Appendix: 'Existing Socialism'	104
Notes	107

Part II: Meta-Political Ideas

4 How to Talk about Values by Talking about Facts   113
Why Shouldn't we Talk About Values by Talking About
   Facts?   114
Why Should we Talk About Values by Talking About
   Facts?   120
Refutation of Emotivism; Explanatory Critiques in Ethics   122
Critique of Moral Absolutism   127
The Relation of Critically Rational, Historical Naturalism
   to Humean and Utilitarian Ethics   132
Notes   137

5 What is Political?   139
The 'Keep Politics out of X' Syndrome   139
The 'X is Political' Syndrome   141
Politics and Other Practices   146
Notes   154

6 Political Sublimation   156
The Concept of Sublimation in Political Contexts   156
'Slave Rebellion in Morals'; Hyndman's Hat   159
Contemporary Instances   165
Appendix: The Historical Uniqueness of the Proletariat   169
Notes   171

Conclusion   174
Bibliography   177
Index   180

Acknowledgements

I am especially grateful to Heather Collier for her support and forbearance while I was writing this book, since most of the work was done during our son's first year.

My debts to published work are acknowledged in the text, but I would like to say that the conception of social science and social being underlying my arguments owes far more to the work of Roy Bhaskar than appears from my brief references to him.

The ideas in this book owe more to conversations and informal correspondence than is usual. Of the numerous friends and comrades to whom I am indebted in this way, I shall mention only those to whom specific arguments in the text are responses – whether by way of developing or replying to their ideas: Mike Westlake, Kate Soper, John Lovering, Stewart Smith, Ganga Pursani, Graham Howard, Eluned Price, Maureen Ramsay, Norman Geras, Annie Williams, Ted Benton, Annie Pritchard. I would also like to thank John O'Neill and Alison Assiter for their comments on the book at manuscript stage.

I am grateful to Methuen London for permission to quote Brecht's poem 'The Abstemious Chancellor' (translated by John Willett).

Foreword

It is well known that Marx's *Capital* (no mean contribution to the argument for socialism) contains scarcely three pages about socialism, and over seven hundred about capitalism. Today, this is often seen as a monumental omission. I believe that it is no accident: it expresses Marx's view about the right way to make a case for socialism. Since he and his audience were, as we are, parts and products of capitalist society, he made his case from the essential defects of capitalist society, visible as such from within that society.

That is not the only sort of case that could be made for socialism. Many claim that socialism is about commitment to certain values – equality, co-operation, sympathy for the underdog. Such values might be seen as eternal, and the case for socialism therefore independent of time and place; or, from a different philosophical conception of ethics, they might be seen as subjective 'value-judgements', which can be preached but not argued for. Marx would see them as deriving their content and force at any time and place from the circumstances, traditions and problems of that time and place. (I shall defend this conception of moral and political reasoning in Chapter 4.) If he is right, then a book such as *Capital* is precisely the right way to argue for socialism.

In part, the term 'scientific socialism' refers to this sort of argument for socialism: the scientific analysis of capitalism *is* the case for socialism. To someone who asks (as people who have seen drafts for this book have asked) how scientific socialism is relevant in the late twentieth century, I would say that the real question is: how is *socialism* relevant in the late twentieth century. If values are eternal, or if they are subjective, the question of relevance *at a given time and place* does not arise. If values are expressions of definite historical needs, then the way to show that socialism is relevant to the late twentieth century is by a scientific analysis of late twentieth-century society, that is by a scientific socialist argument. In Chapter 3 I try to show that concepts implicit in various scientific socialist texts can be used to make such a case for socialism as *increasingly* relevant and indeed urgent in the modern world.

I said that scientific socialism is *partly* a matter of the kind of case which is to be made for socialism. It also includes social scientific hypotheses which can guide socialist politics by indicating which apparent 'roads to socialism' really are such, and which are blind alleys.

The former part of scientific socialist theory can be described as a theory of the constraints on the reproduction of capitalist societies (alias 'contradictions of capitalism') and the latter a theory of the constraints on the transformation of capitalist society. Both kinds of constraint must be shown to exist by empirical and theoretical social scientific work. The theory of these two kinds of constraint (e.g. to take examples from Marx himself, the inability of capitalism to reproduce itself without periodic crises; the inability of the working class to emancipate itself without first taking political power) is the *science* in scientific socialism. In this book, as befits a mere philosopher, I am mostly talking about this theory rather than making contributions to it, though I venture a few original hypotheses in Chapters 3 and 6.

A word about my view of philosophy and its relation to science and to politics may make it clearer what my project is.

I do not believe that philosophy produces any radically new knowledge in the way that science does. Rather, it makes explicit knowledge that was already implicit ('in a practical state', as Althusser puts it) in some other practice. That other practice may itself have cognitive aims (for example science) or non-cognitive ones (for example politics). But in either case, it is the knowledge implicit in the practice itself that philosophy lights up; it does not reflect on the results of a science – the truths that the science discovers – but on the practice of the science. It asks, for instance, how experiment is possible and why it is necessary. (As paradigms of this practice of philosophy in the present century, I would mention (1) Division One of Heidegger's *Being and Time*, as explicating the knowledge implicit in our everyday work-world; (2) Roy Bhaskar's *A Realist Theory of Science*, as explicating that implicit in the practice of the experimental sciences. It is a feature of the notion of philosophy that I am defending, that it makes these two instances *compatible*.)

One effect of lighting up a practice philosophically may be to show how something is done in that practice, which had been alleged to be impossible. For example, many claim that it is impossible to argue validly from factual premisses to practical conclusions; scientific socialism does so argue, and I try to show (in Chapter 4) how this works. But philosophy is not necessarily uncritical of the practices it lights up: it may expose ambiguities or contradictions implicit in the practice, and thereby show the need to transform the practice in some way, or perhaps abandon it.

Political philosophy aims to light up political practice. Scientific socialist politics is a practice which has already been transformed by the application of a theory – not a philosophical theory, but one purporting to give radically new knowledge of society. But this does not mean that this practice is without a residue of merely implicit knowledge. On the contrary, the way in which theory and practice are fused in scientific socialism is itself obscure, and has been the site of many misunderstandings.

I have referred here to political philosophy as lighting up political *practice*, elsewhere as lighting up political *argument*. The (usually misleading) 'action/words' contrast is so often appealed to in politics that perhaps I need to explain this.

The vast majority of political actions consist of argument (and other verbal practices): persuading someone to join a union or a political group, or to come out on strike, or vote this way or that. This applies to many of the activities that are often mistakenly contrasted with 'mere words' – not only such things as selling papers and giving out leaflets, but also the vast majority of demonstrations, acts of civil disobedience, token strikes and 'days of action', antics with the House of Commons mace, etc., which are really not so much 'direct action' as indirect ways of saying something.

Those few political actions open to ordinary people at ordinary times which are not verbal or symbolic (voting, striking, economic boycotts), along with the much rarer physical struggles for power, and the decisions of political leaders and representatives, are nevertheless largely the results of political reasoning, and their results in turn give food for thought to later political activists. Only fascist irrationalism sees unreasoned and unquestioning action as an end in itself.

To illuminate political argument is to show what sort of reasons for a political action or institution are good ones. This is how Hobbes or Rousseau, J.S. Mill or T.H. Green practised political philosophy. But the classics of scientific socialism do not include an explicit political philosophy in this sense; nevertheless, they do give reasons for socialism, and for specific 'roads to socialism'. I hope to make the nature of their arguments explicit, and to show their cogency; also on occasion to remove an ambiguity or contradiction; and finally, to apply the arguments to problems which loom larger now than they did when the classics of scientific socialism were written.

Despite the immense literature both of socialist advocacy and of 'Marxology', I know of very little that does political philosophy in this way. Most often, the scientific socialist tradition is taken to have *evaded* certain questions which I think it has *answered without making the answers explicit*. The implicit answers are missed because the kind of reasoning that they involve does not make any appeal to suprahistorical ideals, such as are the stock in trade of most political thinking. That is their great strength, as I hope to show.

One word about the unfashionable term 'scientific socialism': I think I make it clear in the text why I regard this as the most accurate designation for the tradition to which it refers. But perhaps I should say right away that it differs from the term 'Marxism' in the important respect that it makes no allusion to Marx, who founded it. This is important in the first place because Marx held many opinions which are not part of scientific socialism. Like any scientific discipline, it has a strictly limited scope, and does not tie its practitioners to its founder's views. For instance, it should not sound paradoxical that a Christian may be a scientific socialist, though the term 'Christian Marxist' raises eyebrows. Furthermore, the rejection of any particular doctrine of Marx's (such as my own rejection of the idea of the withering away of the superstructures) provokes unprofitable discussion about whether the theory in question is Marxist or not. And finally, there are those who use the word 'Marxism' for something that has nothing to do with any scientific discipline – from a particular brand of *Realpolitik* to a total world-view.

Introduction

By the term 'scientific socialism' I refer to that tradition of political thought that was inaugurated by Marx and Engels in 1845, when they broke with the Young Hegelians, and with their own Hegelian past; which includes their mature work, and that of the Marxists of the Second International – including, very importantly, those who broke with it at the time of the First World War, Lenin, Luxemburg, Trotsky, Bukharin. The writings of these groups form a sort of canon of 'classical Marxism'. Since scientific socialism, like any scientific project, is necessarily 'revisionist', it has continued to develop since that time, but its developments have been notoriously divergent from one another. Some tendencies, while claiming to originate in the classical Marxist tradition, do not claim and should not be given the title 'scientific socialism'. It should be restricted to those tendencies which continue to uphold the relevance of the scientific project of understanding society to the socialist project of transforming it. But this is compatible both with radical modifications of the scientific findings, and with dissent from the views of the classical Marxists on issues outside the scientific project – for example philosophical, cultural, psychological, moral, religious and aesthetic issues.

At the time of Marx's break with his Hegelian past, he jotted down his eleven theses on Feuerbach, of which the eleventh is perhaps his best-known remark about philosophy: 'The philosophers have only *interpreted* the world in different ways, the point is to *change* it.' If we set this gnomic jotting in its context in the development of Marx's thought, some obvious readings of it are ruled out. It can hardly mark any rejection of theory for a life of action: Marx was already a political activist, and remained a theoretician as well till his dying day. Neither does it mark the beginning of a new, action-guiding philosophy in place of an old, explanatory one; the opposite is nearer the case. Marx's writings of 1844 had been far more obviously prescriptive than any theoretical works he was to write later; their weakness is in their lack of explanatory power. And it is certainly not urging that changing the world is a task for *philosophy*: that is exactly the view from which he is distancing himself in these theses – the view of the Young Hegelian and Feuerbachian circles, which he attacked with all the vitriol he could muster in his writings of 1845–7. Rather, he is saying: since the point is to change the world, it is not to philosophy that we must turn.

This does not only mean that it is not philosophers (or indeed any kind of theoreticians) but workers, who will change the world. It also means that the sort of theory that the workers' movement needs is not a philosophical one. The truth is, that at this period of his life Marx wrote with some animus against philosophy, and thereafter never wrote a word of philosophy except (very briefly) in methodological prefaces to his economic works. The turn marked by the theses on Feuerbach was a turn away from philosophy, towards the objective investigation of society, and more particularly of the 'economic laws of motion' of capitalist society. Thesis Eleven expresses the judgement that the theory required by the workers' movement in order to change the world was not philosophy, but an empirical science of society. Marx clearly believed that this objective knowledge could deliver, not only the 'social technology' necessary for socialist politics, but, in its uncovering of society's inherent contradictions, the *rational motivation* for such politics.

This view, encapsulated in the expression 'scientific socialism', immediately provokes a host of objections. Is objective knowledge of society possible? If so, is it really liberatory, or oppressive? How can objective knowledge motivate action? What is a contradiction? Marx does not give any explicit answers to these questions. He answers them implicitly, by *showing*, in his economic and historical writing, how knowledge of society can uncover contradictions, and motivate, as well as assist, the project of social liberation. The task of philosophy with respect to scientific socialism is to make these answers explicit. Philosophy cannot itself provide the knowledge that makes the case and guides the way for socialism, and in this sense, Marx's rejection of it is correct. But it can render some service to the knowledge that does, if it explicates the answers to these questions.

This task falls to two philosophical disciplines: the philosophy of social science, and political philosophy. The former is concerned with the status of scientific socialist theory as objective knowledge of society. It occupies itself with questions like: What sort of thing must society be, if it is to be investigated scientifically? How do the differences between natural and social realities affect the methods of inquiry appropriate to each? Given that we are part of society, can we ever be objective about it? What counts as a good social explanation? A great deal of good work has been done on these topics, in which philosophers in the scientific socialist tradition find themselves most at home. My own views on them can be found in my book *Scientific Realism and Socialist Thought*.

Political philosophy is concerned with the reasons for political actions – for defending, reforming, transforming or destroying particular social institutions. Traditional political philosophy has tried to clarify notions like 'liberty', 'justice', 'equality', 'sovereignty', 'legitimacy', 'the public interest', 'rights', 'progress', 'the obligation to obey the law' and so on. Such philosophy quite naturally slides into two ways of talking which scientific socialism views as mistaken. It takes these concepts out of the historical contexts in which they are used, and tries to give them general meanings, such that particular institutions in any society whatsoever can be assessed in terms of them; and it rejects or neglects the possibility that questions about these *values* can only be resolved by talking about certain *facts*. Liberal (as opposed to conservative) political philosophy is particularly prone to these mistakes, though there is a Platonistic kind of conservatism of which they are also characteristic. That they *are* mistakes, of course, I have yet to prove.

For the most part, scientific socialists do not feel at home in this area of philosophy. Either they identify the above mistakes, the 'abstractness' of political philosophising, and feel that no more need be said, or they start philosophising in the same way themselves. Thus, the classical Marxists often wrote as if any use of these political value-words was a sign of bad faith, yet no socialist manages to avoid using some of them in every political struggle. If we must use them, and are to avoid using them in a utopian and unhistorical way, we must show what their use is on the basis of scientific socialism. The failure to do so has led to large undigested chunks of classical political philosophy being incorporated into much recent socialist writing, often with groans of vicarious penitence for the scorn with which earlier socialists had treated it.

My starting point in this book is that the turning away from philosophy towards the objective investigation of society was correct, and that it really is such objective knowledge, and not philosophy, which provides the case for socialism. The task of political philosophy is to make it explicit how this is possible. In attempting to do so, I am engaging in three controversies: for socialism against its opponents (mainly liberals); for a scientific style of political thinking against a utopian one (which still survives among socialists); for ethical naturalism, that is arguing from facts to practical tasks, against those who believe the gap between facts and values to be unbridgeable.

In the first chapter I shall defend the style of political reasoning characteristic of scientific socialism; in the second, I shall apply the method defended, in analysing perhaps the most charged concept in political philosophy, liberty; in the third, I shall consider two aspects of the enlargement of human liberties that have been central to the scientific socialist understanding of human possibilities in history: *liberation*, that is the overthrow of various forms of tyranny of one group of people over another; and what Bacon termed *instauration*, that is, the improvement of the human lot by means of the augmentation of human powers over nature – an idea supplemented in scientific socialism by the aim of common control over social processes, which occur 'behind people's backs' in hitherto existing societies.

The remaining three chapters of the book are, each in its different way, second order reflections about political arguments and ideas. In the first, I defend the possibility of doing what, in the first half of the book, I have been doing: talking about values by talking about facts. It may not be obvious that that is what I am doing in the first three chapters; someone may say I have just been talking about words – or, more euphemistically, that I have been doing conceptual analysis. But my aim, as a philosophical realist, is to make the distinctions and connections between words map real distinctions and connections more accurately.

So much for the nature of political reasoning as *reasoning*. I then consider its nature as political. For the question: What is political and what is not? – is itself both philosophically and politically contentious. Finally, I look at some ways in which properly political motives get deflected into non-political aims, in a manner paralleling 'sublimation', in the Freudian sense.

Some points which I make require amplification which is either too technical, or too unphilosophical, or too *ad hominem* in nature to be included in the argument of the chapter concerned; these I discuss in appendices to the chapters.

Part I
Political Ideas

1
Ideals and Contradictions

The Two Styles of Political Thought

The term 'scientific socialism' is very rarely used today. Yet of all the terms by which the classical Marxists referred to their theory, it seems to me to express the case most exactly. Marx's achievement was to equip the working-class movement with a scientific understanding of the society of which it is part, and against which it fights; along with which goes an understanding of the conditions of the overthrow of that kind of society.

One reason for the unfashionability of this term, I suspect, is the elitist assumption that the people are incapable of grasping scientific concepts; it is assumed that socialism can only be scientific if it is dominated by a scientific elite – hence the elitism of the assumption is projected on to advocates of scientific socialism. This projection goes back to Bakunin's *Statism and Anarchy*. In Marx's marginal notes to that text, he comments that the term 'scientific socialism' 'was only used in opposition to utopian socialism, which wants to attach the people to new delusions, instead of limiting its science to the knowledge of the social movement made by the people itself.'[1] The utopian, it seems, is not necessarily anti-science, but may actually *fail to limit* the political application of science. What does Marx mean by this?

Most of the utopians of Marx's era were no less imbued with a scientific world outlook than Marx. The issue between Marx and the 'scientific utopians' such as Saint-Simon and Bellamy is over the question: what sort of political aim are we to pursue scientifically? For the utopians, the answer is: the construction and administration of the best sort of society for human beings. For Marx it is: securing a successful outcome of the workers' struggle against the constraints of capitalism.

It is possible to see these two styles of socialist politics as instances of two traditions of political thinking, both with long histories. One attempts, ostensibly without reference to the contingencies of existing society, to depict an ideal state; the other takes the ends of some existing group or institution for granted, and asks how they can best be furthered. More's *Utopia* and Machiavelli's *The Prince* can serve as examples. The latter is of course 'scientific' in a 'technological' rather than a 'pure' sense – a scientific practice rather than a science. It tells how the political world works, as a condition of telling how to produce certain effects, the effects being the flourishing of an existing political institution. Hence it seems, on the face of it, an unpromising style for anyone who is radically discontented with the existing order. The utopian style, lending itself as it does to flights of fancy, can be used as a medium for the advocacy of socialism or any other unrealised historical vision, but in no way facilitates the production of those or any other desired effects in the real world. Hence the two approaches can coexist: More played an eminent role in the politics of his day – and not a 'utopian' one; this was not hypocrisy, for there was no way in which his ideals and his statesmanship could have engaged with each other.

Along with utopianism in the strict sense, which draws up imaginative blueprints for ideal society, there is the more abstract sort of political ideal: concepts such as liberty, justice, human rights and so on are set forth as principles on which society could be reconstructed; particular instances of these ideals are presented as justified in the name of the ideal, and political thought comes to be the defining of these ideas and their mutual relations.

In advocating a political change, one might say 'here are some ideals, let us find a way of realising them', or one might say 'here is an evil, let us find a way of eliminating it.' The former, which includes both the utopian and the abstract idealist, has more often been the practice of radicals, the latter of conservatives. Conservatives have often recognised particular abuses as evils to be eliminated; radicals are apt to reply: if this is an evil, that is because it violates some ideal – and in that case, should we not reconstruct society as a whole in accordance with that ideal, rather than just reform one isolated abuse? This polemical scenario should be familiar from the controversy between Burke on the one hand, Paine and Godwin on the other. It is a replay – with the authority of reason replacing the authority of scripture – of the controversy among the Protestant reformers as to whether institutions should be retained unless they were contrary to scripture (Luther and the Anglicans) or abolished unless enjoined by scripture (Calvin and the Puritans).

In both these controversies, the 'judgement of history' is undoubtedly on the side of the radicals: they were the ones who paved the way for democracy, civil liberty, universal education, and the first stirrings of the emancipation of women. Philosophically speaking, however, the idealism of the radicals is based on a fundamental mistake – and this mistake is not without its political effects too. The conservative would be quite justified in replying in this vein: 'Principles and ideals don't fall from the sky: they are the products of some aspects of the society in which they arise. We need to know more about existing society before we know whether there are any ways to realise them, and indeed whether anyone really wants to realise them. For ideals often arise from limited aspects of a society, and cause harm if generalised. Public ownership and free access is an excellent way to run a road, but a lousy way to run a bathroom. Individual free choice is the best basis for marriage but the worst for environmental planning. Everyone taking their turn is a good way of arranging annual holidays, but a bit dodgy in surgical operations. Utopias tend to be onesided affairs, one person's dream but another's nightmare; and abstract ideals like justice and liberty are only meaningful when put in context – but then, the context will tell you what is needed, without the ideal.'

This sort of response could equally well be made from the standpoint of the tradition of English conservatism that runs from Burke to Oakeshott, or by a scientific socialist. Both base their programmes on the study of existing society, not of human nature considered apart from history. So far as I know, Marx and Engels are the first 'radicals' to do so. Their refusal to speculate about the future, which has sometimes attracted the charge of evasiveness, and their repeated contemptuous remarks about ideal-words such as 'justice', 'equality' etc., which have sometimes attracted the charge of cynicism, both follow from this principle. They present the principle, not just as more hard-headed than idealist politics, in that it attacks only problems the solution of which has already appeared on the horizon as a manifest possibility, along with the social forces capable of realising that possibility; they present it also as free from the elitist arrogance of utopian thinking, which legislates for the oppressed people instead of studying the direction and conditions of success of their movement. Thus Engels claims that

> modern large-scale industry has called into being on the one hand a proletariat, a class which for the first time in history can demand the

abolition, not of this or that particular class organisation, or of this or that particular class privilege, but of classes themselves

while on the other hand the bourgeoisie 'has become incapable of any longer controlling the productive forces, which have grown beyond its power; a class under whose leadership society is racing to ruin like a locomotive whose jammed safety-valve the driver is too weak to open'.[2] He concludes:

> On this tangible, material fact, which is impressing itself in a more or less clear form, but with insuperable necessity, on the minds of the exploited proletarians – on this fact, and not on the conceptions of justice and injustice held by any armchair philosopher, is modern socialism's confidence in victory founded.[3]

This combination of scientific hard-headedness and respect for the nature of human emancipation as *self*-emancipation is also behind the refusal to legislate for future generations – whose needs and desires we have no means of predicting. As Engels says concerning the sexual morality of communist society:

> Thus, what we can conjecture at present about the regulation of sex relationships after the impending effacement of capitalist production is, in the main, of a negative character, limited mostly to what will vanish. But what will be added? That will be settled after a new generation has grown up. ('Origin of the Family, Private Property and the State', *Selected Works in One Volume*, p. 517)

The same would apply to every other area of social life. The transition to socialism would be a 'Darwinian' rather than a teleological evolution in the sense that every step would be justified by the needs of its time, not indeed irresponsibly towards future generations, but on the basis of already emerged human needs, not some hypothetical New Humanity of the future.

Prior to Marx, the nearest thing to a serviceable theory for radical democracy was that of Rousseau, which was a specific combination of a utopian part and a pragmatic-scientific part. The utopian part is a theory of legitimacy: that no authority or dominion is legitimate unless it is according to law, and all those subject to it have an equal part in the making of the law. This theory, 'the sovereignty of the people', is extremely sketchy compared with most models of utopia. It is sketchy for the right reason too – and the same sort of reason as is behind the sketchiness of Marx's characterisations of socialist society: it leaves the sovereign people to decide *what* laws to pass at any place and time, instead of laying down *a priori* principles. The crucial *democratic* objection to utopian politics therefore does not tell against Rousseau; however, there are other respects in which this theory is objectionably utopian, as we shall see.

The 'scientific' part of Rousseau's theory concerns the conditions conducive to the survival of popular sovereignty in various historical and geographical circumstances. Property must be evenly enough distributed to ensure that no one is economically dependent on anyone else, otherwise the rich will buy out the poor politically too; everybody must be able to get together and argue in the public square – hence the state must be no bigger than one city, and people must have enough leisure for public life. But this last condition has only been fulfilled with the aid of slaves, who are themselves excluded from the sovereign people, and so may wisely and justly take their freedom by force should the opportunity arise. If high technology is offered as an alternative to slaves, Rousseau could reply: it is incompatible with small states and with equal property. Hence, concentrated production must be avoided, even at the cost of preventing the improvement of the human lot by science.

What is missing from Rousseau is any conception of the possibility of equality through common ownership at an advanced level of technology. In the absence of such a conception, popular sovereignty remains an unrealisable utopia; yet Rousseau remains free from the utopian illusion that a society without oppression is always possible granted enough goodwill. Indeed, those of us who live in northern lands might as well give up from the start, since: 'Your severer climates add to your needs, for half the year your public squares are uninhabitable' and so on. I see his point. Having witnessed the degree of popular participation even in a parliamentary election in Greece, I doubt whether Britain can ever have the same potential for democracy as Greece.

Rousseau's recognition of the material constraints on the possibility of non-oppressive political relationships renders that possibility a mere utopia within his thought, while it rescues his thought as a whole from utopian illusion at the cost of a profound historical pessimism, notwithstanding his anthropological optimism. Marx of course fully shared Rousseau's recognition that liberation was only possible in certain conditions, though his socialist answer to the leisure/equality dilemma, and his consequent positive evaluation of technology, frees him for optimism about the future. But I want to focus on the style of Marx's political thought, which I think was scientific in the same sense as was Machiavelli's, Spinoza's or that of book three of Rousseau's *The Social Contract* (independently of whether Marx's particular theoretical achievements warrant the title 'science'). That is to say, his premiss is the existence of a historical agency with definite aims and interests: except that it is neither an actual state nor a hypothetical sovereign people, but a movement and a practice of class struggle: working-class politics. As such, it comes with motives and ends already operating, so the focus of the theory will not be the deduction of ideals, but the analysis of the structure of existing society: in particular, it will seek to discover the structural constraints on the reproduction and on the transformation of that society.

Consider Marx's statement:

> Mankind thus inevitably sets itself only such tasks as it is able to solve, since closer examination will always show that the problem itself arises only when the material conditions for its solution are already present or at least in the course of formation.[4]

When I first read this it astounded me. I had absorbed enough of Marx's thought to recognise that socialism had only become a real possibility since the industrial revolution. But people had been calling for justice, freedom, peace and the end of oppression for millennia – and these could only be realised under socialism!

Nevertheless, Marx was right. In so far as people did sometimes envisage a classless society based on common ownership in earlier times, they were either looking back to primitive equality in poverty and ignorance, or they expected supernatural aid to eliminate scarcity. These were dreams, not policies. And when practical political activists talked about 'justice', 'freedom' etc., they did not mean what a socialist might mean by them. They referred to foreseeable next steps in the direction of extending more powers to more people.

For the most part, the people's sufferings become experienced as of social origin and politically intolerable when they really become so: prior to that, they are accepted as part of the order of nature, not because people are duped into so regarding them, but because they really are part of the order of nature until civilisation has reached a stage at which the power to abolish them exists. That they were part of the order of nature did not remove their character as suffering, but it kept them out of the political arena. I am not simply referring to things like diseases that are now curable but once were not; social inequality and political domination were also part of the order of nature in every society between hunter-gatherer cultures and capitalism. As a result of this, a scientific socialist is bound to read 'people's history' with some ambivalence: our hearts may go out to Münzer and Winstanley, but no programme was a real option that was to the left of, say, Zwingli, or Barebone's Parliament. As Engels remarks, it is a great misfortune to come to power before one's time;[5] at best, one serves the needs of that time at the cost of becoming a 'time server'; at worst – the recent histories of Kampuchea and of Afghanistan illustrate the tragic consequences of trying to implement a policy whose time has not yet come.

Scientific socialism, then, shares with conservatism an approach which is oriented towards the study of existing social realities rather than the projection of ideal ones: it starts from where it is. The term 'scientific' means both less and more than this. Less in that claims that have been made for scientific politics on an anthropological rather than a historical basis are eschewed by scientific socialism, which therefore cannot simply be explained as the addition of science (any science) to socialism, but is a quite specific combination, the scientific element of which consists in the analysis of specific historical conjunctures. More, in that the claim to scientificity is not just a claim to a scientific kind of approach, but to success in applying that approach (for obviously, the scientific *form* of the inquiry is only helpful if it leads to the discovery of truths which would not have been known without it). For the moment, I am considering the approach as such, shared as it is by a number of logically incompatible and politically opposed theories. For want of a better word, I shall call this approach 'realist'. It has sometimes been called 'historicist', but since the Popperian and the Althusserian senses of that word are both better known, and unrelated to this one, I shall avoid it; the term 'methodological conservatism' is closer to the mark, but the political connotations of 'conservatism' make it misleading as a description of any socialist theory. So I stick with 'realism' using it in a sense that is not unrelated to either the philosophical sense or the colloquial one, though it is not identical with either.

The realist style of political thinking has various advantages: that it can sometimes find definite, scientific answers to the questions it asks; that, since it pre-supposes an existing political practice, it can hope for a union of theory and practice such as the politics of ideals has never yet achieved; that its link with people's contemporary strivings reduces the danger of trying to fit the people to the plan rather than the plan to the people; that it does not depend on contentious claims about human nature. But it might look unpromising to someone desiring radical change. What are the specific features of Marx's version of it, for instance, that distance it so far from that of Edmund Burke?

Of course, the existing institutions from which conservative realists[6] take their aims are the powers that be, whereas Marx's standpoint is that of the working-class movement. But in the first place, Marx's choice of that movement needs to be explained, since he started as a liberal bourgeois republican. And secondly, other combinations of working-class politics with a realist political style are possible; an important current in the British Labour Right for example. What distinguishes Marx is the content of his theory, the specific set of conclusions he drew about the nature of existing society: conclusions about the constraints that exist on the reproduction of capitalist society (contradictions), which preclude a conservative politics; and conclusions about constraints on the transformation of that society, which preclude the gradualist politics of 'skinning a live tiger claw by claw'.

Contradictions and Ideals

We have a familiar paradigm for understanding how a theory about the constraints on the possibilities of the *transformation* of a society can influence the practice of a radical political movement: it may show what *means* may be effective and what ineffective in the achievement of an already-projected end. The notion of constraint on the reproduction of a society is not so familiar. It belongs to dialectical thought: the theory of *contradictions* inherent in a structure which make its static self-maintenance impossible, and its necessary development dangerous, or even self-destructive.

The use of the notion of a dialectical contradiction is essential to the thought of all scientific socialists since Marx and Engels, though neither of these two worked it out explicitly in an adequate way. Looking up the references to 'dialectic' and 'contradiction' in *Capital* and in Engels' philosophical writings, one can establish that, for them:

(a) contradictions exist in the real object of thought, not within thought itself; hence they are unconnected with 'contradictions' in the logical sense. Thus, Marx contrasts 'absurd contradictions' which he attributes to J.S. Mill with 'the Hegelian contradiction, the source of all dialectic' with which Mill is at sea (*Capital*, vol. I, p. 596). Engels claims that the conflict between productive forces and modes of production 'exists, in fact, objectively, outside us, independently of the will and actions even of the men that have brought it on' (*Anti-Dühring*, p. 317).

(b) Contradictions are the motors of change in the systems they govern. Thus Marx, and following him Engels, adapts from the Protestant mystic Jakob Böhme a pun on the German word '*Qual*', 'torment': the activating tension of an object which is also its '*qualitas*', that which makes it what it is. (See *Selected Works in One Volume*, p. 382.)

(c) 'Contradiction' is a concept belonging to the *pathology* of systems; hence, where a system in question is a human institution, to identify a contradiction in a system is very often to criticise it. In many instances, this is the case of a once-rational institution which has become irrational at the present stage of development.

In *Capital*, 'contradiction' is sometimes used to refer to an aspect of capitalism that generates its possibility of breakdown in equilibrium (for example vol. I, Chapter 5), sometimes to conflicting tendencies generated by the same mechanism (the best known being the drive to increase surplus value and the falling rate of profit – but the conflict between greater specialisation and greater mobility of labour is also mentioned, p. 487); but dialectic is as often linked to the related concept of *inversion*: dominance of means over ends, product over producers, things over people.

The idea can be summarised: (certain) social structures generate tendencies which damage the structure and prevent it working. Engels' account in *Anti-Dühring* fits this description too: there, the combination of individual appropriation of the product with socialised production is said to be a contradiction, generating as it does both the class struggle and the proneness of capitalism to periodic crisis.

It should be borne in mind here what any social structure necessarily is: a set of relations between people whereby their interaction with their material environment is organised. The dynamic tendency of any given social structure may be quite other than towards the rational use of nature for satisfying human needs; yet it must approximate to that achievement if it is to maintain its physical existence. Capitalism is motored by the drive for the self-expansion of capital; but that does not mean that the conflict between the requirement of capital-expansion and the requirement to satisfy human needs is a conflict between capitalism and some value external to it, an 'external contradiction'. If there were no natural constraints on what humans need, a social structure might make itself immortal by ensuring that people needed only what it provided. But *capitalist* society can only exist among a species which *does* have such constraints. Wage-labour depends on them. And like any human society, capitalism can only survive if, to a considerable extent, it does meet human needs; yet at the same time, its driving force – the self-expansion of capital – is indifferent to human needs. The needs which capitalism overrides are rooted in human nature and hence unsusceptible to elimination; but they are not needs in the abstract, the lowest common denominator of the needs of all people in all societies; they are the needs of the people of specific capitalist societies. As Marx puts it:

> the object (of need – A.C.) is not an object in general, but a specific object which must be consumed in a specific manner, to be mediated in turn by production itself. Hunger is hunger, but the hunger gratified by cooked meat eaten with a knife and fork is a different hunger from that which bolts down raw meat with the aid of hand, tooth and nail. (*Grundrisse*, p. 92)

'Hunger is hunger' (and hunger here can stand in for all human needs) – that is human needs are not infinitely adaptable, and resist any attempt to 'culture them out'. But capitalism is to be condemned, not in the name of human need in general, but of the 'hunger that is gratified by cooked meat eaten with a knife and fork', that is civilised hunger, though that civilisation be capitalist.

This point about taking concrete (and therefore historically conditioned) needs as the datum has political effects. First in that it rules out the sort of ultra-radicalism which, instead of criticising capitalism for its failure to supply people's needs, criticises the needs themselves as the product of capitalism. They are, of course; what else could they be? The socialist movement is also the product of capitalism. The person who, in a capitalist society, holds the needs of humanity under capitalism in contempt, is despising the only human needs that exist, and deserves the enmity of the human race.

Secondly, it forestalls any attempt to set 'absolute poverty' against 'relative poverty' in order to play down the latter. Capitalism thwarts human needs when it deprives the children of the unemployed of the luxuries their school mates expect them to have – and not only when it condemns them to malnutritional diseases.

If scientific socialism includes a political philosophy – in the sense that Rousseau or Mill had a political philosophy – it is all bound up in the concept of contradiction. Where Rousseau might say 'this institution is objectionable since it does not express the will of the people' and Mill might say 'this institution is objectionable because it intrudes on the sphere of private freedom', the scientific socialist will say 'this institution is objectionable since it is contradictory'. On the surface, this may appear more remote from everyday concerns. But in reality it is not, since what is contradictory is always an absolutely concrete institution affecting people's lives, while 'the people's will', 'freedom' etc., are in themselves rather vague terms, which get their concreteness of content precisely from the presence of contradictions to which they (perhaps tacitly) allude. Very often, people talk about contradictions *by* talking about ideals. They demand justice, liberty etc., but only when one understands what contradiction is generating their demands can one know their content. The term 'liberty' has been used, for instance, to mean national independence, political pluralism, private ownership, common ownership, toleration of minority opinions, and many other things. It always (except when simply *misused*) refers to some people having the power to do unimpeded what they might otherwise be impeded in doing. But in order to find out who was impeded in doing what by whom, one has to look at the concrete context in which the cry of 'liberty' was raised: what contradiction was this movement trying to resolve? Likewise, 'justice' (in the distributive sense) generally refers to treating people alike when there is no relevant difference. But differences come to be perceived as relevant or irrelevant for concrete historical reasons. When an institution becomes widely criticised as unjust, we must ask in what way it has become contradictory.

My point is not that we should stop talking about justice, liberty etc. I spend a lot of this book talking about them. I am claiming that when, as part of a real political movement, demands are made in the name of freedom or justice, this is a way of talking about facts (the existence of social contradictions) by talking about values; that in order to understand what is going on, we need to translate back into the language of facts, and ask what contradiction is evoking the ideal as a protest against it; that in general it is better to talk about values by talking about facts; and that the value terms which are used as political ideals ('justice', 'liberty' and so on) are too general and abstract to guide action unless some content is supplied by reference to the contradictions of the time. Any attempt to derive a political programme from these ideals as such would lead to absurdities. One could not make out a coherent programme of treating everyone the same in all respects in the name of 'justice', since, for example, to reward everyone's work equally is not to provide for everyone's needs equally; one could not abolish all restraints in the name of freedom, since freedom for the strong is restraint for the weak (and vice versa). Hence we have to choose between freedoms, and to choose between equalities. But this is never an arbitrary choice; it is always historically placed, and decided on the basis of 'where the shoe pinches'. The idea that the notion of a dialectical contradiction is central to political thought might be found alarming, in that it seems to rest a lot of practical political issues on an obscure and contentious metaphysical notion. There are good reasons to believe that, while the socialist movement needs theory very much, it does not need very much theory; that once a few essential points about the constraints on the reproduction and transformation of societies are established, what is most useful is empirical knowledge of concrete conjunctures; beyond that it is better to travel light, so far as theory is concerned.

In fact, though dialectics – 'the study of contradictions in the very essence of objects' (Lenin) – can have all sorts of interesting philosophical ramifications, the core of the theory required by scientific socialism is easily stated, and in no way mysterious.

The central points are: A. that a contradiction is something wrong with a society, which can be recognised as such within that society, and not just from some external or 'absolute' standpoint, and B. that some contradictions cannot be resolved within that form of society, and hence constitute a motive for transforming it into a different kind of society. These two points are all that is required for this concept to serve its political function.

The typical instances of contradictions in capitalism are (i) irrational use of resources, whether epidemic (as in periodic crises) or endemic (as in planned waste, ecologically shortsighted projects, etc.); and (ii) struggle between classes or groups that are essential parts of the system. Both kinds of case can be seen as centrifugal tendencies in the system: tendencies for the parts of a system to follow a dynamic other than that required of them for the good working of the system, where these tendencies are generated by the system itself. It is a feature of such contradictions that they can be resolved with the resources available to the system, yet cannot be resolved within the system.

(Strictly speaking, the term 'contradiction' should be used to refer to the feature of the system that causes the irrational process or the conflict, rather than the process itself, but the use of the term 'contradiction' for the effects as well as the causes is generally harmless.)

In claiming that the notion of contradiction is the foundation of a political philosophy which can be radical without being utopian, I am referring to contradictions as described in the last two paragraphs; it is not necessary to adopt all Marx's (slightly shifting) uses referred to earlier, let alone the generalised theory of contradictions in everything, postulated by 'diamat'.

Against Utopian Residues

There is a common belief among socialists that sparsity of description of life under socialism in Marxist literature is a serious handicap in making out a case for socialism. It is thought that given the obvious disadvantages of 'existing socialism' (real enough disadvantages – though certainly exaggerated by cold war propaganda to which western socialists often pay too much heed) a full description of the desired society is now needed.

For example, the Pluto Press *Big Red Diary* for 1981, on the theme of utopias, includes the following entry on Marx:

> *Needed*: A Vision of the Socialist Future.
> Marx wrote little about the future socialist or communist society. He seems to have taken for granted a more egalitarian version of the Saint-Simonist and Fourierist utopias of his day. We are left with some extremely vague early statements such as 'communism ... is the genuine resolution of the conflict between man and nature and man and man'. So when Marxists are asked 'what exactly are you fighting for?' they certainly cannot turn to Marx for their answers. Critics then assume that the goal is a society like that of the Soviet Union – the society of a revolution gone wrong. Where are the visions of a socialist future? (facing first week of December)

One would never guess from this that Marx and Engels had made explicit their principled rejection of utopian socialism: it is presented as if it were an oversight, as a result of what they thought they could take for granted (rather as their relative neglect of civil liberties issues might be explained). But aside from all this, the idea that socialist utopian literature might have an apologetic function seems to me quite wrong. The view most frequently encountered among non-socialists, I would suggest, is this: (i) it is taken for granted that socialism is a utopian kind of proposal; (ii) its desirability in the abstract is often conceded ('if only it were possible'); (iii) its possibility is contested, either on the grounds of human nature, or on the grounds that 'if you want to get to socialism, you'd better not start from here'; (iv) it is claimed that the *attempt* to realise this utopia can only lead to disaster (that is to bureaucratic dictatorship, or whatever).

The best response to this view is the opposite of utopian: to concentrate on the next steps, and show how certain immediately practicable socialist measures could remove manifest evils of contemporary capitalism; to describe, not a new society constructed from scratch, but existing society without certain eminently removable features. Marx and Engels have already given us a model for this kind of response, in their answers to objections in *The Communist Manifesto*. To the objector who urges that idleness will overtake us as soon as capital accumulation is abolished, they respond that if this were so, it would already have happened, since those who do the work are not those who accumulate the capital.[7] It is amazing how many people still say things like 'under socialism you'll have to have a police state, otherwise how will you get anyone to do any work? – and are astounded when I reply 'If they don't work, they won't get paid.'

What is really wrong with Marx is not that he said too little about socialism, but that he said too much. For instance, that (in a fully mature socialist society) goods would be distributed according to need (alone), that the state would wither away, and (though this was probably tongue-in-cheek) that division of labour would disappear. Such predictions, unlike the scientific part of Marx's work, *do* make big assumptions about human nature, planetary resources and future technology, all of which assumptions are unproven (and probably false). One of the strengths of scientific socialism is that it makes the case for socialism independent of any theories about human nature, not because (as is often stupidly said) there is no such thing, but because it shows the possibility of socialism with people as they are now.

Certainly, there is reason in the structure of capitalism and of the workers' movement, to suppose that, among the first steps of a workers' government, along with the transfer of capital to public ownership, would be measures that broke down certain forms of division of labour (for example workers' participation in management), those which increased the use of the criterion of need in the allocation of resources (the 'social wage'), and those which cut down the coercive machinery of the state, since the repression of the working-class majority was no longer among its functions. So does the projection of these tendencies in socialism towards a final state do any harm?

Very great harm, in fact. It licenses the most destructive idea in the history of modern socialism: the teleological conception of the transition to socialism. The view, that is, that treats the transitional period and its institutions as a means to an as yet unrealised end, rather than as governed by its own structural laws and moved by currently existing needs. On the one hand, this view excuses present evils by the promise of future perfection, and on the other, it leads to measures being introduced which are currently unnecessary and even unworkable, because they prefigure the supposed goal.

Take the example of the Russian Revolution. Much of what Lenin wrote in 1917 is admirably free of utopian elements. In the *April Theses* he states – and repeats in his polemic against Kamenev – 'It is *not* our *immediate* task to 'introduce socialism' (*The April Theses*, pp. 10 and 23); 'I build *only* on this, *exclusively* on this – that the workers, soldiers and peasants will deal better than the officials, better than the police, with the difficult *practical* problems of producing more grain, distributing it better and keeping the soldiers better supplied, etc., etc.' (p. 24). Measures of nationalisation are advocated on pragmatic grounds: 'measures which have been frequently resorted to during the war by a number of bourgeois states, and which are absolutely indispensable in order to combat impending total economic disorganisation and famine' (p. 42). And indeed, in the months following the October revolution, nationalisations were undertaken in a piecemeal and pragmatic way. Lenin warns against forcing the pace of the revolution: 'The Commune, i.e. the Soviets, does not "introduce", does not intend to "introduce", and must not introduce *any* reforms which have not absolutely matured both in economic reality and in the minds of the overwhelming majority of the people' (p. 37). He was quite clear about the class nature of the coming revolution: that though the proletariat must lead, it could do nothing without the support of the 'petty bourgeois' majority of the Russian people, the peasantry.

The use of scare-quotes around 'introduce', which occurs also in

The State and Revolution, indicates that socialism is not the sort of thing that can be introduced (cf. 'The State and Revolution' in *Selected Works in One Volume*, p. 334). And the view of the withering away of the state in that work, is exemplary: no one can *promise* that the higher stage of communism will arrive; but meanwhile 'the proletariat needs only a state which is withering away, i.e., a state so constituted that it begins to wither away immediately, and cannot but wither away.' (ibid. p. 280). Withering away is thus a structurally determined tendency in the workers' state, not a goal for the future.

Unfortunately, Lenin retained a utopian streak, inconsistent with these positions. His renaming of the Bolshevik Party 'Communist' was in part an allusion to the 'higher stage' for which Lenin always reserved the term 'communism'. Once in power, the temptation to 'introduce' a bit of prefigurative politics with the aid of coercion was too strong. Bolshevik policy from the Spring of 1918 was all too dominated by the desire to leap straight to socialism; the monopoly of the grain trade was a particularly disastrous instance, not only for that generation, but for the world ever since. I think that any objective account of the Russian Revolution must recognise that the seeds of Stalinism were sown by the Civil War; by its destruction of people and resources, its erosion of Soviet democracy, and its militarisation of Bolshevik ideology (not to say the brutalisation of the Bolsheviks' sensibilities). Yet the war might have been avoided had not Lenin and the Bolsheviks treated private trade as treason, at a time when the alternative was not socialised trade, but mass starvation. Lenin the scientific socialist knew that in peasant Russia workers' power could not survive without the 'petty bourgeois' majority behind it; but Lenin the utopian (and a myriad of lesser, more utopian, Bolsheviks) hated the private proprietor and trader as a reprobate of deepest dye. Since the material basis did not yet exist to replace private trade by more advanced economic forms, mass coercion was used, criminalising the majority of the Russian people, and wrecking the chance of a 'state of the vast majority'.

Even the gentle Winstanley would have done the same: humane as his proposed legal code is by the standards of the time (indeed of the following two centuries), he too treated private trade as treason, worthy of death.[8] Terrorism is the practical expression of a politics which is out of step with its time, as utopianism is the theoretical expression of it.

Politics without Teleology

Marx's rejection of utopias and 'ideals' can be summarised in the slogan: scientific socialism is a politics without teleology. It is easy to amass quotations from the classical Marxists to prove that they thought of themselves as anti-teleologists. As Marx put it:

> Darwin's book is very important and serves as a basis in natural sciences for the class struggle in history ... Despite all deficiencies, not only is the death-blow dealt here for the first time to 'teleology' in the natural sciences but their rational meaning is empirically explained.

A point taken up by Trotsky, when he wrote: 'If we were to use the language of biology, we would say that the rational law of history is realised through a natural selection of accidental facts.'[9] Bukharin devotes the first chapter of his book *Historical Materialism* to the opposition between causation and teleology in social science, defending the former in the following terms:

> the legislation of bourgeois governments pursues the goal of strengthening, extending, perpetuating the rule of capital; the decrees of the proletarian state pursue the goal of overthrowing the rule of capital and safeguarding the rule of labour. Now, if we should wish to understand scientifically, i.e. to explain these phenomena, would it be sufficient simply to say that the purposes are different? Everyone will at once see that this would not be sufficient, for everyone will ask: but why, why should 'men' in one case set themselves one goal, and in another case a different goal? This brings us face to face with the answer: because in the one case the proletariat is in power, in the other case the bourgeoisie; the bourgeoisie desires one thing, because the conditions of its life cause it to have one set of desires; but the conditions of life of the workers cause them to have a different set of wishes, etc. In a word, as soon as we wish really to understand social phenomena, we immediately find ourselves asking the question: 'why?' i.e., we ask concerning the *causes* of these phenomena, in spite of the fact that these phenomena may be the expressions of certain human purposes. In other words, even if men should regulate everything consciously, and even if everything should be accomplished in society just as these men

desire, we should still need an explanation of social phenomena, not teleology, but a consideration of the causes of the phenomena, i.e., the determination of a cause and effect relation, as their law. And for this reason there is no difference at all in this regard between the social sciences and the sciences concerned with nature. (pp. 28–9)

Before saying what sort of thing the rejection of teleology excludes, it is necessary to mention three things which are *not* being rejected. It is not being denied that people have purposes, and while such purposes are not explanatorily ultimate, they are real, and effective. Suprapersonal purposes are certainly denied, but not individual purposes:

> 'history' is not, as it were, a person apart, using man as a means to achieve *its own* aims; history is *nothing but* the activity of man pursuing his aims ...
>
> ... men (plural), in the concrete sense, are necessarily subjects (plural) *in* history, because they act *in* history as subjects (plural). But there is no Subject (singular) *of* history. And I will go even further: 'men' are not 'the subjects *of* history'.[10]

The non-existence of supra-personal purposes, subjects or agents does not mean that the nature of people's purposes determines the course of history. People do not, as is sometimes cynically said, get the government or the society that they deserve. The way to hell is paved with good intentions – not because the intentions are unfulfilled, but because the effects of their fulfilment are determined by the structure of the society. Purposive human action is the matter of history but not its form.

Secondly, it need not be denied that there is a place for *functional* explanation. G.A. Cohen has made a strong and influential case for functional explanation as part of the Marxist conception of history (see Appendix A to this chapter).

Thirdly, it need not be denied that, in certain respects, human history tends to move in a definite direction. World population tends to increase, knowledge tends to accumulate, technology tends to advance, units of social organisation tend to get bigger. The power at the disposal of the human race is augmented, and such augmentation is not easily given up: hence it is a cumulative process. And since this means that more freedom is possible for more people, it can be called 'progress' with the evaluative weight that this word carries. There need be no teleological assumptions behind this 'conviction that humanity, at least at the present moment, moves on the whole in a progressive direction',[11] as Engels calls it. It may involve some notion of functional explanation, but that is another thing (see Appendix A).

The rejection of teleology means that, to find out where we are going, we must investigate the synchronic structure of society to determine what developmental tendencies it generates; we can't make forecasts on the basis of some conception of an end at which history must inevitably arrive. It is well known that scientific socialists have sometimes talked as if we could – as if socialism were inevitable. I suspect that this has usually been loose talk indulged in for the sake of 'cheering on the troops' – which is not to excuse it, since, in political argument as in war, 'careless talk costs lives'. But the central theoretical claims of scientific socialism do not entail any such optimistic predictions.

They do, however, entail something that, on the surface, looks equally teleological: the inevitable *breakdown* of capitalist society, with the consequent disjunction of outcomes, 'a revolutionary reconstitution of society at large' or 'the common ruin of the contending classes', as Marx and Engels put it; in Luxemburg's slogan 'socialism or barbarism'. But this sort of forecast has several differences from the 'end of history' one. It postulates an end, not of 'history', but of a specific type of society; an 'end', not in the sense of a goal, but of termination; it makes the prediction not on the basis of trans-societal tendencies, but of tendencies of an existing structure, to develop in ways that are self-destructive. A man who predicts that he will die some day would hardly be accused of teleological talk – the less so if he already had a terminal disease. It may be said: we know something about the processes of human aging, but do we know anything about the processes of societal aging? I shall argue that we do, in Chapter 3. Here it is enough to point out that the slogan 'socialism or barbarism' belongs with the politics of contradictions, not the politics of goals.

The rational motivation of polity – whether conservative or revolutionary – is the resolving of contradictions. Revolutionary theories are those that discover contradictions that cannot be resolved within the system, and are sufficiently grave to make its replacement worthwhile. If it can be shown that the combination of technical progress beyond a certain point with the continuance of the market economy and the nation-state generates a tendency towards the destruction of civilised life, that is a sufficient motive for socialist politics (granted that technical regression within capitalism is not a live option). This is very different from a theory that claims that a socialist goal is somehow written into human history in advance.

Now suppose somebody says: granted that functional explanation, laws of tendency and the like are not teleological, nevertheless, the adherence of the socialist movement to its goal is, and the foremost goal of any socialist government is to work for a socialist society. This is very easily taken as obvious, but it is wrong. The goal of a socialist government is to govern the country well, as representatives of the oppressed. Inevitably, this will mean far-reaching measures of socialisation of the economy, in any modern society. But these are dictated by the practical tasks of the government, given its class nature, and not by its aims. Marx was quite aware of this when he described the Paris Commune as a workers' state; it did not have a socialist strategy; but insofar as it was a form of workers' power, it would have been bound, had it survived, to introduce socialist measures. Likewise the Bolsheviks won the Russian Revolution on the basis of demands expressing the immediate needs of the exploited (for land, peace, security against a Tsarist restoration and so on) – and lost it when they tried to introduce socialism by decree.

A workers' government will of course have purposes. The point is (first of all, objectively) that these are only effective insofar as they arise out of the actuality of the workers' movement and are rooted in its structure. So that the question to ask about any putative socialist government is not 'what are its goals?' but 'what relations of class power does it represent?'. So far as the 'subjective aspect' is concerned, this will mean that the purposes of a workers' government are all going to be rather short term. Their time scale might be that of a five year plan, but nothing so long as a lifetime. On this matter if no other, Bernstein was right: the movement is all, the end is nothing. Bernstein's mistake was thinking that you can skin a live tiger claw by claw; the case against social democracy generally is not that it does not establish socialism, but that it does not secure jobs, decent housing etc., for all. But it cannot secure these things, because this cannot be done without taking the main economic institutions into public ownership; and that cannot be done without destroying the apparatus of the bourgeois state; which in turn can be done only on the basis of relations of class power quite unlike those which give rise to social democracy. [12]

The key to a 'political ethics' of scientific socialism (see Appendix

B to this chapter), is that there can be no great temporal distance between means and ends. This is, of course, only a starting point, but it is a necessary starting point. On this basis, we can understand the mistakes – often, the crimes – that have been committed by socialist leaders in the past, and guard against them in the future.[13] What should be avoided at all costs is the opposite response to these mistakes: the demand that we should spell out the ethics of the future, and start applying them now. I think that Steven Lukes, in an important book that raises very serious issues about 'political ethics', falls into this error. He seeks out those moments of weakness in which Marx says too much about future society, and points out that the picture is incomplete – that lots of questions are left unanswered. They are – the mistake was to start describing communism in the first place. Thus, Lukes asks:

> What, then, does emancipation promise? What are the distinctive virtues embodied in the realm of freedom? As we have seen, Marx and Orthodox Marxism systematically avoid explicit answers to this question as 'utopian'. Yet, as we have also seen, the marxist views of justice and injustice, exploitation and the unfreedom of alienation all suppose an ideal of freedom. They all employ a radical critical perspective, the standpoint of 'human' society, or the realm of freedom, that cannot be adopted unless the question is answered, unless some content is given to 'communism'. (*Marxism and Morality*, p. 86)

But Marx does not in fact adopt any such perspective: his perspective is that of the exploited proletariat within capitalism. Lukes wants to 'focus' (p. 86) on mature communism, but to do so one would have to be (if I may extend the metaphor) so longsighted that one might trip over a tank. We do not know – cannot remotely guess – what institutions a society in which working for one's living had been marginalised would require. Perhaps productive work done for pleasure in 'spare time' would become the major sector of material production, as William Morris (and sometimes Marx) seemed to think – perhaps not. Perhaps increased free time would cause immense social problems – for example a plague of personal violence and oppression, to curb which, powerful new social authorities would be needed; of course, we all hope not, but it cannot be ruled out. Even the political forms of such a society cannot be adumbrated. Proletarian democracy is based on the co-operative nature of the labour process; when the work situation ceases to be so central to life, *that* material foundation of democracy vanishes – and democracy cannot exist without *some* material foundation: it cannot be had simply because most people think it is the best way of organising things. Who is to say that the leisured people would not be atomised, happy in their atomisation, and given to the politics of atomised classes hitherto: leave it to the experts? At least this might be so in 'northern climates' – assuming anyone still lived in northern climates.

Anyway, the distant future, which we cannot foresee, cannot be a moral authority for us. Indeed, if we could foresee it, we would almost certainly find it so unlike our own life as to be repulsive.

To sum up: the case for socialism is independent of any projections of the future. It is to be made entirely on the basis of the remediability, with existing resources but given a changed social structure, of existing ills, perceived as such by existing people with their existing values.

Appendix A

Cows' Tails and Capitalists

I want here to defend my claim that functional explanation need not be teleological. I have in mind explanations such as: 'cows have long tails because it enables them to flick away flies', or 'discrimination against women takes place because it is conducive to the maximisation of profits.' I am assuming that these are not covert purposive explanations. The former is not to be interpreted as meaning that God, benevolent to Sister Cow but caring little for Brother Fly, ordained it so; and the latter does not imply any sort of conspiracy.

At an ordinary, pre-scientific level, we take it for granted that some such explanations are true; yet at first they appear to have the paradoxical feature that the effect of some state of affairs causes it: a sort of backwards-running causality, though not symmetrical with 'ordinary causality', as understood by the empiricists, since not just any 'ordinary' effect could be presented as a functional cause. Birds have hollow bones because that facilitates flight; they don't have hollow bones to make it easier for cats to eat them, though a feline theologian might think so.

In his book *Karl Marx's Theory of History: a Defence*, G.A. Cohen defends functional explanation as a species of what he calls 'consequence-explanation'. The form of a consequence law explaining an event (it can easily be generalised to other explananda) is:

IF it is the case that if an event of type E were to occur at t_1 then it would bring about an event of type F at t_2,
THEN an event of type E occurs at t_3.

Cohen points out that such explanations do not purport to explain causes by effects. 'They are not mirror-images of ordinary causal explanations. Rather, and very differently, it is the fact that *were an event of a certain type to occur, it would have a certain effect*, which explains the occurrence of an event of the stated type' (p. 261).

It should be clear, I think, that there are at least two kinds of consequence-explanation that are generally accepted, namely purposive explanation (for example it is the fact that having a cup of tea would quench my thirst that motivates me to make a cup of tea); and Darwinian explanation (cows' tails, birds' bones, etc.). Cohen goes on to consider the idea that all plausible consequence-explanations are functional explanations, though it is logically possible that there could be other sorts. What makes a consequence-explanation a functional one? I think the most informative thing Cohen has to say about this is:

> The background against which consequence-explanation is offered in biology or anthropology or economics is a conception of species or societies or economic units as self-maintaining and self-advancing, and consequence-explanations are accordingly accepted only when they are also functional explanations. (p. 264)

Thus, Darwinian explanations are certainly included, and the Darwinian model extended to other areas: wherever anything competes for existence. 'Social Darwinism' has got a bad name because it has usually meant that sort of brutal liberalism which treats the downfall of the weak as something to be desired. But *that* social Darwinism is not a theory of social evolution (that is of the evolution of social institutions), but of the biological evolution of social (that is human) beings. And since social change occurs at too fast a pace for genetic change ever to catch up, such a theory is without scientific credibility. Human evolution is exosomatic, and the 'struggle for existence' which propels it takes place between tools, and between institutions, not between people. That this struggle *does* also destroy people is for Marx and Engels a feature of some societies only – a feature which it is the task of socialism to abolish: only when the powers of production have been subjected to common control, says Marx, 'will human progress cease to resemble that Hindoo pagan idol, who would not drink nectar but from the skulls of the slain'.[14]

Cohen takes his notion of functional explanation right to the heart of Marx's theory: the explanatory primacy of the base over the superstructure, of technology over economy and economy over politics and ideology. The latter case – Marx's so-called economic determinism – surely cries out to be interpreted in this way. It is precisely because of the effects that politics has on economics that political structures have to be changed under pressure from the economic. Hence 'economic determinism' has nothing to do with Popper's ludicrous notion that Marx believed politics to be powerless. Consider the dispute over the statutes of the First International. Marx had written:

> That the economical subjection of the man of labour to the monopoliser of the

means of labour, that is the sources of life, lies at the bottom of servitude in all its forms, of all social misery, mental degradation and political dependence; That the economical emancipation of the working classes is therefore the great end to which every political movement ought to be subordinated as a means.

To Marx's great annoyance, the French translation omitted the phrase 'as a means': a prescription for syndicalism which follows from a reading of Marx such as Popper's. (See G.D.H. Cole's *History of Socialist Thought Vol.II: Marxism and Anarchism*, pp. 101–2, where the English and French versions are quoted.)

This sort of means–end relationship proposed by Marx is within the framework of purposive explanation: since it is the economic structure which generates other social goods or ills, the chief purpose must be to transform this structure; but political power is an effective and unavoidable means of doing so. It is because the economic interests that motivate the class struggle require political power for their promotion that political power is to be sought. But in cases where the means–end relation is not part of a conscious strategy, the same structure of consequence-explanation of political revolution would be available to the historian; the bourgeois revolutions of the seventeenth and eighteenth centuries, which gave rise to the Dutch, English, American and French republics, were not made with the purpose of promoting capitalism. But the ultimate triumph (through temporary setbacks) of the movement of which they formed a part is explained by the fact that the institutions they set up had that effect.

More controversially, Cohen wants to apply the consequence-explanation analysis to the relation between the forces of production (that is resources, tools, workers with their skills, productively applicable knowledge, etc.) and the relations of production (relations between worker and exploiter, exploiter and exploiter, worker and worker, etc.). The forces and relations of production are separable only in thought, since the forces are what are related in the relations. Marx claims that 'Social relations are closely bound up with productive forces. In acquiring new productive forces men change their mode of production; ... The hand-mill gives you society with the feudal lord; the steam-mill society with the industrial capitalist' (*The Poverty of Philosophy*, quoted by Honderich, p. 452). It would be possible to interpret this as meaning that for example steam mill and capitalist were inextricably linked, such that steam mills could not exist except as owned by capitalists; there would then be, so to speak, too tight a connection between state of forces and type of relations of production for any question to arise about causal relations between them, except perhaps to say that the explanation for change lay in the technological aspect, not the social. Such an interpretation of Marx would not only strain the text somewhat: it would yield a theory so obviously false as to be uninteresting. For societies have often had different relations of production with very similar forces of production. I therefore work on the assumption that the steam mill 'gives you' capitalism on some causal account of 'gives you', and hence that a *ceteris paribus* clause can be assumed. The question is, is that causal account, as Cohen claims, a functional one?

In an article called 'Against Teleological Historical Materialism' (in *Inquiry*, 25, 1982), Ted Honderich attacks Cohen's view. Part of the attack is the familiar

Ideals and Contradictions 27

attempt to make consequence-explanation collapse into reverse causality: 'The steam mill, if taken as the effect of the rise of the industrial capitalist, cannot conceivably explain the rise of the industrial capitalist' (p. 460).

If this is meant as a proof of the incoherence of all explanations which meet the formal requirements of consequence-explanations as set out by Cohen, it would surely prove embarrassingly much: that Darwinian and purposive explanations have to go too (which Honderich explicitly denies). But it seems to me that the appearance of reverse causality stems from the type/token indeterminacy of expressions such as 'the steam mill', 'the industrial capitalist'. Clearly *this* steam mill does not give you *this* capitalist (who in fact built it). The steam mill claim has to be read as shorthand for something like:

> Take any society of which it is a fact about its technological level that steam mills have become the most efficient way of producing the requisite goods; industrial capitalists will tend to become more numerous and influential in it, since they run steam mills more efficiently than they could be run under feudal relations of production.

But this looks compatible with the sort of account that Honderich supplies *instead of* Cohen's purported consequence-explanations, claiming not that they are a clarification, but an alternative – a 'wholly better' account:

> *Birds have hollow bones because that enables them to fly better.* What that comes to is best described as the claim that there *is* or *exists* an explanation of birds' hollow bones, and that the explanation has as an essential part the fact that hollow bones have a causal role with respect to better flight. (p. 462)

But the admission that the causal role of hollow bones has an *essential part* in their explanation seems to indicate that the functional explanation, while it may be further explained when its mechanism is spelt out, is not thereby explained *away*. The dispute has shifted ground: reverse causality is nonsense, but the claim about birds' bones is not nonsense; it is true, but not (thinks Honderich) an explanation – no more than a marker indicating what kind of explanation there must be. Honderich tells us:

> It is said by Cohen, seemingly not consistently with the view that explanation-claims are themselves uncompressed explanations, and that what remains is only the question of *how* they explain as they do, that Darwin gave a *fuller* explanation of what is given in the claim about the birds, a *more complete form* of the explanation given there. My difference with this should now be clear. Someone, perhaps Darwin, may have contemplated and indeed confirmed the relevant explanation-claim. What Darwin principally gave was something different, an explanation where there was none before. (p. 465)

This is wrong on two counts:

(1) If a pre-Darwinian biologist discovered what the (previously unknown or misconceived) function of an organ was, had they [15] not explained it? Surely, yes.
(2) When that explanation had been filled out with the aid of Darwin's discoveries, must it bow out like a regent when the prince comes of age, since it never had the royal blood of explanatory power anyway? Surely not, since what had needed to be explained, and later was explained, was precisely how this functional explanation worked; an explanation which bypassed the functional question and simply gave an account of how a certain bit of matter came to be in a certain place in an animal would be inferior in many ways to the 'unexplained' functional explanation.

What we require here (and what is lacking in both Honderich and Cohen) is a notion of stratified explanation: an explanation can itself become an explanandum; and its own explanation, so far from explaining it away, acquires its place in science just by being the explanation of that explanation.

Certainly, we select between consequence-explanations partly on the grounds of ideas about how they might themselves be explained – as indeed we do with any kind of statement registering a regularity. Honderich talks about 'historical materialism naturally understood', and 'standard causal understanding' of Marx's claims, intending thereby some non-functional kind of causal explanation; but if there is any connection between steam mills and capitalists it is difficult to see what it could be if not a functional explanation. A constant conjunction statement such as 'wherever there are lots of steam mills, you will soon find lots of capitalists about' is not much of an explanation because it is so unpromising as an explanandum: are capitalists spontaneously generated from steam? Do they move to steam-mill-ridden areas to admire the view? The functional account of such a correlation is a good explanation precisely because it immediately presents itself as a possible explanandum.

Appendix B

Trotsky on Means and Ends

I shall comment only on some points made by Trotsky in the last four pages of his essay 'Their Morals and Ours', and shall say nothing about the rambling and sometimes unfair *ad hominem* arguments which form the bulk of that essay. The points are as follows:

1. 'A means can be justified only by its end'.
2. 'The end is justified if it leads to increasing the power of man over nature and to the abolition of the power of man over man.'
3. 'That is permissible ... which *really* leads to the liberation of mankind ... Precisely from this it flows that *not* all means are permissible.'
4. 'These criteria do not, of course, give a ready answer to the question what is permissible and what is not permissible in each separate case.'

Ideals and Contradictions 29

5. 'Dialectic materialism does not know dualism between means and end. The end flows naturally from the historical movement. Organically the means are subordinated to the end. The immediate end becomes the means for a further end.'

Comments:

1. I take this to be analytic. A means is whatever is justified only by its end.
2. This end (hereafter referred to simply as 'liberation'), is not introduced as an end to which everything else is a means, but as what justifies the *end*.
3. The clearest example of a means which cannot lead to its intended end and so is not permissible, is *substitutionism*, the replacement of soviet democracy by a bureaucratic apparatus. This was meant as a means of defending workers' power in adverse times, but because it replaced the structures in which such power was incorporated by ones incorporating the power of a bureaucracy over the workers, it created a new self-reproducing system, incompatible with workers' power.

    The question remains open, however, whether means that did *not* in themselves involve such structural changes, could be nevertheless ruled out as defeating their own end. To this I shall return.
4. A fair enough observation: everything depends on the factual question whether a given means can lead to a given end.
5. At first sight these rather cryptic points might seem to undermine the terms of the whole discussion. I think they do indicate that the means/ends problematic is not Trotsky's chosen ground. He is rebutting his opponents' charges in the means/ends language that *they* set up. Why is he dissatisfied with it? 'The end flows naturally from the historical movement', i.e., the historical movement is not a means to an end, but is the cause of its end: its (the movement's) motives are immanent in it, not an external teleology.

This, I think, clarifies the importance of the point I note in my comment on 2.
It is not: means = civil war
            end = liberation
    but: means = civil war
         end = defence of soviet power
Why soviet power? Because it is conducive to liberation.

The point here is that liberation is not a future state of affairs to which all current activities are means: the means/end distinction is made only within current practice; the ends – that is the immediate goals of current practice (for example victory for the soviets) – are justified if they *increase* liberation. Liberation is not a once-and-for-all matter.

These immediate goals are ends, but they generate further development, and in that sense become 'the means for a further end'. It is not for the sake of this further end (classless society?) that they were pursued, but for reasons present in existing life (the workers' desire to control their conditions of life, the peasants' to retain their land). Hence, Trotsky's view does not countenance the temporal distancing of means and end, the promise of bread in the shed when you're dead. And this disarms a great deal of the criticism of his position (which is in this respect the position of classical Marxism, I think).

This is of the first significance, if we consider what is really at stake in arguments about whether 'the end' justifies 'the means'; for no one thinks that any old good end can justify any bad means whatsoever ('father, fetch the hammer, there's a fly on baby's head'), nor yet that no intrinsically bad means is ever justified by a good end (like the man in *Dr Strangelove* who would not rob the Coca-Cola machine to phone the President and stop the nuclear holocaust). The real question is whether there are some means so evil that they should not be used for any end, however good; and conversely, whether there are any ends so good that they justify any means whatsoever. It is commonly believed that Marxists think that there is such an absolute end, namely, bringing about a communist society. I would not deny that some Marxists have sometimes talked and acted as if they thought this; but the whole critique of utopia and teleology precludes such a view.

There remains the question about whether there are some means that should be absolutely excluded. The Bolsheviks in 1918 thought that there were. Steven Lukes refers to the case of Bruce Lockhart, a British diplomat who was expelled from Russia for heading a conspiracy against the Soviet regime. The *Cheka Weekly* published a letter urging that he should have been tortured for information about anti-soviet terrorists. The Party leaders were indignant, and reacted by closing the *Cheka Weekly*, dismissing the authors from their jobs, and barring them from government office. The Praesidium referred to the measures advocated as 'despicable, dangerous and contrary to the interests of the struggle for communism'.

Can this admirable attitude of the Bolshevik leaders be justified on the basis of Trotsky's principles? The torture of an isolated foreign conspirator can hardly be thought to transform the social or political structure in the way that, say, the substitution of top-down appointment for bottom-up elections did.

Yet many of us would want to say that means such as torture are paradigm cases of unacceptable means. Even substitutionism might be justified on the grounds that, though it could not lead to its intended end, it was a lesser evil than counter-revolutionary victory. But the Bolsheviks rightly rejected the lesser-evil argument for torture. Suppose someone were to say: torture corrupts its agents and those who consent to it; socialism needs leaders who have not been so corrupted. Without going into the question of the relative effectiveness of 'good structures' and 'good people' (I would give 'good structures' clear priority), it can be recognised that the corruption-argument has some force. The Russian Civil War undoubtedly had a callousing effect on the Bolsheviks, that eased the way for Stalin's reign of terror. But it is impossible to understand why torture is corrupting without also understanding that what is wrong with torture is not primarily that the torturer is corrupted, but that the victim is tortured.

This indicates that the means/end relation is not the right concept for thinking about this matter. The cause/effect relation is the other way round: it is not that torture is an ineffective means for liberation, but that a movement which proposes the use of torture thereby shows that it is already moving in a direction other than that of liberation.

It should go without saying that this view of the matter has nothing in common with that primitive superstition 'prefigurative politics': if politics is non-teleological, there is nothing to prefigure.

Notes

1. *The First International and After*, p. 337.
2. Does Engels underestimate the bourgeoisie's capacity for recovery? Perhaps – but recovery at what price? Not only are periodic economic crises still with us; the intervening century of bourgeois rule has given us two world wars, Nazism, Hiroshima, the impoverishment of the southern hemisphere and the spoliation of the planet. Was Rosa Luxemburg wrong to call this alternative to socialism 'barbarism'?
3. *Anti-Dühring*, p. 189.
4. *Selected Works in One Volume*, p. 183.
5. Of Münzer, Engels says:

   > The worst thing that can befall a leader of an extreme party is to be compelled to take over a government in an epoch when the movement is not yet ripe for the domination of the class which he represents, and for the realisation of the measures which that domination implies. What he *can* do depends not upon his will but upon the degree of contradiction between the various classes, and upon the level of development of the material means of existence, of the conditions of production and commerce upon which class contradictions always repose. What he *ought* to do, what his party demands of him, again depends not upon him or the stage of development of the class struggle and its conditions. He is bound to the doctrines and demands hitherto propounded which, again, do not proceed from the class relations of the moment, or from the more or less accidental level of production and commerce, but from his more or less penetrating insight into the general result of the social and political movement. Thus, he necessarily finds himself in an unsolvable dilemma. What he *can* do contradicts all his previous actions, principles and immediate interests of his party, and what he *ought* to do cannot be done. In a word, he is compelled to represent not his party or his class, but the class for whose domination the movement is then ripe. (*The Peasant War in Germany*, pp. 138–9)

6. Of course, conservative utopias have also existed, Plato's *Republic* being the most brilliant example. Occasionally, conservative governments have even conducted themselves with a utopian political style. In

the British context, the Stuart monarchs and Margaret Thatcher are the obvious examples.
7. *Selected Works in One Volume*, pp. 47–9.
8. Winstanley, *The Law of Freedom and Other Writings*, ed. C. Hill, p. 383.
9. Trotsky, *My Life*, p. 515.
10. Marx and Engels, *Collected Works vol. IV*, p. 93; Althusser, *Essays in Self-Criticism*, p. 94.
11. *Ludwig Feuerbach*, in *Selected Works in One Volume*, p. 610.
12. Social democracy representing, roughly speaking, a situation in which the dominant capitalist power is limited by an industrially well-organised working class, which is nevertheless politically atomised, and hence unable to take power on its own account.
13. In speaking of 'crimes' I am not only referring to Stalin, whose crimes were largely directed against the workers, peasants and the revolutionary leadership. I refer the reader to the writings of Victor Serge and Roy Medvedev for documentation, from a socialist perspective, of crimes authorised by Lenin, Trotsky, Dzherzhinsky and others, while these were the authentic defenders of workers' democracy.
14. Marx, in *New York Daily Tribune*, 8 August 1853, quoted in *Reader in Marxist Philosophy*, p. 271 (Selsam and Martel eds).
  A similar metaphor of Engels occasioned one of the sillier remarks in that farrago of blown-up trivia, Lewis Feuer's introduction to *Marx and Engels Basic Writings* (London: Fontana, 1969):

> Engels at the end of 1893 comforted himself with a myth: 'But history is the cruellest of all goddesses, and she drives her triumphal car over heaps of corpses, not only in war, but also in "peaceful" economic development.' One remembered the cities depopulated and the countries denuded, and wondered how Engels could still in masochist fashion worship 'the cruellest of all goddesses'. (pp. 28–9)

  This one wonders at the mentality that could read such remarks as expressing worship of these idols, rather than proclaiming their twilight.

15. I have adopted the convention of using 'they' as a gender-indeterminate third person singular, as we all do every day in spoken English ('If you see one of my students, tell them tomorrow's lecture's cancelled'). Janet Radcliffe Richards claims the precedent of Jane Austen in adopting this convention; it also occurs in the Authorised Version of the Bible.

2
Liberties without Liberalism

The conclusions of the last chapter suggest that it is possible to demystify political value-concepts, that is to show how they can mislead, and how they can be used without misleading, given a contradiction-oriented rather than an ideal-oriented style of political thought. In this chapter, I try to do this with the concept of liberty. Though I shall have various things to say about other concepts which have also served as political keywords, I shall not discuss any at such length. For although, as with so many much-revered words, it has sometimes been only the *word* 'Liberty', rather than any meaning of it, that has remained constant, it can be said that ever since the great bourgeois revolutions of the seventeenth and eighteenth centuries, liberty has been *the* political ideal. This is true, not only of liberal and anarchist political thought, but of Rousseau and Hegel – and indeed, a case can be made for thinking that scientific socialism, while debunking other political ideals, retains this one alone. For example, Trotsky's formula (to which I shall return in the next chapter) of 'the increase of man's domination over nature, the abolition of man's domination over man', is about liberty, that is enabling us to do what we were previously prevented from doing. But such a general conception of liberty can serve only the very general political function of marking the direction of human progress. If scientific socialism's legacy from Hegel was the idea of *progress through contradictions*, 'progress' here means the enlargement of liberty.

But if liberty is to be the sort of aim that can generate a definite political programme, upholding some laws and institutions and rejecting others in its name, it has to be defined more narrowly than 'being able to do something unhindered'. The task of demystification is largely a task of making explicit the narrowing of the concept; for it can be narrowed in various ways, and in some, the appearance is created that it has not been narrowed at all.

Liberties and Liberty

First, a word about terminology. A word is required for a partisan of liberty. Clearly 'liberal' will not do: this word, in its political sense, was originally a term of abuse meaning 'lax' or 'wet' and was adopted by liberals with the idea of liberality, that is magnanimity in mind. Liberal political movements are characterised primarily by belief in parliamentary government, a market economy and a secular state. Whether these things are conducive to liberty is a moot point. I shall use the word 'libertarian'; but I warn in advance that I do not intend either of two meanings that this word has acquired in different times and places: when I was a boy, 'libertarian' had distinctly left-wing connotations. It was often used in conjunction with 'socialist' or 'communist', to mean 'leaning towards anarchism'. Sometimes it was a synonym for 'anarchist': 'I am as good a Libertarian republican as thou' says one anarchist peasant to another, in between beating the local fascists to death with flails, in Hemingway's *For Whom the Bell Tolls*. More recently, the word 'libertarian' has been hijacked by the so-called 'libertarian right', to refer to unrestricted capitalism. I am not using the word with either right or left connotations.

When people are being prevented from doing what they believe they are entitled to do, they will often attack the laws and institutions that are restraining them, in the name of liberty. In a given context, it is usually clear what they mean by this. The historian *may* be able to say with some degree of confidence what, say, the Girondins or Jacobins or the signers of the American Declaration of Independence meant by 'liberty' – that is to say what they meant *extensionally*, to list the measures they would have regarded as entailed by their demand for liberty. But these lists would be different at different times and places, and for different parties. In his book *The Dutch Revolt*, Geoffrey Parker notes that the French ambassador to the Dutch Republic observed that the Dutch were 'a people who believe that freedom of speech is a part of liberty' (p. 270). No doubt the ambassador took it for granted that all right-thinking people would agree that this eccentric opinion of the Dutch was absurd. Yet for many modern liberals, freedom of speech is not just a part, but the paradigm case of liberty.

Probably most people would feel no difficulty about determining whether an issue was a libertarian one or not, even though cross-cultural agreement would be lacking. The *Guardian*-reader in the Clapham omnibus would probably list: my freedom to read and write whatever I like, to hold and express my opinions about politics, morality etc., to travel abroad, to engage in whatever sexual activities I like with consenting adults, to indulge my own tastes in the arts, to worship or refrain from worshipping whichever gods I choose, to refresh myself with beer or wine. Any interference with these freedoms (all of which we – more or less – possess in Britain, while they are lacking in, for example, Iran) would be resented by most of us (certainly by me) as infringements of 'liberty'. Moreover all these freedoms are liberties in the same sense of the word. In each case, it is a matter of being able to do something unhindered. And I take it that, other things being equal, any liberty in this sense is a good thing just because it is a liberty. It is important to note this in order to get out of the way two issues with which I am *not* concerned in this chapter. I am not discussing different *senses* of the word 'liberty', nor am I discussing whether liberty is good in itself. But aside from this, the above definition and positive evaluation of liberty get us nowhere, since other things never are equal. Freedom to walk about the streets in safety is incompatible with freedom to murder at will. Freedom to own slaves is incompatible with the free disposal of their own persons by those who would be slaves. Libertarians other than anarchists have therefore generally wanted to define liberty more narrowly, so that freedom to murder or enslave is not included, while the freedoms listed above are.

One can of course defend any of the above liberties without reference to any general principle of liberty. One may think that freedom of thought and expression is good, not because it is a case of freedom, but because it is conducive to intellectual progress. That after all is the character of Mill's defence. And the pilgrim fathers who emigrated in search of freedom of worship and denied the same freedom to others were not actually being inconsistent, since they demanded freedom for Puritan worship, not for the sake of freedom, but for the sake of Puritan worship. Of course, the word 'liberty' may be used in such cases, but it is not a general principle of liberty which is being defended, but some particular liberty or set of liberties. Such is the usage of most of those who we think of as the first libertarians. For instance, in her biography of the Leveller leader John Lilburne, Pauline Gregg says of the Levellers:

> Their frequent use of the word 'liberties' or 'freedoms', in the plural, indicates the specific and positive content which they gave to the term. Freedom was understood by them to imply powers and rights, as well as the absence of coercion. Consequently, the cry for

liberty was accompanied by the constantly expressed desire to check the strong and to protect the weak. Though this involved the infringement of liberty in the sense in which that idea was interpreted by some of the individualist thinkers of a later age, it was in complete accord with the positive content which the Levellers gave to the term. (*Free-Born John*, pp. 350–1)

It will emerge that the Levellers had reason, as well as humanitarianism, on their side here.

Nevertheless, if we describe someone as 'libertarian', we mean at least that they are prepared to defend someone's liberty to do something, not because it is a good thing to do, but just because it is that person's liberty. Indeed, Lilburne advised his Royalist fellow-prisoners on how best to defend their liberties in the courts of the Commonwealth. But partly because of this need to distinguish a specifically libertarian element in the defence of liberties – an element present in the Levellers but not in the pilgrim fathers, for instance – it is very natural for a libertarian to want to define a general principle, 'liberty', in terms of which particular liberties can be defended, which can serve as a criterion by which we can judge what is a libertarian issue and what is not. The search for such a general principle is not just motivated by the desire for an intellectually satisfying subsumption of cases of liberty under a single principle. It is also politically desirable to have such a principle, if one can be found, to prevent people from appealing to liberty when what they actually want is the particular activity for which they are demanding liberty. In other words, it would sort out the opportunistic from the principled libertarian appeals to liberty.

More than this; it might be possible to subsume *all* political values under the single principle 'liberty', on the grounds that, whatever people's personal moral ideals were, they would need freedom to pursue them, so this could perhaps become an agreed political ideal, under the shelter of which a variety of moral ideals could compete. I must admit to finding this idea of liberty as the overarching political principle, obviating the need to decide moral disputes before political decisions can be agreed, an immensely attractive one. I would like to be able to reply to the question 'why is socialism better than capitalism?' quite simply by saying 'because it can provide more liberty'. There are particular contexts (as I shall show below in my discussion of the relation of private to public choices) in which one *can* show that socialism adds to the possibilities open without subtracting from them. If such an argument could be generalised, and supplemented with a proof that everyone must desire freedom, we would have the perfect naturalistic argument for socialism, in the form of the assertoric imperative: 'since you desire freedom, seek socialism and pursue it!' Unfortunately, things are not so simple.

In the following four sections I shall discuss four ways in which liberals have tried to delimit the notion of liberty in such a way as to make it a workable political principle, generating a definite, plausible and internally consistent set of liberties.

Liberty to Do What Does Not Harm Others

> ... the only purpose for which power can be rightfully exercised over any member of a civilised community, against his will, is to prevent harm to others. (Mill, *On Liberty*)[1]

The above is supposed to be a 'simple principle' which can set the limits to legislation. It is a simple principle only on the assumption that there is no problem about what constitutes harm. The claim that there are such problems, and no generally applicable solution to them, is not new; but I think it is demonstrably true, and fatal to Mill's project. Even to cite a list of things which might, or might not, be considered harms, goes a long way towards dispelling the obviousness of this principle.

Does someone harm me if they destroy my favourite work of art? Or if they buy it and withdraw it from public display? Or if they build a motorway through my favourite landscape, close my favourite footpath or install games machines in my favourite pub? Or if they put stonecladding on their house in the brick-built terrace where I live, or scrawl offensive graffiti on a wall which I pass, or play loud music when I want silence? Or if they tell me a lie, or a truth which damages a friendship, or if they tell lies or such truths about me? Or film me without my consent, or *with* my consent when unclad? Or convince me that I am predestined for hell, or persuade me to join a monastery? Or ridicule my Queen, country, church, politics, race, sex, sexuality or hairstyle?

Suppose someone says, *a propos* of the last sentence: 'It is obviously criminal to ridicule someone's race, sex or sexuality, and obviously acceptable to ridicule their religion or politics; and it is alright to ridicule my country, but not other people's; and alright to ridicule other people's hairstyle, but not mine.' This may represent some sort of muesli-belt consensus, but I defy anyone to produce a general principle which will justify this judgement. The same applies in all the other cases: to know whether it is a harm one must know about the society and subculture and even the individuals concerned. This is perhaps most obvious in issues involving sexuality. In order to answer the question whether it harms someone if you sleep with their wife or husband, or whether it degrades women to publish photos of naked, or topless, or unveiled women, you have to know in what society the event occurs, and to understand something about the moral traditions of that society.

A historically sophisticated defender of Mill might reply: 'indeed you do, but in framing legislation for any given society, you should not forbid anything that is not a harm in that society'. This might be a good principle in a culturally monolithic and stable, slow-to-change society. Mill, of course, deplored such societies, and welcomed pluralism. But in a pluralistic, multi-cultural society, it is absolutely inevitable that some people will be prohibited from doing what they regard as manifestly harmless to others, and/or that some people will be permitted to do what others will regard as harming them. Insofar as this is a matter of the contingent co-presence of different cultures, it certainly presents a problem to public authorities (to which there is no satisfactory solution), but raises no particular issues for political philosophy. But it is also the case that a society's customs, morals, conceptions of harm etc, *change*; that intra-societal differences are partly an effect of change, of old versus new; that changes can be for better or for worse; and that legislation can speed up or slow down or, within limits, alter the direction of change. The legislator therefore has to ask: 'what sort of society do we want?' The answer will determine which things are to be regarded as harm by the law, and which not. Of course, this question can be asked in a utopian way, and the answers will then be a bad guide for legislation, but it can also be asked in a practical way, and cannot be avoided, since laws have to be either retained or changed, and unavoidably have effects on the way society develops. But to support a law which forbids certain actions, in order to bring about a desired kind of society, is to fall foul of Mill's doctrine of liberty. Mill makes this clear in his polemic against the American prohibitionists.

I shall criticise Mill starting with an example about which every reasonable person's first reaction will be to defend him. Someone demands, appealing to the principle of liberty, the right to play cards on Sunday. A representative of the Lord's Day Observance Society replies: by playing cards on a Sunday, you are interfering with my liberty to live in a society in which the Sabbath is observed. One may be tempted to reply: 'Tough!' This may be the correct reply. But the Millian reason for thinking it correct is the wrong one. The Millian would tend to reply that freedoms that can only be formulated: 'freedom to live in a society in which ... ' are not cases of liberty at all. As Mill puts it:

> ... a religious bigot, when charged with disregarding the religious feelings of others, has been known to retort that they disregard his feelings, by persisting in their abominable worship or creed. But there is no parity between the feeling of a person for his own opinion, and the feeling of another who is offended at his holding it; no more than between the desire of a thief to take a purse, and the desire of a right owner to keep it. And a person's taste is as much his own peculiar concern as his opinion or his purse. (p. 215)

This looks so right in the examples at hand that opposition might seem perverse. But let us look at some other examples, for if we are dealing with a general principle, it should work for all specific cases:

In modern Britain, I lack the freedom to live in a society in which no one is so economically unequal with me as to make relations of friendship difficult. This seems to me one of my most important lacks of freedom. So much so that I envy the citizens of some Eastern European countries this freedom,[2] even though they lack one of the freedoms listed early on in this chapter, namely to express dissenting opinions on political matters. This is not a matter of my valuing something else – say equality or fraternity – more than liberty. It *is* an issue of liberty for me, since it is where the chain chafes, preventing me from doing what I want to do.

The need to allow in freedoms of the 'to live in a society in which ... ' kind is perhaps best seen in the case of environmental issues. If we discount at the outset claims for freedom to live in a town where there is no litter, or pollution of the atmosphere by traffic, or danger of aesthetic amenities being removed by private irresponsibility, then all the evaluative weight of the idea of liberty will be put on the side of permitting these environmental harms. Someone might want to argue that that is quite correct: that maybe we should restrict liberty for the sake of the environment, but that if we do so, we should admit that that is what we are doing. To be consistent, I think, the adherent of this position would have to say the same about laws against murder: that they increase our security, but reduce our liberty. And this position can only be maintained if we allow the stipulative definition: restraints on our activities only diminish our liberty if they are imposed by the state. This arbitrary definition directs us away from theories about liberty towards theories about the state: I shall follow this up later in the discussion.

Here I want to outline the case against counterposing liberty to the public sphere – a case which is to be elaborated later in the chapter. It follows from the general definition of liberty given earlier that the more possibilities that are open to you, the greater liberty you have – that is that if you can choose between A, B, C and D, you are freer than if you can only choose between A and B. This would hardly seem contentious. Now suppose that as the citizen of a hypothetical democracy, you can choose what to do within the law, and also choose how to vote as between different laws. When voting, you may put the questions to yourself (in this order): (i) 'What possibilities have we got?', and (ii) 'Which of them do I want?' In this case there will be, among the various possibilities, some which can be realised only by a collective decision, that is which could not have come about by the accumulation of private choices outside the political process. For instance, town planning laws which restrict private motor traffic, and institute a comprehensive and cheap public transport system, and better facilities for cyclists.

Suppose on the other hand you first consider your private wants, realisable aside from matters requiring collective decision, and then ask yourself which collective decisions would promote their satisfaction. You will say: 'I need a car since that is the only way to get around town; so I shall vote for more facilities for motorists – roads, car parks, etc. – even though this will naturally be at the cost of losing some other amenities (children's playgrounds, clean air, safe passage for walkers).' The possibilities of collective action which would have obviated the need for private cars will simply remain invisible when the question is put in this way.

Note that the first sort of relation between private and collective choice does not prejudge the issue against private traffic in the way that the second prejudges it in its favour. The people may consider the possibility of a traffic-free town and choose private cars. Hence such an ordering of the decision-making process is unambiguously an extension of liberty relative to the latter ordering. Hence any proposal to remove some issues from the sphere in which the writ of public action runs, is a reduction of freedom: it closes some options. Leaving the public sphere unrestricted however does not in itself restrict private choice. It opens up possibilities, but does not close any. For it is always possible for collective choice to leave a particular matter to each individual to decide, and any liberty-loving people will leave as much as it can to private choice. But it will recognise that that is what it is doing: that the private sphere is the product of its collective choice, not something naturally outside its scope.

If this is not recognised, options which cannot be secured by private choice on the basis of existing public institutions will be lost. Such non-recognition prevails as a pre-theoretical ideology underlying liberal ideas of minimal legislation – the assumption that public *inaction* can never be a threat to liberty. I encountered an amusing instance of this a few years ago. In Wales there is a plebiscite in each locality every seven years, if enough voters call for it, on whether pubs should be allowed to open on Sundays. The landlord of my local had got me collecting signatures to call such a plebiscite, our area being 'dry' at that time. I explained carefully to one lady that if we had no plebiscite we would remain 'dry', but that to sign was not to vote, but to call for the opportunity to vote. She replied: 'Well, I won't sign, and that will leave everyone free to do as they like, isn't it?' Not a piece of random unreason, this, but an instance of the common liberal prejudice that where no political decision is taken, there is liberty. Her views were no more unreasonable than those of other liberals who think that since the right to drink on a Sunday is an inalienable natural right, the issue should never come before the electorate anyway. Open pubs, like correct ideas, do not drop from the sky.

In short: we should recognise the privative character of the private. Some social power is at work everywhere; only by understanding this and subjecting it to democratic control is it possible to create that social space which is 'individual liberty'. This is not an argument against there being a 'private sphere', but in favour of recognising that such a sphere can only exist because of a social decision (explicit or implicit) to draw a line round it and restrict entry by others.

Some people on the left express this recognition by denying the public/private distinction altogether; this is a mistake. Political struggles about the public/private boundary are in fact about where to locate that boundary, not about whether it should exist. Most people on the left would want certain things to be treated as public that are now treated as private, and also certain things to be treated as private that are now treated as public. Marital violence would be an example of the former (of course the law does not treat it as private, but the enforcers of the law and staff of the social services often do); cohabitation (as affecting welfare benefits) would be an example of the latter. It is one thing to insist that the question where this boundary should be drawn is a political one; quite another to reject such a boundary – implicitly if not explicitly refusing to limit the public sphere and squeezing the private sphere out; modern capitalism is intrusive enough into the private sphere, without its opponents seeking to remove such limits as have from time to time been set to it.

But all this does mean that the legislator has to decide between incompatible liberties without the aid of Mill's principle, and that among these liberties will be some of the sort which can only be described as 'freedom to live in a society in which ... '. And this in turn means that the sabbatarian can claim to be as good a libertarian as the rest of us. The opening of pubs changes the character of an area on Sundays, for those who don't frequent them as well as those who do. Many people in Wales, without the slightest tendency either to religious sabbatarianism or to temperance, voted 'dry' for just this reason. The case of card-playing is different only in degree. If the correct response to the sabbatarian's sense of injury is 'Tough!', that is not because their liberty has not been affected; it is because they lack the virtue of tolerance.

Someone might allege that tolerance and liberty are not independent issues, that tolerance is a specifically libertarian virtue. It is true that where this virtue is widespread, more freedom is possible than where it is not. In a community composed of Sunday drinkers and tolerant Sabbath-keepers, all can be free – though it does *not* follow that in a community of Sunday drinkers and intolerant Sabbath-keepers, the freedom of the latter is not infringed by the former. But it is possible to defend both tolerance as a private virtue and toleration as a public policy without any reference to libertarian concerns. And whoever heard of a tolerant anarchist?

If it is thought that I should not have taken sabbatarianism so seriously, let me introduce another example which has to be taken seriously – pornography. The National Council for Civil Liberties – Britain's main libertarian pressure-group – has had motions to its conference urging both more and less censorship of pornography. This indicates that some of the advocates of censorship see their grounds as libertarian ones. Typically, the more traditional case for censorship would be that while liberty is good, public decency also needs protection, and some compromise must be worked out between the two values. But recently, censorship has been defended on the ground that pornography is an infringement of the liberties of women. It follows from what I have been saying that there can be no *a priori* objection to this type of argument. Even without any reference to the question whether there is a causal relation between pornography and sex crimes (on which the empirical evidence is inconclusive, but probably on balance tends to show that there is no such relation), it is perfectly in order to enter the claim for freedom to live in a society in which there is no pornography. One can easily think of cases where this could be a plausible libertarian claim, i.e. not counter-intuitive, in the way that, for most of us *Guardian*-readers, the environmentalist's libertarian claims are plausible, while the sabbatarian's are not. Suppose that with the coming of satellite and cable television, several of the 30-odd commercial channels were devoted to non-stop pornographic films. Existing standards of television should be enough to convince us that, once the ban on pornography was lifted, it would be likely to take a violent and sadistic form. There is some evidence that pornography is addictive. Possibly it would become a major part of the entertainment of a large number of people. The debasement of attitudes in such a society could make it a nightmarish one, from which a perfectly reasonable and tolerant person might want to emigrate. Could not such a person claim that some measure of censorship would increase their freedom?

Here it is perhaps necessary to deal with a certain objection that the 'conservative' advocate of censorship might raise against the 'libertarian' one. It might be said – and with reason – that insofar as pornography is experienced as degrading to women, the conservative's values are being presupposed. It is after all a matter of social convention, and not of nature, what degrades and what does not. Hence the claim that, in a given society, there are libertarian grounds for banning pornography, is parasitic upon the possession by that society of the sort of values in the name of which the conservative wants to ban pornography. So far, this claim is absolutely correct. However, it does not follow that the libertarian case against pornography is weaker than the conservative one. For it might reasonably be claimed, both that (1) within a given society which (in fact) has certain values in virtue of which it cannot but regard certain acts or images as degrading, there are good libertarian reasons for banning these acts or images; for 'regarding as' here is not something which might be mistaken; that society regards, say, striptease as degrading, and that it is degrading, are the same fact, just as it is the same fact that people use the word 'bastard' as an insult, and that it *is* an insult; and (2) the values of existing society, which give rise to the reasons why there is a *bona fide* libertarian case for banning pornography, could change. It they did, that case would have to be reassessed. Possibly, things that are now degrading would not be. And this might be an altogether better state of affairs.

Thus the libertarian might simultaneously oppose the values of existing society which constitute pornography as degrading, and oppose pornography, within that society, because it is degrading. The conservative defender of censorship, on the other hand, is typically defending precisely those values of existing society against change; in so far as they appeal to the argument that pornography degrades women (as they often do) they are merely restating these values, not defending women's liberty to live in a society in which they are not degraded; for that liberty would be just as well served by society's ceasing to live by those values which define degradation in a particular way – and this solution would be anathema to the conservative.

Libertarians who aim both to transform societal norms and to defend liberties which are defined in terms of those norms, are likely to find themselves confronted with practical contradictions in implementing both programmes at once. For banning an image that is currently found degrading serves both to defend freedom from degradation, and to defend the status of that image as degrading. But such practical contradictions are no objection to a position. They reflect the fact that not all good (or bad) things are compatible.

This is not a defence of censorship, but merely an argument that it cannot be ruled out *a priori* on libertarian grounds. The case for or against any specific measures of censorship will be peculiar to the society in question. The case for censorship in the West today is that it sets limits to the commercial exploitation of sensitive areas of human life. In the countries of 'existing socialism', where the evils of commercialism are much less pronounced, but the ill effects of bureaucratic intolerance are severe, there is a good case for abolishing censorship altogether.

To sum up my case against Mill's principle of liberty: on any plausible definition of liberty, there will be incompatible liberties, so the liberties available in any society are necessarily *selected* (explicitly or implicitly) by that society. Any decision-making procedure which excludes from its purview certain liberties that might have been selected reduces the choice of possible liberties to be available in that society, and so reduces the 'liberty' of that society. One kind of such restrictive procedure is that which excludes from purview possibilities which are only available through collective action (either because such action is necessary to effect the requisite changes, or because the possibility in question is intrinsically of the kind that exists for all or none, for example to live in a nuclear-free world).

Mill's principle of liberty tends to reinforce such restrictions, in so far as it involves defining interests, and therefore harm, too narrowly. Mill himself recognises that if the distinction between *direct* and *indirect* effects of one person's action on another breaks down, the class of cases falling within his 'province of liberty' would be empty, for all actions can affect others (see *On Liberty*, p. 137). But this distinction can only be made in a principled way if some form of social atomism is true.

It is against the atomistic conception of interests and harm that my defence of liberties of the 'to live in a society in which...' type is directed. Mill holds up as a 'monstrous' and 'dangerous' principle, that which 'ascribes to all mankind a vested interest in each other's moral, intellectual and even physical perfection' (pp. 221-2). Socrates, Spinoza and Hume (the three greatest moral philosophers of all time) could not have begun to get their moral theories off the ground without some such principle. And Mill himself accepts it whenever he passes from the narrower to the broader conception of consequences. His best arguments for particular liberties presuppose it. For it is a curious fact that the 'principle of liberty' is superfluous to most of Mill's defences of its 'applications'. It is not to that principle, but to the 'monstrous' principle of our interest in the improvement of mankind that he then appeals, in arguments akin to Milton's 'I do not praise a fugitive and cloistered virtue'. It is this that explains why Mill is so often right in his conclusions (about liberties), despite the weakness of his general principle of liberty, and the perniciousness of the narrow conception of interests and harm with which he sometimes supplements it.

The Minimal State

Liberals have typically seen state power as the main, if not only, threat to liberty, and it is this opposition 'liberty/state power' that implicitly circumscribes the liberal set of liberties – which selects among possible liberties those with which the liberal is concerned. Sometimes this circumscription becomes explicit: liberty is identified with the minimal state. Liberalism claims that 'that government is best which governs least', and on this basis presents its credentials as the unique politics of liberty.

The libertarian claims of minimal state theory may rest on the contingent proposition that the state is, in fact, the chief threat to liberty; or it may rest implicitly or explicitly on the (Hobbesian) *definition* of liberty as that whereof the law is silent. Take the following example, from Professor Raphael's essay 'Tensions between Equality and Freedom': 'If Topsy inherits a million dollars, she has more power than Mopsy who inherits nothing ... An inheritance tax that takes away from Topsy a good slice of her million dollars is a restriction on freedom' (*Justice and Liberty*, p. 57). In the unrestricted sense of 'freedom', it is a restriction on Topsy's freedom, but an extension of Mopsy's (who *ex hypothesi* benefits from the redistribution). But Raphael is using the example to illustrate conflict between freedom and equality. Redistribution of money is seen not as a redistribution of freedom, but a reduction of it in the interest of equality. The assumption seems to be: 'The reduction of somebody's power by state action is a reduction of freedom; the increase of somebody's power by state action is not an increase of freedom; the reduction of somebody's power other than by state action (for example by the economic processes which have allocated great wealth to Topsy, none to Mopsy) is not a reduction of freedom.' In which case, it seems that freedom is being defined in terms of state inaction, and 'minimal state theory = libertarianism' becomes, not a hypothesis, but a prescription for redefining words, uninteresting unless it is misleading.

Even so, this theory has problems. How small is minimal? A minimal state is not the same as no state at all. Minimal state theorists must hold that there is some limit below which state activity should not fall. One answer might be: it should not fall so low that it is unable to *protect* citizens' liberties. This answer is only available to someone who has *not* defined 'liberty' in terms of state inaction, since state inaction is clearly maximised by anarchy. If we take 'liberty' in the unrestricted sense, however, and say that a minimal state is one that cannot be further reduced without diminishing liberty, nor increased without diminishing liberty, i.e. an optimal state from a libertarian standpoint, then of course minimal state theory = libertarianism' once again becomes true by definition; only this time it is 'minimal state' which is defined in terms of 'liberty' rather than vice versa. On this definition, even a theory which claimed that a massive increase in state power would be conducive to liberty could call itself a minimal state theory.

I suggest that we drop the search for any philosophically rigorous concept of minimal state theories, and discuss under this heading theories that say: 'reduce state activity and you will increase liberty'.

Such programmes generally rest on two assumptions about liberty and authority: (i) that the alternative to authority is no authority; (ii) that (in any given matter) no authority means more liberty than authority does.

With regard to the first assumption, it should be evident that, on what I shall call the vertical axis of politics – relations of domination and subordination and the struggles they generate – the alternative to one authority is often another. Free enterprise does not mean no (or less) authority over the worker, but the absence of outside limits to authority within the firm (hence often more subordination of the worker). Removal of state regulation within capitalism largely allows boss-regulation to take its place. This point is common ground of socialist and anarchist criticism of capitalism.

However, even the second assumption, shared by the liberal and the anarchist, is false. Sometimes, the removal (or non-establishment) of an authority does leave no authority. But this does not necessarily mean more freedom. It may mean that something which might have been done, and which most people wanted done (for example footpaths maintained) is left undone because no one is in a position to do it. Even the existence of an undemocratic and 'authoritarian' authority may in this way increase the total liberty available for distribution, even though at the same time it holds that liberty back from the people and hogs it for itself. And this *may*, provided there are outlets for the expression of public opinion, increase the people's freedom too, relative to the case in which there is no competent authority, since the people may be able to bring pressure to bear even on unelected authorities. In some cases, for example the prevention of disease, an authority may have the same interest as the people even without any method of popular pressure existing, and so may of itself act to increase the people's freedom. If, for example, an hereditary body of people was endowed with the powers necessary to prevent the pollution of the environment, then, on condition that its members were prohibited from owning shares, it is certain that we would be freer to enjoy an unpolluted environment than we are now, even if no public pressure on environmental issues existed, or were permitted.

At this point it is worth noting that the liberal type of 'minimal state' theory is not the only kind: whereas the liberal generally means minimal *legislation* (in accordance with Hobbes' definition of the liberty of the citizen as that which the law does not forbid), there is also the view of Rousseau, who, while leaving open the question whether more or less laws are desirable as a question to be decided by the vote of the sovereign people, taught that the *state apparatus*, the 'government' as opposed to the 'sovereign', ought to be as small as possible. The distinction between this and the liberal view is sharply brought out by Rousseau's dictum 'I hold enforced labour to be less opposed to liberty than taxes' (*The Social Contract and Discourses*, p. 77). His point is that if everyone has to serve their turn at performing state functions, there will be no need for a specialised apparatus of government, financed out of taxation, which would have its own sectional interests – and the means to further them – and hence would be a permanent threat to popular sovereignty.

> As soon as public service ceases to be the chief business of the citizens, and they would rather serve with their money than with their persons, the State is not far from its fall. When it is necessary to march out to war, they pay troops and stay at home: when it is necessary to meet in council, they name deputies and stay at home. By reason of idleness and money, they end by having soldiers to enslave their country and representatives to sell it. (*ibid*)

Hence a law imposing service in the militia, by obviating the need for a professional army, preserves the minimal state in Rousseau's sense, though it departs from it in the Hobbesian sense, which is also that of the liberals.

Modern libertarians often use Rousseauite criteria alongside liberal ones for a minimal state. Thus, the *World Human Rights Guide* (1983) reports as indices of civil liberties in a country both things like freedom of association and number of police and military per 100,000 citizens.

The classical Marxists belong to the Rousseauite tradition in this matter. Among bourgeois states, they preferred those with small bureaucracies; they opposed standing armies and proposed arming the people instead; and they assumed that a workers' state, right from the outset, would have a smaller state apparatus than a bourgeois one. Marx's and Engels' writings against the anarchists make it clear that they did not expect either *public authority* or *representative bodies* to 'wither away'; what they did expect was that specialised bodies of full-time coercive and administrative agents would wither away.

It is not in fact clear that either the Rousseau-Marx theory of the minimal state or the liberal one is correct. Repealing laws against child-battering would not increase liberty – and neither would making social workers redundant and abolishing their office. In fact, minimal state and minimal law theories are most plausible in a specific combination, which requires that we make a distinction between different sorts of state activity. The distinction is not new; here is J.S. Mill's version of it:

> Government may interdict all persons from doing certain things, or from doing them without its authorization; or may prescribe to them certain things to be done, or a certain manner of doing things which it is left optional with them to do or to abstain from. This is the *authoritative* interference of government. There is another kind of intervention which is not authoritative: when a government, instead of issuing a command and enforcing it by penalties, adopts the course so seldom resorted to by governments, and of which such important use might be made, that of giving advice and promulgating information; or when, leaving individuals free to use their own means of pursuing any object of general interest, the government, not meddling with them, but not trusting the object solely to their care, establishes, side by side with their arrangements, an agency of its own for a like purpose. (*Principles of Political Economy*, p. 309)

Mill goes on to say that authoritative intervention requires much stronger necessity to justify it than unauthoritative intervention.

Using this distinction, a reasonable sort of minimal statism might urge that authoritative interference be kept low, and the coercive machinery needed to enforce it small, if this can be done by increasing other state activities in such a way that the evils which it would otherwise be necessary to suppress coercively would be removed. For instance, the state might establish good education facilities, youth clubs, full employment, etc., and in consequence not need to increase the size and powers of the police force in order to prevent hooliganism by unemployed young people.

But this reasonable minimal statism is not, of course, minimal statism as such. It means the state doing more for people's welfare in order to obviate the need to prohibit and to police. Hence one could construct, out of intellectual curiosity, an exactly opposite theory, 'perverse minimal statism', according to which the welfare-providing function of the state should be minimised, at whatever cost in terms of extending its coercive functions. Thus, state support for youth clubs would cease, even if this was known to have the effect of increasing crime, and hence necessitating expenditure on police staff increases far in excess of the cost of maintaining the youth clubs – not to speak of the cost in slashed faces and broken skulls. It might be difficult to imagine anyone seriously defending perverse minimal statism; actually, it is not necessary to imagine it since it has in fact been defended by the Thatcher government, and implemented by them so far as they can get away with it.

Many psychiatrists have held that madness, though irrational, is intelligible. Let us try to understand the mental processes behind perverse minimal statism. The assumption must surely be that while taxes are a restraint on liberty, punishment is not. This is not an alien doctrine to the liberal tradition, however odd it may seem from a humanitarian point of view. It was 'no taxation without representation' not 'no coercion without representation' that inspired the American revolution, and this was also Locke's view.

The idea is that the state has a single legitimate function within its territorial boundaries: the maintenance of law and order; the economic and the ideological functions that all states have in fact to some extent exercised in addition to coercion, are abdicated and left to commercial interests subject to the laws of the market.

The sort of social metaphysics underlying this position might be:
(a) law and order means the suppression of crime; crime is a voluntary act, so punishment can be avoided by keeping the law. Hence the coercion necessary for law and order is no violation of liberty;
(b) taxation on the other hand is the plundering of the 'tax-payers' money' by the state – money, that is, that 'naturally' belongs to the tax-payer, and would continue to do so if the state did not take it away.

However plausible this idea that the state's revenue is 'the tax-payers' money' might have seemed to Locke or the American colonists, there is no excuse for it today. Many tax-payers get their money from the state in the first place, directly in salaries, grants or benefits, or indirectly by providing goods and services to those who do; others carry on businesses which rely, not only on police protection, but on the use of state-maintained roads and state-researched information; have employees who learnt to write in state schools, live in council houses, travel to work on state-subsidised transport, and have not died of cholera because of state-maintained sewers. Not to mention the fact that 'the tax-payers' money' consists of bits of worthless paper, deriving its value from the state's imprint. Even before modern times, it had been said 'Shew me a penny. Whose image and superscription hath it? ... Render unto Caesar the things that be Caesar's ...'

The idea that wealth could be an independent creation of an individual, such that anyone else's claim on it is robbery or parasitism, is senseless outside the exceptional circumstance of a shipwrecked mariner. The idea that money-wealth or capital could be produced or held independently, not just of other people, but of a state, is just as absurd. Any claim that transfers of wealth to or by the state without consent are unjust in themselves falls along with such claims.

What about the idea that punishment, when just, does not violate liberty, since crime is voluntary? In the first place, it seems to suppose (as Locke, indeed, did hold) that we know by nature what is crime, so we have no need of a state to define it before we can be said to have "consented" to punishment. I take it no one now holds this view of Locke's.

Secondly, while in a certain sense it has to be conceded that crime is (except in psychopathic cases) voluntary, the fact that certain social arrangements *other than* punishment can prevent (and cause) crime, shows that the responsibility for crime is shared by society, as well as the criminal.

Naturally, perverse minimal statism appeals to classes confident that they will never fall foul of the police, but with much to fear from the Inland Revenue. But is is not *rational*, even for them; it is their prejudices and resentments that it gratifies, rather than their interests. Let us hope it soon becomes a thing of the past.

The position that I described as reasonable minimal statism should, I suggest, replace the utopian notion of 'the withering away of the state', which the classical Marxists retained.

Positive and Negative Liberty

I am concerned here only with the use of the distinction between positive and negative liberty to circumscribe a privileged set of 'liberal' liberties: the negative ones. This use originates, so far as I know, with Isaiah Berlin's essay *Two Concepts of Liberty*. Of course, he did not invent the terms: his polemic is directed against those who already make this distinction, and give precedence to the 'positive' liberties; and some of his accusations really do stick to some of the defenders of 'positive liberty'. Nevertheless, considering the influence that the essay has had, it is remarkably full of confusions; some of these originate with the people Berlin is criticising, but he fails to clear them up, adding, instead, a few of his own. What emerges is, more or less, an identification of the acceptable ('negative') liberties with state inactivity. Not that he always favours state inactivity, but he justifies his departure from it on grounds other than liberty.

Berlin characterises negative liberty in the following way:

> I am normally said to be free to the degree to which no man or body of men interferes with my activity. Political liberty in this sense is simply the area within which a man can act unobstructed by others. (*Four Essays on Liberty*, p. 122)

Concerning positive liberty, he tells us:

> it is this – the 'positive' conception of liberty: not freedom from, but freedom to – to lead one prescribed form of life – which the adherents of the negative notion represent as being, at times, no better than a specious disguise for brutal tyranny. (*ibid.*, p. 131)

But the contrast between 'freedom from' (negative liberty) and 'freedom to' (positive liberty) will not do the work that Berlin wants it to. Notice his gloss on positive liberty: 'to lead one prescribed form of life'. That would indeed be like freedom to have any colour car you like so long as it's black – no freedom at all. But that gloss is not required by the phrase 'freedom to'. The point is rather that 'freedom from' and 'freedom to' are both incomplete phrases, which denote freedom only as long as they are left incomplete. As soon as I am told what I am to be free to do *or* free from, my freedom has been restricted. It is not the positive form, but the specification of the content of freedom, which takes away with one hand what it has given with the other. Hence, when Berlin characterises negative liberty, not just as 'freedom from' but as freedom from *deliberate interference*, he is restricting the scope of freedom just as surely as if he had advocated freedom to lead a prescribed form of life. Maybe it is not deliberate interference that is restricting me; maybe deliberate interference is the only thing that could remove the restriction, so that any general presumption against such interference would keep me unfree. Consider the example of two states: one has been very active, in ways which necessarily involve all sorts of interference in people's activities, to promote literacy and public education generally. It also practises censorship of literature that it regards as ideologically unsound. The other state deliberately abstains from the legislation, expenditure, etc., which would lead to a high rate of literacy, because it believes that by keeping the people ignorant it will prevent subversion – that is, it has a different means of keeping ideologically unsound literature from the people, so it need not bother with censorship. Is there more freedom in the second state? At least the people of the first state can read the literature that is *not* banned. Now suppose it is not a matter of deliberate policy in the second state to keep the people ignorant; it just wants to save money. Does that make the people any freer?

Berlin's setting up the issue in terms of 'from' and 'to' has hidden a real bias towards non-interventionism. In fact, freedom is always both freedom *to* do something and freedom *from* what might prevent you. It is always possible, by a purely syntactic operation, to translate one into the other. There is a story of a young catechumen who promised 'to keep my body from temperance and chastity'; negative liberty, or positive?

Berlin himself recognises that positive and negative liberty are (or seem) 'at no great logical distance from each other – no more than negative and positive ways of saying the same thing' (pp. 131-2). But of course, in that case, they cannot conflict; so why all the fuss? He goes on to say: 'Yet the "positive" and "negative" notions of freedom historically developed in divergent directions not always by logically reputable steps, until, in the end, they came into direct conflict with each other.'

However politically disreputable the conclusions, if the argument is logically disreputable, no suspicion is thrown on the premises. Many of the ideas criticised by Berlin in the later parts of the essay have nothing to do with positive freedom. But one important instance has sometimes been defended under that heading: the idea of freedom as rational self-direction. This is an issue on which C.B. Macpherson's excellent – in many ways, definitive – reply to Berlin[3] concedes too much. Berlin's account of the anti-libertarian potential of this idea is as follows: rational self-direction is interpreted as the direction of one part of the self (the irrational part) by another (the rational part); this essentially moral ideal is claimed to be *directly* realisable through politics; it is assumed that one part of society is governed by reason, another not, hence that this ideal will be realised when the rational people rule the irrational ones. It is recognisably Plato's political ideal. But first, not all advocates of the ideal of rational self-direction mean to imply any split in the self between rational and irrational parts. Plato and Kant do, but I take it that Aristotle and Spinoza don't. Secondly, these ideals (whether in their dualistic versions or not) are not necessarily political ideals at all, but ideals for personal morality. Political measures may be conducive to them, for example a freer society may give more scope for the development of its citizen's characters along these lines than a paternalistic one, but that can hardly be supposed to make this idea a danger to liberty. Finally, someone might hold that this ideal could be realised directly by politics, without dividing society into rational rulers and irrational ruled. The civic self might be regarded as more moral than the private self. This idea sometimes crops up in Rousseau. But the conclusion is that all should be thus improved by participation in public life – that is extreme democracy. The specific combination of individual and social dualism and the identification of morality with politics that generates the conclusions that Berlin deplores, is in no way implicit in the ideal of rational self-direction, and is rare outside Plato. So far as I know, no modern dictatorship has defended itself in this way. One might think better of them if they had: Stalinist dictatorships have generally defended themselves by the fiction that the whole proletariat ruled, while fascist dictatorships have generally taken a frankly dim view of rationality.

Curiously enough, even the Platonist version conflicts with democracy rather than liberty – two ideals which Berlin is usually careful to distinguish. Of course, Plato was no libertarian, but the idea that government by reason is best achieved by government by a rational elite is in principle compatible with commitment to private freedoms; I suspect that such is the utopia of many liberal academics.

Can anything be rescued from the positive liberty/negative liberty distinction? I think not. I am not arguing that we should retain the distinction and rehabilitate positive liberty. I think that those socialists who do argue the latter generally mean to make a different distinction from Berlin's. They may be defending positive liberties in the sense of specific liberties established by law, as opposed to an abstract, supposedly unitary ideal of liberty. It is in this sense, I take it, that the Levellers' conception of liberty was said to be positive (pp. 35-6 above). That is all well and good, but this sense of 'positive' is not the one that contrasts with 'negative'.

Or they may be contesting the distinction between liberty and the conditions of liberty, a distinction that Berlin tries to keep separate from that between positive and negative liberty. This is the distinction highlighted by questions like: is an unemployed worker in Britain free to send her son to a public school?[4] Berlin's answer would be: she is *free* to, but lacks some of the *conditions* of that freedom. This is a very odd use of the notion of conditions. What can it mean to say that one has a freedom while lacking its conditions? It sounds like a piece of sophistry, and a gift to the worst kind of hypocritical politician.

If a brother or sister be naked, and destitute of daily food and one of you say unto them, Depart in peace, be ye warmed and filled, notwithstanding ye give them not those things which are needful to the body: what doth it profit? (Epistle of James, 2, 15-16)

What would we make of a dictator who announced the release of all prisoners of conscience – only one of the conditions of their liberty, namely the opening of the prison doors, would not be supplied? And why should lack of money be less of an impediment to liberty than lack of a key?

Surely what the unemployed worker in my example has are the *legal* conditions of a liberty, but she lacks the *financial* conditions of it, and since both are necessary conditions, she lacks the liberty. [5]

Are these two sorts of condition relevantly different? The case for answering 'yes' would seem to be that laws are deliberate restraints of liberty, financial arrangements not so. But such arrangements are not the gift of nature. They are both the result of, and alterable by, human actions. Here it is necessary to challenge Berlin, not on the grounds of his values, his definitions or his logic, but of his (usually tacit) *theory* about how human affairs operate. It is odd that Berlin says that his opponents on the present issue must have some theory, presumably implying that his own views are independent of any theory, and that a theory is perhaps a slightly disreputable thing to have.[6] Such a claim only needs to be stated to be seen to be absurd. The question is: which theory is true? Perhaps, since Berlin refers to Christianity and utilitarianism in this connection, he has in mind a moral rather than a sociological theory[7] – for example the Christian and utilitarian denial of any morally relevant difference between positive and negative responsibility, killing and letting die: 'Is it lawful on the sabbath to do good or to do harm, to save life or to kill?' (Mark 3, 4). But in the context of the ethical naturalism that informs the present work, and is defended in Chapter 4, the issue must be resolved at the level of theories making factual claims about societies.

Berlin's definition of liberty in terms of deliberate interference is made plausible by the contrast between natural events and human actions:

> 'The nature of things does not madden us, only ill will does' said Rousseau. The criterion of oppression is the part that I believe to be played by other human beings, directly or indirectly, with or without the intention of doing so, in frustrating my wishes. (p. 123)

Suppose we grant this for the moment. It means that, in order for a case of lack of power to be a case of lack of liberty, it would have to be an effect of the power of other people. What sort of powers can people have, that limit the powers of others? Berlin's model is that of classical mechanistic atomism: political power appears as one person bullying another, rather as, for Newtonian mechanics, causal power is understood on the model of one billiard ball hitting another. And Berlin explicitly counterposes freedom to 'bullying' or 'coercion'.

But most power in society is not like that at all, and could not be in any stable society. Most power takes the form of power over 'things' rather than over people – but an essentially *social* power over things, in that it involves the capacity to withhold them from other people. Such a capacity does involve the possibility, when necessary, of resorting to direct force, 'bullying', for example of calling in the police to eject workers who have occupied a factory. But bullying is the exceptional, not the only, or even a major, way in which some people's power causes other people's lack of power. If a mad monopolist buys up the entire banana crop and tips it into the sea as a sacrifice to Poseidon, he has deprived people of the freedom to eat bananas as surely as if he had hired thugs to beat people up in greengrocers' shops.

To return to the case of public schools: the son of a rich family who goes to public school is not of course physically preventing the son of the unemployed worker from going. But this does not mean either that the latter is free to go, or that there is no causal relation between the one's power and the other's lack of it. Indeed, the existence of public schools reduces the liberty of those who cannot afford to go to them, for the public schools are not simply an alternative to the state system, but derive much of their function and their attraction from their exclusion of the proletariat, and the privileged access to positions of power in the state and the world of big business which they provide. They close certain politically significant career possibilities to the children of the proletariat, as surely as the mad monopolist closes their possibility of eating bananas.

This is true of property generally, and the power it gives its owners. Not only does the power over property necessarily involve the exclusion of others from such power over it; it is also the case that much of the power that property brings, it brings only because there are others who lack similar property. Ownership of the means of labour only enables the capitalist to exploit the labour of others, granted that those others do *not* own the means of labour.

To sum up: in order to see the true relations between various kinds and instances of liberty, it is necessary to break with that 'social metaphysics' which sees power in terms of the domination of one person by another – and hence sees *liberty* and *power* as contraries. Such a metaphysics may indeed be stretched to include powers exercised without stopping anyone from doing what they *tried* to do – since, knowing that 'you can't fight City Hall', they don't try. Steven Lukes' valuable essay *Power: a Radical View* takes such stretching as far as it will go, to include powers which (to invert an expression from the realist theory of science) are realised unexercised. But such stretching remains stretching; we remain within Berlin's perspective according to which senses of 'freedom' other than 'absence of bullying' are 'extensions' or 'metaphors'. The paradigm-shift which enables us to see the realities of social power and possibilities of freedom as they are, comes when we start from the etymological sense of *power* as *pouvoir*, 'being able' – the missing infinitive of the English verb 'can'. In this sense, power and liberty become near-synonyms, and instead of the question how much power and (conversely) how much liberty is there in a society, we have to ask how the social power/liberty is organised, distributed and exercised. *Domination* or 'bullying' can then be seen as a special case, by no means the most important one, of *uneven distribution* of power. As Lenin says somewhere: freedom is a very valuable commodity – we must ration it very carefully.

Individualisms and Collectivisms

It may be thought that my differences with the liberals could be summed up in another familiar contrast: individualism and collectivism. The position that I am defending certainly stresses collective action, collective decision-making and collective responsibility in ways that liberal thought typically does not. And I do think that what appears in Berlin's essay under the heading 'collective self-direction' as one of the mutant varieties of positive liberties, is in fact the sort of social arrangement capable of securing the most, and the most valuable, liberties to individuals.

Nevertheless, I believe that the individualism/collectivism disjunction is one of the most confusing in political discourse. There is a spurious obviousness to these two terms, and even otherwise clear-headed political philosophers often use them without further definition. Yet the word 'individualism', even if one limits it to evaluative contexts (leaving out, for instance, methodological individualism), can mean any of the following distinct things: (a) egoism (that is selfishness), (b) egotism (that is vanity), (c) competitiveness, (d) eccentricity, (e) originality, (f) the capacity for critical judgement, (g) belief in the value of diversity, (h) belief that each person should be independent of others (economically or emotionally) that is, what is called 'self-sufficiency' in various senses, (i) belief in the moral value of every individual, (j) belief in the special value of a few exceptional individuals, (k) belief in individual rather than collective responsibility for certain social arrangements (for example, education, insurance), (l) belief that there can be conflicts between the interests of individuals, on the one hand, and interests which are irreducibly those of institutions on the other, and that in such cases the former should prevail, (m) belief that there are certain areas of the life of an individual which should be nobody else's business.

I think it is true to say that no two of these individualisms are strictly incompatible (though in conjunction with some plausible empirical premises, some are); and that none entails any other. It would be hard to find anyone who would defend all, or none, of these individualisms. (Personally, I favour e, f, g, i, l, and m, and am generally indifferent or opposed to the others.)

To illustrate the political ambivalence of the term 'individualism', consider the classical defence of *laissez faire* economics: while it is hard on the weakest that they go to the wall, it serves the national interest in the long run. This clearly violates individualisms i and l, and it would be quite natural to say that what is wrong with *laissez faire* is that it sets at nought the interest of the individual. Yet it is sometimes called 'economic individualism', and in senses a, c, h and k, so it is.

These ambiguities ease the path of anti-socialist propaganda. Appeals to individualism evoke a favourable response because people rightly abhor uniformity and the persecution of dissent; and such appeals are used to support surrender to blind market forces which punish the dissenter with insolvency and crush the rich differentiation of tradition into the uniformity of the profitable.

At the theoretical level, the most serious confusion over individualism is the conflation of one or more of the above evaluative senses of the term with the explanatory principle of 'methodological individualism' in the social sciences, that is with the principle that only facts about individuals are explanatory. The attraction of methodological individualism rests partly on the failure to understand the alternatives, and partly precisely on the confusion of it with some value-judgement that it is desired to uphold. Take for example Isaiah Berlin's statement that: 'Conservatives and socialists believed in the power and influence of institutions and regarded them as a necessary safeguard against the chaos, injustice and cruelty caused by uncontrolled individualism' (*Four Essays on Liberty*, p. 5). 'The devils also believe, and tremble.' Socialists – at least those in the scientific socialist tradition – have not upheld the power of institutions as an end in itself, as some conservatives have. On the contrary, they have aimed to organise every institution which is a locus of social power in a democratic fashion, so that such institutions do not acquire aims independent of those of the people affected by them: 'an association in which the free development of each is the condition for the free development of all' (*Communist Manifesto*). But socialists *have* recognised that powerful institutions will not go away if you ignore them. But 'institution' is also a pretty vague term, and it should be pointed out that scientific socialism's alternative to methodological individualism is not 'methodological collectivism', if that is taken to mean that social explanation is ultimately in terms of *groups*; it is in the *set of relations* between various social agencies (individuals, groups, apparatuses) that social explanations lie. Methodological individualists tend to see 'methodological collectivism' as the only alternative, and so to read Marx as vacillating between the two, rather than presenting a third alternative. Their response to Marx is like that of a peasant who sees a steam train for the first time, describes it as something between a horse and a kitchen stove, and predicts that it will come to no good because it is neither one thing nor the other. But this is not the place to discuss the foundations of social science;[8] I only wish to warn that not all individualisms (or collectivisms) are the same.

Certainly, scientific socialism has never been committed to a blanket preference for everything collective over everything individual. It has no tendency, for instance, to favour collective living or collective artistic or intellectual production, as some utopian socialists (including Maoists) have.[9] When scientific socialists have referred to themselves as collectivists, as they sometimes have, this has always been a shorthand way of saying that they stand for ownership of productive wealth by the whole community of producers, whereas capitalism consists in ownership by a privileged class of non-producers.

> Capital is a collective product, and only by the united action of many members, nay, in the last resort, only by the united action of all members of society, can it be set in motion.
> Capital is therefore, not a personal, it is a social power.
> When, therefore, capital is converted into common property, into the property of all members of society, personal property is not thereby transformed into social property. It is only the social character of the property that is changed. It loses its class character.
> (*Communist Manifesto*)

A socialist may perfectly well hold that it is a fact about human nature that people tend to look after their own affairs better than common affairs, and that 'too many cooks spoil the broth.' But socialism is not about cooking broth, it is about mining coal and making computers and building hospitals, and these things can only be done as a collective effort, whether under collective or individual control.

I think we can understand the way the individualism/collectivism disjunction works in liberal ideology if we look first at the question in what way individuals in society are interdependent and in what way independent; and then at the practical consequences of this, in projects of *solidarity* and *atomisation*.

Independence and Interdependence

Liberal thought inherited from contractualism (and, at the more rarified levels of ideology, from the philosophical and religious cults of late antiquity) certain assumptions about individual independence: that we are not *essentially* dependent on the external world (including other people), and hence that we can be free without having power over that world, just so long as it lets us be. The curious thing about this claim is that it is not in itself a 'value-judgment', it is a factual claim of the sort that can be true or false – and that practically everybody, liberals included, would agree that it is false. Nevertheless liberal arguments continue to proceed as if it were true. The positions I have criticised in Mill, classical minimal state liberalism, and Berlin all have the idea of the originally independent individual as their implicit assumption – yet Mill knew very well that the contractualists were in error to make such an assumption, and that the individuality which he valued was a very late flower of human history; Berlin criticises what he aptly terms 'the retreat to the inner citadel', the prizing of an inner freedom immune to the buffets of fortune because requiring no external conditions.

If we seriously reject the myth of the pre-social and self-sufficient individual – 'trollish individualism' as we might call it, with reference to Ibsen's contrast 'man, to thine own self be true', 'troll, to thine own self be enough' – we must recognise that freedom involves *power* over those things on which we are dependent, which includes both material resources and *social resources*, that is social institutions and other people. Relations of power between people are often, as we have seen, equated with relations of *unfreedom*. But to the extent that people are interdependent, there can be no freedom without power over others. There need be nothing sinister about this; it need not be 'bullying', or any other kind of one-sided power. It includes such things as the power of reasoning, and the ability to evoke an emotional response; participation in the making of binding collective decisions; the ability to make use of the labour of others to satisfy needs one could not satisfy on one's own – something we do every time we go shopping. So Trotsky's formula, which occupies such a prominent place in the present work, 'increasing the power of man over nature and ... the abolition of the power of man over man',[10] is acceptable only on condition that 'the power of man over man' is interpreted as meaning the structured, unilateral and persistent holding of power by one class or group, thereby withholding it from another. Power over others, while it may take the form of oppression and exploitation or alternatively of collective control of social (including human) resources, is itself an ineliminable social invariant.

Now the first question this raises is, what form does the distribution of this social power take in bourgeois society, and how does it come about that the pervasive ideologies of that society can deny this reality, and include the belief that an individual's powers/freedoms have nothing to do with anybody else, being, so to speak, a natural or self-made possession.

I shall for the moment pass over the manifestly oppressive forms of power, in order to point out the universality of power-relations. That power over others which every individual must have in order to live, is, in capitalist society, embodied in *money*. That will come as no surprise to readers of *Capital*; in money, social relations are *reified*. To possess a given quantity of money is to possess rights over a given quantity of social labour. We should not see this as a form of oppression of one part of society by another. In any society, people can only live with the aid of power over others, whether the mechanism for the exercise of this power is money or something else. The *unequal distribution* of money, and the class monopoly of capital that underlies it, is another question. One can imagine an egalitarian market society (though such a social structure is not a durable one, and has probably never existed). In such a society, there would be no relations of oppression, but there would be relations of power over others. 'Money is power': this is not a figure of speech. The total social power would not be exercised in a *gathered* fashion, as it would in a commune or in Rousseau's ideal democracy; but the dispersedness of the power among individual agents does not mean that each one has power only over their own affairs; it is not that, in the gathered society, individual powers are aggregated, but that, in the dispersed society, social powers are divided up.

Reification – the appearance of a relation as if it were a thing – hides the reality of social power: power, which is a relation, appears as money, which can be chinked or rustled in your pocket. 'I have the right to do what I like with my own money'; it does not sound so plausible if rephrased as 'I have the right to do what I like with my own power over the labour of others.' The illusion of independence is an effect of this reification. 'A man of independent means' is one who possesses a tidy sum of money. He can only have obtained that money in a social process involving the labour of others, and it will only be of any use to him as long as there are others producing, and social mechanisms for the use of money to acquire their products. That is what is forgotten by the old person who thinks that to collect their pension would be to be a burden on the community, whereas to live on their savings would not. In either case, that person has (we may assume) worked to produce wealth in the past, and is dependent on the labour of others now.

As for the real, *relative* independence of the bourgeois, it is an effect of his or her privileged position in the class structure of society, and relatively great power over the labour of others.

Solidarity and Atomisation

Let us now consider the ways in which the term 'individualism', understood in senses conditioned by the ideology of individual independence, is used as a weapon against socialism and movements of the oppressed generally.

The real repressive function of 'individualism' as a component of liberal ideology in bourgeois society is its role in securing the atomisation of the exploited. The organised collective power of the ruling class is anyway ensured in the first place by the fact that the relation of capitalist enterprise to workers is one-to-many; and secondly, by the bourgeois character of the state. These concentrations of power are 'given' with the system, and hence appear 'natural'. The workers on the other hand have to organise consciously before they can take collective action (though such organisation is made easier by the social nature of the productive process – in the case of oppressed groups other than the proletariat, it is more difficult to win through to collective action, and 'individualist' ideology is consequently always stronger than solidarity).

In order to keep the exploited classes politically impotent, it would be enough to prevent the formation of effective collectives among them. So the worker who refuses to join a trade union or participate in a strike is upheld by the media as a freethinking individual while those who unite and take common action are lampooned as sheep. Coercion of an individual worker by a union is treated as unambiguously an assault on individual freedom. (It is of course a restraint on freedom, in just the sense in which, as liberals recognise, any law is; yet liberals have correctly held that some laws increase the aggregate liberty.) The fact that the dominant form of power in the capitalist workplace is necessarily with the bosses, that the union is the only instrument of the oppressed within that workplace to limit that power, and that anything that weakens the union enhances the oppressive power – these facts are rendered conveniently invisible by the appearance of an original independence, arising out of the cash nexus and the labour market.

The 'individualist' in this sense is not the person who stands up to authority or uses his or her critical faculty in relation to the staus quo, but the one who abstains from participation in collective action, though that abstention leaves intact existing institutions that are antagonistic to his or her liberty. The implication is that there are alternative solutions to the predicament in which an individual is placed by his or her position in the social order: a collective solution (which is supposed to diminish individual freedom) and a solution which can be achieved in isolation (which is supposed to enhance it). But in reality there are only collective solutions to problems created by social structures and institutions. To abstain is to submit. It is easy to make this submission look like heroic 'individualist' integrity.

> Casey Jones, he got a wooden medal
> For scabbing on the workers of the S.P. line.

The idea that individuals have their destiny in their own hands is a heady one, and people are apt to forget that they are being asked to renounce individual liberty so that the institutions that exploit them can remain intact and powerful.

This is most clear in the case of the controversy over the closed shop. Many people who are in other ways sympathetic to the labour movement oppose the closed shop, seeing it as straightforwardly a violation of obvious individual rights. Yet the status of this rule is clear: as a result of bargaining between union and employer, union membership becomes a condition of employment at a given firm. It is *one* condition, among many to which the worker must submit without any say in the decision-making process, such as he or she will have in the case of *union* rules. In order to get a job in a capitalist concern at all, a worker must 'consent' to the exploitation of his or her labour, which means among other things that part of the worker's product may be used for ends abhorrent to the worker. If a union wishes to use its money for political purposes, it has to establish a separate political fund, but an employer can donate money to the Tory Party, or invest it in South Africa, without any consultations with the workers. The worker's life in the workplace is one long violation of his or her personal freedom, the only limit to that violation being the collective power of the unions, whether directly through bargaining and the threat of strikes, or indirectly through pressure on the state. If the closed shop strengthens that countervailing power, it can only yield a nett gain in freedom for the worker.

Conclusion

I have been defending what may seem very disappointingly meagre conclusions from the standpoint of assessing legislation, that is that each liberty conflicts with some others, and that there is no general principle of liberty that could arbitrate between them. How much use is such a result, politically?

In the first place, it involves a recognition of the place of *tradition* in determining which liberties are important. T.H. Green, at the end of a lecture on liberal legislation, advocates a more stringent liquor law, and refers in this connection to 'the not very precious liberty of buying and selling alcohol'. In a Moslem country, that would make perfect sense. But in Europe, where drink has been the focus of social life for three millennia, and is enjoined as part of worship by the major religion, it makes none at all.

Of course, the reformer or revolutionary, in making space for new freedoms, will necessarily violate old ones. But in deciding between a new and an old freedom, one should not treat them as on an equal footing. The old freedoms are the ones that have formed the social needs and capacities of the people, and their restraint will be rightly resented. The scientific socialist should be a conservative (with a small 'c') on these matters. Only when the demand for a new freedom has so matured in the people's hearts that they willingly abandon the old one, has its time come. This recognition is part of what it means to start from contradictions rather than from ideals in one's political practice. In this way, perhaps scientific socialism can shake off the puritanism that has always seemed to follow revolutions and radical movements, like a hyena in the tracks of a lion, from the banning of the theatre and the maypole in our last Republic, through Lenin's promise that soviet state industry would make everything 'except icons and vodka', to Clare Short's bill to ban the pictures of unclad women that grace the pages of the gutter press. My case against such puritanism is independent of the moral value or disvalue of the items banned, and I am not questioning the right and duty of public authorities to care for the moral welfare of citizens; my point concerns the unrootedness of these puritan projects in the people's existing values.

All this applies so far as we are concerned with conflicts between freedom for one thing and freedom for another; conflicts between the freedom of for example one class and another are a different matter (though of course the cases will overlap). Here the issue will be decided by the relative strength of the contending classes, and one's class standpoint will determine one's selection of liberties.

But there are also things which can be said about the particular freedoms which are necessary to or incompatible with a given political or economic structure, and others which are made easier to exercise by one such structure, more difficult by another. For example, socialism makes it impossible to buy and sell slaves or to buy and sell capital; it entails the freedom to work for a living; it facilitates the cultural self-development of the worker; it makes it difficult to amass personal wealth.

Two groups of liberties are especially worth mentioning in this connection. (1) There are certain liberties which are essential to democracy, in the sense that, if they are removed, democratic institutions, even if retained in name, cease to have any significance. Freedom of public debate, political association, assembly and propaganda, and a degree of freedom of information, fall into this category. They have quite rightly had a special place in programmes for political liberty. This is not because they are, so to speak, more of liberties than others, but because they are necessary to democracy. Even here, however, we are not dealing with all-or-nothing 'rights'. A threatened democracy can extend such liberties to a variety of allies, including critical and even lukewarm allies, while denying them to its enemies, and yet can remain a democracy. And it is unavoidably the *government* that decides who to regard as its enemies. There can be no *a priori* rule for deciding this. Generally, it is better to err on the side of tolerance, since the danger of losing democracy through the suppression of opposition is generally greater than the danger of its overthrow by internal dissidents. But no serious libertarian can object *on principle* to the detention of British fascists during the anti-Nazi war, or to the suppression of *La Prensa* by the Sandinistas.

(2) Socialism focuses on the freedoms and lack of freedoms inherent in the work situation. Any socialist economic plan must treat as fundamental desiderata the extension both of free time, and of control by workers of their working lives. And these freedoms are the foundation of the extensions of political and spiritual liberty which are to be hoped for as effects of socialism. A 'socialist culture' and a 'socialist character' (in the psychological sense) can only be a culture and character which emerge on these foundations. They cannot be promoted by any 'cultural revolution' enacted from above. Something Trotsky said about the arts is applicable here:

The heart of the matter is that artistic creativity, by its very nature, lags behind the other modes of expression of a man's spirit, and still more of the spirit of a class. It is one thing to understand something and express it logically, and quite another thing to assimilate it organically, reconstructing the whole system of one's feelings, and to find a new kind of artistic expression for this new entity. The latter process is more organic, slower, more difficult to subject to conscious influence – and in the end it will always lag behind. (*Trotsky on Literature and Art*, p. 66)

Clearly this is true, not only of artistic productions, but of the life that they express. Not only is it impossible to prefigure under capitalism the lifestyle of a socialist commonwealth; even under socialism, the first generation or two can hardly be expected to 'postfigure' it. Hence, scientific socialism teaches us to use political power to transform the 'base' of society, the forces and relations of production, 'workers' power plus electrification'; and, while not abdicating collective responsibility for the 'superstructure', to take it easy in this area.

Appendix A

Equalities

Much of what I have said about liberty can be applied, *mutatis mutandis*, to other political value-words. Perhaps I should say a few words about equality, though, since there are those who think that 'socialism is about equality.'

The scientific socialist tradition is in general far more negative in its view of the slogan 'equality' than it is of 'liberty'. It has good reason to be. Both words, of course, can bear quite acceptable meanings in context, but in the abstract they are misleading for the same reason: one liberty conflicts with another, and one equality conflicts with another. For instance, the equal right to one's property may conflict with the right to equal property, equal pay for equal work may conflict with equal provision for equal needs, and so on. As Marx puts it:

> A right can by its nature only consist in the application of an equal standard, but unequal individuals (and they would not be different individuals if they were not unequal) can only be measured by the same standard if they are looked at from the same aspect, if they are grasped from one *particular* side, e.g., if in the present case they are regarded *only as workers* and nothing else is seen in them, everything else is ignored. Further: one worker is married, another is not; one has more children than another, etc., etc. Thus, with the same work performance and hence the same share of the social consumption fund, one will

in fact be receiving more than another, one will be richer than another, etc. If all these defects were to be avoided rights would have to be unequal rather than equal. ('Critique of the Gotha Programme', in *The First International and After*, p. 347)

In the case of liberty, however, it can at least be said that a liberty is a good (other things being equal) just because it is a liberty; that an increment in human powers may increase the total liberty available; that this provides a criterion of progress, that is changes which increase the total available liberty are progressive. Can anything similar be said about equality? It might be said: the formal principle of equality at least demands that treating one person more favourably than another be justified in terms of some relevant difference between them; of course, the conflicts between different equalities will still occur, in the form of different ideas about which differences are relevant; but the onus will be on the defender of unequal treatment to place a claim for some difference as relevant. Such a principle does, I think, have some use. But it should not be thought that we could first identify a case of unequal treatment as such and then ask about its justification. Take the man in the parable who pays all the workers in his vineyard a denarius for the day, whether he hired them early in the morning or late in the evening (Matthew 20). Does he treat them equally or unequally? In order to answer that, one would have to have already decided whether availability for work or work actually done was the relevant criterion. And something of the sort applies in every instance. Making expensive hospital equipment available to all equally instead of only those who can pay increases equality in one respect – but, from another point of view, reduces it by treating the sick more favourably than the healthy. Hence there can be no progress in the degree of equality, only changes in the respects in which we are to be treated equally. Different freedoms and different equalities are characteristic of capitalism and socialism; but socialism potentially provides *more* freedom than capitalism; it does not provide more equality.

Socialism is not about equality, but it is about some equalities rather than others. It is worth saying something about the specific equalities characteristic of socialism. The classical Marxists held that the call for equality was only acceptable if it was understood to mean the abolition of classes. If 'the abolition of classes' is to be rephrased as a proposal for an equality, it would have to read something like: 'equality of access to, and power over, the means of life'.

So far so good. It cannot be expected, however, that there can be perfect equality in this respect, any more than any other. A manager – even one who is hired and fired by the workers – inevitably has more power over the production process than an average worker; and the sort of fact which distributes power unevenly between different groups of workers within capitalism – which, for instance, makes assembly-line workers a more industrially powerful group than shopworkers – would continue to operate for the foreseeable future. These things depend on objective conditions, and not on anyone's decision or value-judgement.

Finally, scientific socialism can say something about the two equalities most often demanded in modern political debates: equality of opportunity, and equality of income. Like any two equalities, these sometimes conflict. But it is sometimes claimed, usually by advocates of equality of opportunity who reject equality of income, that they necessarily conflict. I think this claim is based on a familiar liberal mistake: the assumption that opportunities of for example great wealth or prestige are somehow naturally there, unless the state comes and takes them away. In fact, such opportunities exist, when they do, by virtue of certain social arrangements, which might be altered. The demise of absolute monarchy deprived people of the opportunity to become courtiers, and the end of arranged marriages closed the career of marriage-broker. A citizen of a socialist commonwealth could not make a fortune by speculating on the stock market, not because the police would come and confiscate his piggy bank, but because there would be no stocks and shares to speculate in.

The fact that opportunities are social products, not gifts of nature, also undermines the case for making equality of opportunity some kind of basic right, as many liberals do, rejecting in its name policies such as reverse discrimination (or as it is often confusingly called 'positive discrimination', or, even more evasively, 'affirmative action'). If it is socially desirable – as it undoubtedly is – that the racial composition of the police force should reflect that of the community, or that the sexes should be approximately equally represented among those who make and administer the law, or that a majority of those admitted to university should be the sons and daughters of manual workers, then society has the right to promote such outcomes, by quota-systems or whatever, even though this makes opportunities unequal as between individual members of these groups.

A similar consideration applies to income distribution. No share of the social product belongs naturally to any individual or group. There is no way of *identifying* any individual's share – it has to be *decided*. Further, there is no way of deciding whether different kinds of work are 'equal work' or not. As Marx puts it, in a socialist society

> individual pieces of labour are no longer merely indirectly, but directly, a component part of the total labour. The phrase 'proceeds of labour', which even today is too ambiguous to be of any value, thus loses any meaning whatsoever. (*ibid*., p. 345)

So, if it is socially advantageous to pay a research scientist or a lavatory attendant or a remedial teacher ten times what anyone else is paid, no one can call this unjust or exploitative. However, there are three sorts of reason why the limitation of income differentials within narrower bounds is socially desirable.

First, it is desirable that poverty be eliminated. Since some of the determinants of what constitutes poverty are absolute, this is mainly an argument for a lower limit to income, but since some are relative, it is also an argument for an upper limit.

Secondly, it is undesirable from the standpoint of democracy that differentials be so great as to create significant imbalance between the political power of different groups of citizens (though as I have said, some imbalance is unavoidable). This is mainly an argument for an upper limit to income, though it is an even stronger argument against anyone's income being so low that they are dependent on some other individual for the means of life.

70 *Socialist Reasoning*

Thirdly, inequalities of income are invidious.

In short, when equalities are important, they are not important because they are equalities, but as necessary conditions for welfare, or democracy, or fellowship.

Appendix B

Fellowship

The French Revolution – which, after all, formed the political culture in which scientific socialism was born – conjoined a third watchword to 'liberty' and 'equality': 'fraternity'. Since, in English, 'fraternity' or 'brotherhood' sounds male-biased, I shall follow William Morris's John Ball, and use the word 'fellowship'. This idea is indefinite in a rather different way than liberty and equality are. They can be defined accurately enough, but since they are highly abstract concepts, they require much further specification before they can generate political programmes. 'Fellowship', however, is an essentially and acceptably vague concept, since what it denotes is an indeterminate cluster of states of affairs. It is sometimes said to be out of place as a political slogan, since it cannot be realised by political means. This is not entirely true. Of course, it cannot be decreed, as one can decree the nationalisation of the banks. But I take it that fellowship has something to do with feeling enough in common with the strangers that most other people are in any large community, to be confident that the possibility of friendship is far greater than the possibility of hostility. That such a state of affairs can be fostered or obstructed by political arrangements is clear as soon as we consider its opposite – mutual suspicion and hostility, whether between specific groups such as nationalities, races, sexes or sexual orientations, or the generalised assumption of mutual predatoriness which is the air we breath in market societies, or again the mutual fear, diffidence and complaisance which is secreted by totalitarian regimes.

In choosing which of incompatible liberties we want instantiated, we should take it into account that certain liberties are conducive to fellowship and others opposed to it. A socialist state will have a rational interest in creating conditions favourable to fellowship, and, in the absence of class exploitation, that interest will be shared by the whole people. This interest will lead, as a matter of policy, to the fostering of certain institutions and the weakening of others, and consequently to the facilitating of certain liberties and the inhibiting of others. The socialist state cannot be neutral, as liberal states pretend to be, towards institutions of 'civil society' such as those listed by Althusser as 'Ideological State Apparatuses': schools, clubs, families, churches, etc. Its different attitudes to different such institutions will be determined – not by any metaphysical dogmas – but by each institution's relation to fellowship. Thus, the state should not treat a religion which teaches the subordination of women, or the inferiority of one race to another, or the damnation of homosexuals, with the same favour that it should treat a religion which teaches that there is something of God in all people. The state should not authorise its own set of dogmas – whether these are the 39 Articles of the Church of England or the official atheism of Stalinist Albania – but it cannot be 'secular' if that implies indifference towards all world-outlooks.

I refer to religion here as a particularly important instance. A similar principle applies to all the institutions of 'civil society'. Snooker is preferable to boxing. No doubt it would be a 'puritan' error to ban boxing, but measures fostering the climate of opinion in which it became unacceptable would not.

Liberal theories of liberty have tended to link that concept, not only with a minimal state, but with an ideologically neutral state. But the ideological committedness of a state is not necessarily antagonistic to the people's freedoms. Rather, it may determine which out of a number of incompatible liberties it promotes, and certain such choices may bring about a society in which more liberties are compossible than others.

The 'secularity' of the liberal state is not neutrality as between world views, but commitment to a particular one – commercialism – which can only be presented as ideology-free because the institutions in which it is embodied are not specifically 'ideological apparatuses', but the economic apparatuses of capitalism. A liberal state which weakens the specifically ideological apparatuses and abstains from blatant propaganda for its own world view, may present itself as neutral, and be believed, while in fact delivering the task of producing world views entirely to the commercial apparatuses which can be trusted to produce commercialist ideology – the ideology most antagonistic to fellowship. 'Nothing is sacred' is the formula, not only for secularity, but for the removal of limits to commercial exploitation. Socialists may have to reconsider the question where to look for allies in these matters.

If the socialist use of technology leads to the massive expansion of free time for all, the scope of specifically 'ideological' or cultural apparatuses outside the economic apparatus is correspondingly increased. It is undesirable that the state should organise all these free time activities itself. But if it can succeed in promoting fellowship–enhancing rather than fellowship–destroying ones, the consequent development in the public spirit would not only be good in itself, but conducive to liberty, since incompatibilities between different people's wants would be likely to be reduced.

Appendix C

Epitaph on Contractualism

The disavowed premisses of liberalism are, I think, the same as the avowed premisses of contractualism. Let me explain.

For the last 200 years everyone has recognised that there is something mythological about the idea of a contract as the origin of political society, preceded by a 'state of nature'. The question is, what is wrong with it? – and therewith, how much of contractualist political philosophy can be retained?

Of course, contractualist political philosophers often have ideas which do not depend on their being contractualists. One can follow Hobbes' case for the unification of power in a single agency, and the impossibility of placing any external limits on that agency, while discounting all talk of an original contract, and Hobbes himself is compelled to do so, since he knew perfectly well that all actual sovereigns are such by acquisition, not by institution. One need not even know that Rousseau mentions contracts in order to understand his account of the tendency of government to usurp sovereignty, and its remedies. But what of the ideas that are, in the contractualists, tied to the notion of an original contract?

It seems to be a common assumption that so long as we avoid thinking that the contract was an historical event, we are clear of mythology. In that case, Hobbes and Rousseau are more or less in the clear anyway. Hobbes' state of nature is best seen as a premiss of a *reductio ad absurdum*: take away political sovereignty, and what would life be like? It wouldn't last long. Rousseau, at the outset of *The Social Contract*, disclaims knowledge of the actual origins of states; but more importantly, he says in his *Discourse on the Origin of Inequality* that of those who go back to a state of nature 'not one of them has got there', since they attribute to pre-social man moral ideas, property and social vices, which can only exist in society, and he goes on to say that talk of states of nature should be hypothetical and explanatory, not claiming historical truth. He has hit the nail on the head. The mythology lies in the idea of human nature that is presupposed in talk about people in a state of nature making political contracts: the idea that prior to their membership of any political society, people could be proprietors and traders, moral agents and legislators. Neither Hobbes nor Rousseau makes such assumptions; their only assumptions about human nature are that we have needs for potentially scarce resources, and that we are vulnerable to each other's violence (Hobbes), or able to do more things together than we can separately (Rousseau). These no one can deny. This is a far cry from Locke's anarcho-Whig oligarchs, having turf-cutting servants and using money, but lacking laws and public authorities.

The fallacy that Rousseau identifies in such as Locke could be called the fallacy of incomplete abstraction: thinking away certain aspects of something, while retaining others which make no sense without them. But *this* fallacy is not just committed by poor Locke, in a work which is after all only a political squib on behalf of William of Orange, as riddled with inconsistencies and non-sequiturs as most of its genre, and which it does Locke no service to treat as political philosophy. It is also committed by neo-contractualists like Rawls and Nozick. It is for this reason that I see no reason to engage in a sustained critique of their work. Once their feet of clay are exposed – that is their fallacies of incomplete abstraction – they might as well have brought their impressive batteries of analytical techniques to bear on the problem of squaring the circle.

Notes

1. p. 135 of the collection *Utilitarianism*, ed. Mary Warnock.
   All references to Mill are to this volume, unless otherwise stated.
2. I am aware that there are regrettable inequalities in Eastern Europe too. Nevertheless, according to *The State of the World Atlas* (Michael

3. Kidron and Ronald Segal, Pan Books, 1981), there are (or were at that date) only five countries in which the richest 5 per cent of the population earned less than the poorest 20 per cent. Four of them were in Eastern Europe.
3. I refer to his essay 'Berlin's Division of Liberty', in *Democratic Theory*.
4. For the benefit of readers outside the United Kingdom: the English Public Schools are not the state schools, but high-status private schools.
5. Cf. Mill 'Every increase of cost is a prohibition, to those whose means do not come up to the augmented price' (p. 233).
6. Maybe I am mistaken about this implication, but it is really hard to tell from the text. Berlin is by no means insensitive to the case for economic freedom, and puts the case for it quite well – but then turns round and says that the slogan 'freedom for an Oxford don is a very different thing from freedom for an Egyptian peasant' is 'claptrap' – though the peasant may have more urgent needs than for freedom. Yet if the theories he refers to are true, it is not claptrap, but a simple fact. One is left with the impression that he thinks that Marxists, Christians and utilitarians know at heart that their theories are *really* 'only theories'.
7. 'The Marxist conception of social laws is, of course, the best-known version of this theory, but it forms a large element in some Christian and utilitarian, and all socialist, doctrines' (footnote to p. 123).
8. I have done so in *Scientific Realism and Socialist Thought*.
9. For example: 'When the futurists propose to throw overboard the old literature of individualism, not only because it has become antiquated in form, but because it contradicts the collectivist nature of the proletariat, they reveal a very inadequate understanding of the dialectic nature of the contradiction between individualism and collectivism' (*Trotsky on Literature and Art*, p. 58); 'Communism in the means of *production*, after which the modern social democrat strives, is quite compatible with separate family life' (Kautsky, *Communism in Central Europe in the Time of the Reformation*, p. 15) (the contrast is with the communism in consumption, characteristic of pre-proletarian communist movements).
10. I trust that readers will not commit the anachronism of attributing sexism to past writers and translators using the word 'man'. Only recently has it come to imply maleness – and the German 'Mensch' and Russian 'chelovyek' cannot be read as implying maleness.

3
Liberation and Instauration

The Two Goals and Their Connections

I have already had occasion to refer to Trotsky's principle whereby political programmes are to be judged: 'the end is justified if it leads to increasing the power of man over nature and to the abolition of the power of man over man.' Both aims have been inherent in scientific socialism from the beginning, and each has a fundamental role in the theory. The former is technological progress, the growth of the productivity of labour through new means of production, which is, explanatorily speaking, the basic form of progress. This might be called the horizontal axis of Marx's theory of history. The latter aim would conclude the class struggle, of which Marx and Engels said: 'The history of all hitherto existing society is the history of class struggles' ('Communist Manifesto', *The Revolutions of 1848*, p. 67). This may be called the vertical axis: oppression, and the struggle of the oppressed against it.

These two aims have not always gone together. The idea of a society without classes or oppression goes back at least to the Hebrew prophets, but has usually meant either equality in poverty, or reliance on a miraculous accession of abundance in nature. The idea of progress through science, lightening labour by increasing human control over nature, enters the history of thought with Bacon's project of the Great Instauration, lifting the curse of Adam 'In the sweat of thy face shalt thou eat bread' by fulfilling Adam's mandate 'replenish the earth, and subdue it'.[1]

Assuming that both aims are possible, one might expect all partisans of human freedom and welfare to support both, for weakness in the face of nature and weakness in the face of other people are both fetters to our freedom, and both sources of misery. And I have already made a case for treating both as stakes in politics. The characteristic liberal doctrine that it is only the power of others that constrains freedom is to be rejected. People's freedom may be curtailed, not because there are institutions powerful enough to stop them doing what they want, but because there are no institutions powerful enough to enable them to do what they want: freedom to travel is restricted not only by closed frontiers, but by closed railways. Political institutions which increase people's power in relation to nature may increase their nett freedom, even if they also subtract from it in some degree.

For scientific socialism, moreover, it is not just a question of supporting *both* liberation from oppression *and* 'instauration' with regard to nature. The two are linked in all sorts of ways. In fact, it is not a bad description of scientific socialist theory to say that it is a theory about how the two principles – technical progress and class struggle – are articulated to each other. For instance, the great 'modes of production', feudalism, capitalism, socialism etc., are each appropriate to a particular level of technology, and each constitutes a particular class structure; and one might expect a smooth transition from one mode of production to the next in the wake of technological progress, were it not for the powerful class interests that protect obsolete modes, and can only be overcome by the struggle of classes whose liberation is bound up with transition to the next mode. Finally, scientific socialists have usually held that there can be no liberation without instauration and no instauration (beyond a certain point) without liberation. Thus Marx and Engels wrote in *The German Ideology*:

> that it is only possible to achieve real liberation in the real world by employing real means, that slavery cannot be abolished without the steam engine and the mule and spinning jenny, serfdom cannot be abolished without improved agriculture, and that, in general, people cannot be liberated as long as they are unable to obtain food and drink, housing and clothing in adequate quality and quantity. 'Liberation' is an historical and not a mental act, and is brought about by historical conditions, the development of industry, commerce, agriculture, the conditions of intercourse. (p. 61)

Thus, no liberation without instauration – but the converse is also true, in that particular relations of production form 'fetters' to the development of the forces of production beyond a certain point, which fetters can only be broken when a new class liberates itself:

> At a certain stage of development, the material productive forces of society come into conflict with the existing relations of production

or – this merely expresses the same thing in legal terms – with property relations within the framework of which they have operated hitherto. From forms of development of the productive forces these relations turn into their fetters. Then begins an era of social revolution. ('1859 introduction', in *Early Writings*, pp. 425–6)

Lord Bacon, though the author of the aphorism 'wealth is like muck – only good if spread', did not concern himself with liberation which he thought (rightly enough) would involve civil disorder. The 'easement of man's estate' was to be achieved by instauration alone. Such political proposals as he made were merely means to the advancement of science and its application in industry. If instauration and liberation were causally unconnected ideals, that might be an admirable option – serving humankind by the enlargement of knowledge rather than by struggle against the oppressor, with the casualties that such struggle inevitably brings. However, once we have got away from the liberal-humanist model of social power as 'one person bullying another', we can see that if one institution or group or individual acquires more power over nature (which is what, for Bacon, knowledge is all about), while another does not, then granted human dependence on nature, the freedom of others is affected. If my neighbour acquires a car while I don't, my freedom may of course be enhanced if he gives me lifts. But it may be reduced in various ways without any *domination* of me occurring. I may be kept awake by his engine, I may have to build a fence or risk my child being run over, the loss of his (and other's) custom may bankrupt the bus company and leave me without any means of getting into town. This is clearer still in the case of production. If I am a hand-loom weaver and my neighbour acquires a power-loom, my prices will be undercut and I will go broke. And perhaps it is clearest of all in military matters. The Earl of Grab loses much of the power his castle gives him when Lord Smash acquires cannon, without a shot being fired or a stone being dislodged. In international affairs, of course, this still applies: 'Poor Mexico, so far from God, so near the United States' – and not only Mexico. One cannot begin to understand, not only the foreign policy, but the economic and even cultural policy of the Soviet Union from Stalin to the present, except in terms of the military implications of the West's technological superiority.

In short, inequalities in power over nature reduce the freedom of the less powerful, not only relatively but absolutely, no less than direct domination of the master–slave sort. In capitalism, this indirect domination of people – mediated through domination of things – is the typical form of oppression (and this goes for the relations between nation-states in the post-colonial forms of imperialism as well). As Marx puts it (in a passage where he is attacking the Gotha Programme's slogan 'labour is the source of all wealth'):

> Man's labour only becomes a source of use-values, and hence also of wealth, if his relation to nature, the primary source of all instruments and objects of labour, is one of ownership from the start, and if he treats it as belonging to him. There is every good reason for the bourgeoisie to ascribe *supernatural creative power* to labour, for when a man has no property other than his labour power it is precisely labour's dependence on nature that forces him, in all social and cultural conditions, to be the slave of other men who have taken the objective conditions of labour into their possession. He needs their permission to work, and hence their permission to live ('Critique of the Gotha Programme', in *The First International and After*, p. 341)

I have not yet broached the question whether instauration without liberation is actually *self*-defeating. But it is clear that, uncoupled with liberation, it is not necessarily *neutral* with respect to liberation, but may be adverse to it. It may aggravate rather than ease the human lot.

It is well known that Rousseau, the first democratic philosopher, was suspicious of technical progress, which he saw as actually antagonistic to liberation. His reasons for this are mixed: partly that attitude so natural to the non-proletarian oppressed which condemns superfluities, not just as badly distributed, but as inherently corrupting; partly the belief that civilisation, by creating new needs for more material goods, made people more and more vulnerable to enslavement by those who controlled these goods. This is a more serious point; a worker with a huge mortgage will be likely to think twice about going on strike. But at worst, this reduces the room for manoeuvre of those already oppressed; it does not *cause* oppression; in a society without oppression, 'new needs' could be seen, as Marx saw them, as unambiguously an enrichment of human potentiality. And as Marx also noted, even under conditions of oppression, 'new needs' may make the oppressed more discontented, and so bring liberation nearer. Thirdly, Rousseau takes it for granted that material progress exacerbates inequality of wealth, which is both morally corrupting and fatal to democracy. No doubt he saw such exacerbation going on all around him, and would have to have lived another 100 years, that is become contemporary with Marx, to see the imminent possibility of greater material equality as a result of material progress.

I have already alluded to the great problem that Rousseau's anti-progressism leaves him with. The high degree of participation in public affairs that is required of everybody if popular sovereignty in Rousseau's sense is to survive the tendency of governments to usurp sovereignty, is only possible on the basis of considerable free time, made possible for citizens of the ancient republics that are Rousseau's model by the possession of slaves. And if we are to have any chance of approaching popular sovereignty in a complex modern society (as maybe Rousseau would argue we have not), people will need the time, not just to attend meetings and debate public affairs, and do their stint in the militia and on juries, but also to acquire the *knowledge* necessary for a conscious practice of political and economic management.

As soon as humankind emerged from the classless society of hunters and gatherers, social management became the reserve of the few, whose leisure was based on the fact that the technical means for producing a little more than subsistence were present, and on the lack of leisure of the oppressed majority. If any movement for a classless society had succeeded prior to about the middle of the nineteenth century, it would have been at the price of the destruction of the arts and sciences, and the cessation of technological progress, and could not have led to democratic political forms.[2] Doubtless even Rousseau would have been unwilling to pay that price, though Pol Pot was willing. The socialist project in modern proletarian movements rests on the success, up to a point, of Bacon's instauration, the application of science to industry. This has made possible universal participation in public life and in the education necessary for it. I labour this point, which has long been a commonplace to scientific socialists, partly because there is still a species of socialist historiography which proceeds as if, had Spartacus only taken Rome, or Cromwell handed legislation over to the likes of Gerrard Winstanley instead of to the likes of Praise-God Barebone, or Babeuf's conspiracy of equals ousted the *Directoire*, we would have been saved 2,000, or 300, or 200 years of oppression. But more seriously, because there is a tendency within the new left, and more pronouncedly within the Green movement, to return to Rousseau's opinion that liberation and instauration are antagonistic goals. And this is not just an intellectual fashion, but has its roots deep in the real contradictions of our time – in the fact that, for the first time since the ice age, the existence of life on earth is threatened, and not by our weakness in the face of nature, but by the power over nature that science has given us. The onus is on those of us who retain the goal of instauration to explain what has gone wrong with it, or else abandon it, even at the price of jettisoning the project of liberation too.

In defending it, I shall be introducing another aspect of scientific socialism's commitment to the enlargement of human powers, and its critique of capitalism: the 'sorcerer's apprentice' aspect of capitalism – that it brings into being social powers that it is constitutionally unable to control, so that while human power over nature is enlarged, human power over that power, so to speak, is diminished.

Powerlessness over Social Forces; Gatheredness/Dispersedness

In *The German Ideology*, Marx and Engels wrote:

> The social power, i.e. the multiplied productive force, which arises through the co-operation of different individuals as it is caused by the division of labour, appears to these individuals, since their co-operation is not voluntary but has come about naturally, not as their own united power, but as an alien force existing outside them ... *All-round* dependence, this primary natural form of the *world-historical* co-operation of individuals, will be transformed by this communist revolution into the control and conscious mastery of these powers, which, born of the action of men on one another, till now overawed and ruled men as powers completely alien to them. (*Collected Works*, vol. V, pp. 48 and 51–2)

So the augmentation of the powers of humankind is not just a matter of technological progress, of making two blades of grass grow where one grew before, and the goal of instauration comes to have a whole new dimension: increasing social power over social power. This sounds paradoxical, and some might say that it is a survival of the pre-scientific socialism of texts like Marx's *Economic and Philosophical Manuscripts* of 1844, where the dominant theme is that of 'alienation' or 'estrangement'. Certainly, Marx refers there to 'the relationship of the worker to the *product of labour* as an alien object that has power over him', and 'the relationship of the worker to his own activity as something which is alien and does not belong to him' (*Early Writings*, p. 327). In those manuscripts, however, alienation and exploitation are not clearly distinguished; thus Marx goes on to say: 'If the product of labour does not belong to the worker, and if it confronts him as an alien power, this is only possible because it belongs to *a man other than the worker*' (p. 330). The 'alienation' that I am referring to here is not of this kind; people's powers are 'alienated', not in favour of other people, but of wholly impersonal social forces; alienation, one might say, on the horizontal rather than the vertical axis.

This theme, often under the heading of 'inversion' (that is, of product and producer), rather than of 'alienation', survives into the mature works of Marx and Engels:

> In bourgeois society capital is independent and has individuality, while the living person is dependent and has no individuality. ('Communist Manifesto', *The Revolutions of 1848*, p. 81)

> ... this complete inversion of the relation between dead and living labour, between value and the force that creates value ... (*Capital*, vol. I, p. 310)

> The law by which a constantly increasing quantity of means of production, thanks to the advance in the productiveness of social labour, may be set in movement by a progressively diminishing expenditure of human power, this law, in a capitalist society – where the labourer does not employ the means of production, but the means of production employ the labourer – undergoes a complete inversion ... (*Capital*, vol. I, pp. 644–5)

In what follows, I want to separate out this theme of inversion from the theme of exploitation, so that the two can be seen in their distinctness, and thereby also in their interaction. To this end, I shall consider Engels' argument in *Ant-Dühring* Part III, Chapter 2 (which was reprinted as part of *Socialism, Utopian and Scientific*).

Engels' argument is as follows: the fundamental contradiction of capitalism is between collective production (that is in the factory – production that can occur only through the organised co-operation of many individuals) and individual appropriation (by the capitalist – who may not, of course, be an individual). It is implied that where not only appropriation but also production is individual (that is in a community of independent artisan–proprietors), there is no contradiction. Certainly there is no exploitation;[3] which there must be when many are producing and few appropriating. So it is no surprise that: 'The contradiction between socialised production and capitalistic appropriation manifested itself as the antagonism of proletariat and bourgeoisie' (p. 321).

But alongside this, there is another manifestation of this contradiction: 'The contradiction between socialised production and capitalistic appropriation now presents itself as an antagonism between the organisation of production in the individual workshop and the anarchy of production in society generally' (p. 324). The 'now' indicates that this horizontal contradiction becomes increasingly acute with the development of capitalism, with 'modern industry and the opening of the world market' (*ibid.*). So the issue is not *just* the 'anarchy' of the market – that would exist also in a community of individual proprietors exchanging their products. It is contradiction *between* that anarchy and the increasingly large-scale planning within the increasingly large-scale firm. It is an anarchy in which the 'atoms' are powerful, and of unequal and variable power. The possibility of competition leading to overproduction, for instance, is limited in the economy of small proprietors, by the limited physical capacity of any individual producer to increase their output. A capitalist concern which can take on new workers and/or install new machinery (and conversely lay off workers and underuse capacity) is a different case. The contradiction is produced by the combination of the greatly augmented powers of capitalist industry with the determination by market mechanisms of what the capitalists can and must do. This combination generates, not only the periodic crises, and the fact that 'labour-saving' machinery serves, not to lighten labour, but to destroy jobs (the chief forms of irrationality in the capitalist economy noted by Marx and Engels), but also such twentieth-century phenomena as planned waste, and global ecological damage, and the specific social irresponsibility of capitalism in its promotion of armaments and instruments of torture, and of medically and morally unhealthy products.

All these irrationalities are intelligible granted that the increasingly great powers over the material world that have become available to us are used – and can only be used – in ways dictated by the competition for survival and expansion of individual units of capital; hence we do not *use* these powers, but are *used* (without there being a user) for the development of these powers. (I hope that the sort of functional explanation discussed in Appendix A to Chapter 1 will explain the content of this metaphor of usedness without a user.)

Engels puts it in this way:

> Active social forces work exactly like natural forces: blindly, forcibly, destructively, so long as we do not understand, and reckon with, them ...
>
> But once their nature is understood, they can, in the hands of the producers working together, be transformed from master demons into willing servants. (*Anti-Dühring*, p. 331)

Of course, an individual artisan or trader, if they have the misfortune to live in a free market economy, is also subject to the compulsion of competition. In the absence of laws regulating shop opening hours, for instance, shopkeepers may be compelled to work unsocial hours on pain of going broke. So even in an economy of individual proprietors, public regulation yields more personal freedom than laissez-faire does. But the sheer material efficacy of the tools (and correspondingly concentrated labour forces) of modern capitalists means that the social feedback of their economic activities is increased out of all proportion – in terms, for instance, of environmental destruction, or political and ideological manipulation. Peasants, through many generations of woodcutting, have sometimes deforested their region and caused erosion of their soil; modern capitalists would be capable of making the world's atmosphere unbreathable, by massive deforestation, within the span of a few years. It is like the difference between giving water-pistols to children in an unsupervised playground, and giving them hand-grenades.

Engels never doubts that the solution to the two contradictions is one and the same.

> The proletariat seizes political power and turns the means of production in the first instance into state property ... With the seizing of the means of production by society, production of commodities is done away with, and, simultaneously, the mastery of the product over the producer ... The whole sphere of the conditions of life which environ man, and which have hitherto ruled man, now comes under the dominion and control of man, who for the first time becomes the real, conscious lord of nature, because he has now become master of his own social organisation. (*Anti-Dühring*, pp. 332 and 335–6)

Proletarian liberation and social instauration are achieved at one stroke. This is a possible, and attractive scenario. But it is not a *necessary* one. One can conceive of the solutions of the two contradictions coming apart. Consider the possibility of a fully-fledged 'market socialism', in which separate workers' co-operatives, some of them perhaps huge multi-nationals, compete on a free market system. It is not inconceivable: it is the Yugoslav system with the remaining constraints of state regulation and communist ideology removed. The major form of exploitation as it exists in capitalist societies would seem to be abolished. But there is no reason to suppose such a society more capable of providing full employment, or adequate housing, or a pollution-free environment, than capitalism is. Imagine on the other hand a country conforming to the classical Marxist model of state-capitalism: an oligarchic state with an economic monopoly; it might be a very efficient exploiter, yet free of many of the irrationalities of capitalism.

This suggests that the classical Marxists saw the two contradictions as more closely tied than they are. Certainly, they interpenetrate so much that it is impossible to say anything concrete about one without talking about the other too. One cannot discuss class struggle, for instance, without specifying which classes are struggling (lord and serf, or bourgeois and proletarian), and that brings in the 'horizontal' dimension. But the vertical and horizontal contradictions are not simply different descriptions, or different aspects, of the same thing. That workers are exploited is not the same fact as that social forces operate blindly. For the rest of this section I shall abstract from the vertical axis, putting in brackets the question whether anyone is being exploited or not, and concentrate on contradictions on the horizontal axis. This is best done by looking at human progress focusing on the *gatheredness* or *dispersedness* of social powers. Inevitably, we will have to keep peeping inside the brackets to see what happens when the dimension of relations between oppressor and oppressed is superimposed on the dimension of the gathered or dispersed character of power. But certain features will be shared by gathered power, whether oppressive or not, and likewise by dispersed power.

Take the following examples: (i) the Hobbesian 'war of all against all' versus sovereignty; (ii) a market economy versus a planned economy; (iii) nation-states versus world government. (Of course, the Hobbesian sovereign may be monarch, oligarchy or sovereign people; a market economy may be capitalism, an egalitarian economy of self-employed artisans and peasants, or Yugoslav-style self-management; a planned economy may be totalitarian or democratic socialist; a world government may be an empire or a free federation.) Certain structural features of gatheredness or dispersedness apply across the bracketed distinctions. In particular, dispersed power is characterised by (1) the necessity of each unit to compete with others if it is to continue existing, and (2) the disappearance of certain consequences of the use of power from the motivation of that use; consequently (3) the disappearance of certain technically available powers altogether. Thus (1) the nation-state does not (without exceptional circumstances) have the option either of isolationism or of entering world politics unarmed; the enterprise does not have the option (beyond a certain point) of retaining staff who do not increase its profits; (2) a military commander does not (as a rule) count the cost in terms of enemy casualties; a business does not calculate 'social costs' in making its decisions; these are not personal failings: not every war-wager need rejoice at the drowning of enemy sailors; the point is that such considerations could not carry their weight in action-guiding deliberations in these practices – that would be a recipe for defeat, or bankruptcy; (3) certain aims can only be achieved by a powerful agency *not* subject to constraints (1) and (2); the care of the environment, and the assignment of useful work to all, for instance.

On the other hand, Hobbes' claim is not completely mistaken, that an absolute monarch measures their wealth by the wealth of their realm. In general, any agency will want to conserve whatever is valuable within the boundaries of its power; within these, power will be used to care and tend (though of course there are oppressive as well as co-operative modes of caring and tending). In relation to external agencies, however, power will be exercised in a competitive way; most powerful agencies are both 'particular wills' in relation to outside powers (dispersed power) and 'general wills' in relation to their parts (gathered power). Both uses of power are directed towards the enhancement of the power of the unit; but internal uses towards power over what pertains to the unit (the farmer's power over the land, the monarch's over the resources of the nation etc.), external uses towards the power to damage, or ward off damage from, other powerful agencies. The former may be called *dominion*, the latter *relative strength*.

Unbracketing, for a moment, the question of oppression: either use of power may occur onesidedly as between people – that is both can be forms of oppression. But by and large, being oppressed by the relative strength of another in a dispersed situation is a worse fate than being oppressed by the dominion of another in a gathered situation. Slavery and serfdom are oppressive forms of dominion, but armed robbery, plunder and pillage are generally worse, since the plunderer has no self-interest in the non-destruction and ablebodiedness of the victims, as the master has. England fared better ruled by Canute than raided by Vikings.

Neither sort of power is necessarily oppressive to other people, and the distinction between the two has other sorts of effect – for instance, on the structure of the agency itself (where another analogy from Rousseau springs to mind: the distinction between self-love and vanity). But here I shall refer only to the power of human agencies (people and institutions) over nature. In this instance, of course, there can be no case of oppression, since nature has no feelings or designs.[4] But nature – *at least* organic nature – can be damaged, that is reduced in its variety and fecundity. We necessarily exercise some degree of power over nature in order to live, but this power too can take the alternative forms of dominion (with the care for future resources that that involves), or raiding and plunder, caring nothing for the devastation left behind – since it is left behind. The dispersedness of human power over nature between competing capitals and between antagonistic nation-states ensures that there will often be plunder where there could have been dominion.

Take the case of a bit of new technology that, for instance, makes it possible to kill twice as many whales in the same time as before. If this new power is in the collective hands of humankind, then in so far as people are rational, it will be used only to the extent that this serves human interests (that is species will not be hunted to extinction) and furthermore, in so far as people's aesthetic commitment to natural variety, and/or moral commitment to animal welfare, is developed, stricter controls might be placed on its use, or it might be discontinued. Suppose the power is in the hands of the single authority of a worldstate. The decision is transferred from all to a few, but it can still be made. Probably, a single bureaucratic state of this sort would be no more likely to fish to extinction than a democratic one. But if the new machine is dispersed among separate, competing units, the compulsive force of the market will cause its use willy nilly. In this sense one could say (parodying Hegel) that in a free market economy none are free, in a bureaucratic state economy some are free, and in a democratic socialist commonwealth all are free. In practice of course, the pure forms do not exist: even free market capitalism is subject to some degree of state restraint, and no stable bureaucracy can be completely unresponsive to public opinion, as the success of the Greenpeace campaign against whaling shows; and no democracy can be completely without bureaucratic distortions.

But the example illustrates that, not only democratic control, but gatheredness of control whether or not democratic, both increases the options open for the use of human powers, and makes the responsible use of power more likely. (Dispersedness among competing nation-states naturally has much the same effect as dispersedness among competing capitalist concerns.)

As Marx put it:

> From the standpoint of a higher economic form of society, private ownership of the globe by single individuals will appear quite as absurd as private ownership of one man by another. Even a whole society, a nation, or even all simultaneously existing societies taken together, are not the owners of the globe. They are only its possessors, its usufructaries, and, like *boni patres familias*, they must hand it down to succeeding generations in an improved condition. (*Capital* vol. III, p. 757)

The judgement which, I think, emerges from this discussion can be summed up as follows:

(a). Other things being equal, it is good that human powers be increased; one of the 'other things' is the question whether the social structure in which human powers are increased cause those powers to be exercised in a gathered or a dispersed fashion; the augmentation of gathered powers can never be bad; the augmentation of dispersed powers often is, since the powers will be exercised without there being any mechanism whereby people can arrive at a reasoned decision as to how they should be exercised; they will be exercised in accordance with mechanisms which are systematically indifferent to certain of the effects of their exercise.

At this point, perhaps, I should parry one possible objection. It might be said – and rightly so – that since planetary resources are limited, the unlimited expansion of consumption is impossible. The inference might then be drawn that the augmentation even of *gathered* powers is undesirable. But this does not follow. First, because technical advance does not necessarily increase the expenditure of scarce resources – compare the petite machines of the present day with the Satanic mills of the industrial revolution. And secondly, because there is no reason why we should use our increased powers to increase the quantity of consumption, rather than, say, increasing leisure, or improving the *quality* of consumption.

(b). Hence, other things being equal, it is better that powers should be gathered than dispersed. In this case, one of the most important 'other things' is the 'vertical axis': oppression or liberation. In some cases gatheredness and liberation may go together, but in others they may be independent variables, and in others still, antagonistic. The division of landed estates among the peasants which accompanied the Bolshevik Revolution was at once a liberation and a dispersal. It freed the peasants from their oppressors, but lost some of the advantages of more centralised land-care. Had a voluntary collectivisation into democratic co-operatives been possible (which given the ideology of the peasants it was not), that would have realised the advantages of both gatheredness and liberation; forced collectivisation was a re-institution of oppression, and, in this case, a crime and a disaster. But one cannot say *a priori* whether the advantages of gatheredness or of liberation are greater when they conflict; it will vary from case to case; a peaceful empire may be better than a collection of chronically warring tribes; almost anything would be better than the nuclear war with which the present dispersedness of nation-states threatens us, or the rendering of the earth uninhabitable by the ecological irresponsibility of great capitalist enterprises.

(c). The dispersedness of powers does not do too much harm when the powers themselves are small. The example of the egalitarian market economy of individual producers versus capitalism has illustrated this. And – just as Rousseau said that, if there must be factions in the state, better many small ones than a few big ones – so if we have to have nation-states, it would be better if none were bigger than, say, Wales, since then none would be able to afford nuclear weapons. Dispersed powers are made more dangerous, both by increases in the share of the total social power held by particular units (as, for instance the share of the market held by a capitalist corporation, or the share of military force held by the great powers), and by increases in the absolute power possessed by particular units, which may be augmented by new technology. Furthermore, the augmentation of human powers over nature tends to cause the enlargement of the agencies of that power, for example as technology advances, and capital costs increase relative to labour costs (in Marx's terms, the organic composition of capital increases), so firms become bigger (though it is as yet unclear what the long-term effects of the newest technology will be in this matter).

To return to Engels' two contradictions of capitalism, and the question what the conditions of their resolution would be: (1) as human powers increase, there is an *inevitable* increase in their gatheredness since the increased power *cannot* be exercised without the gathering together of individual human powers – for example the factory replaces the backyard workshop. In this situation, oppression can only be avoided if *control* of the exercise of that power and disposal of its fruits is correspondingly extended. Co-operatives under workers' self-management would meet that requirement. (2) The same increase in human powers extends the range of people and things affected by their exercise far more widely than the extension from solitary artisan to large factory; the operation of a highly technologised factory has a great many effects, most of them unintended, on a great many people not involved in that operation, or even knowingly connected with it in any way. The artisan's work had far less (probably negligible) 'escaped effects'. To bring these effects under rational human control, power would have to be gathered on a much larger scale than the factory itself (whether privately owned or a co-operative). The degree of gatheredness which is *inevitable with the increase of human powers is much less than the degree required to subject those powers to rational control.*

Where we are concerned with small-scale and relatively untechnological economic activities, the need for social control is very limited; laws regulating working hours, and quality of goods for public sale, and so on, are the sort of thing required. The fact that the bakery at the end of the street is privately owned, and the greengrocer's round the corner is run as a co-operative by the people who work there, does not contribute appreciably to the runaway character of dispersed social powers, and gives both workers and consumers more choices than a state monopoly of trade would. But the great corporations in engineering, metallurgical and chemical industries would need to be the common property of all humankind: only such a degree of gatheredness would be commensurate with the range of effects of the exercise of their powers.

Socialism or Barbarism: the Augmentation of Dispersed Powers

We are now in a position to clarify that part of the case for socialism inherent in the scientific socialist tradition, which is *not* based on the fact that it would liberate the workers from oppression: the part that Marx tended to describe in terms borrowed from Feuerbach's critique of religion, and ultimately from the Hebrew prophets' denunciation of idolatry – the transformation of human powers into alien forces, the domination of the producer by the product, and so on; it is also the part which has often been expressed in terms of the *necessity* of socialism, and, since Rosa Luxemburg, in terms of the disjunction: 'socialism or barbarism'.

If a doctor were to tell an alcoholic patient with cirrhosis of the liver that it was necessary that he stopped drinking, no one would read 'necessary' as 'inevitable' (unless, with morbid humour, meaning that there's no drinking after death). But for some reason, when scientific socialists say that socialism is necessary, their opponents, perhaps bemused by Calvin or Laplace, think they are saying that socialism will come about whatever happens. Perhaps a few quotations are in order:

> Freeman and slave, patrician and plebeian, lord and serf, guild-master and journeyman, in a word, oppressor and oppressed stood in constant opposition to one another, carried on an uninterrupted, now hidden, now open fight, a fight that each time ended, either in the revolutionary reconstitution of society at large, or in the common ruin of the contending classes. (Marx and Engels, 'The Communist Manifesto' in *The Revolutions of 1848*, p. 68)

Once, after having been endlessly accused by his reformist opponents of deterministic dogmatism, Kautsky confronted the issue directly: 'if we speak of the necessity of the victory of the proletariat and of socialism that follows therefrom, we do not mean that victory is inevitable, or perhaps, as many of our critics perceive it [that victory] must come of itself with fatalistic certainty, even if the revolutionary class does nothing. Here necessity is understood in the sense of the only possibility of further development.' The ascension to power by the proletariat was a necessity, it was inevitable, according to Kautsky, only in the sense that without such progress, modern society would 'stagnate and rot.' (Gary P. Steenson, *Karl Kautsky*)

Necessity (outside the contexts of logic and mathematics) is always 'necessity *if* ...' Socialism is necessary if what? If the contending classes are to escape mutual ruin, if society is not to stagnate and rot, if we are to avoid barbarism. Scientific socialists have said very little about what such ruin, stagnation or barbarism would consist in – probably because, like Queen Victoria, they were not interested in the possibility of defeat. Today, we are compelled to be interested in it; barbarism is odds-on favourite.

It is quite clear that socialism and barbarism are not symmetrical alternatives. It is not like the board game of 'Class Struggle', where the alternative outcomes are 'socialism wins' or 'barbarism wins'. 'Barbarism' is Luxemburg's name for 'ruin' and 'rotting'. One image of barbarism is: capitalism collapses into a terminal crisis, into complete chaos; the workers' movement is not strong enough to take over, so chaos remains. But of course, there can never be *total* chaos, a Hobbesian war of all against all. If powers become *completely* dispersed, they cease to be powers – just as, in St. Augustine's theology, the devil cannot be perfectly evil, because if he became so, he would cease to exist (since evil is a privation of being). The agents of 'barbarian' destruction would not be powerful enough to cause chaos if they were not internally ordered. If the Vikings were not loyal subjects, faithful comrades, loving parents and industrious farmers, they could never have got it together to murder, loot, rape and burn their way through these islands.

At the other extreme from the chaotic image of barbarism is the 'iron heel' image. The threatened capitalist class get together, in Jack London's novel *The Iron Heel*, and they overcome the *dispersed* nature of capitalism, while maintaining its *exploitive* nature by means of the same authoritarian state. In the novel, this regime lasts centuries and takes civilisation to new heights, while crushing opponents with the utmost brutality, until eventually the oppressed overthrow it. What internal cracks in the regime made this possible we are not told; surely, a regime with only vertical contradictions could last for ever.

The iron heel, while barbaric, is not truly barbarian. If this is really a possibility, it should be seen as a third alternative outcome to the history of capitalism. Fortunately the nearest approaches to it hitherto – fascist dictatorships – have never covered enough of the globe, or sufficiently overcome their nationalistic narrowness, to attain such stability. Fascism in fact is not only barbaric, but to a large degree barbarian as well – hence its weakness.

Since neither of these models of barbarism – neither total chaos nor the iron heel – has come to prevail, the critic of Luxemburg and of scientific socialism generally may say that the socialism/barbarism disjunction is just scare-mongering propaganda, without scientific justification. If one were to reply by pointing to the list of barbarities perpetrated in the seven decades since Luxemburg's murder, it could be objected that there is no single, permanent or developing feature of late capitalism that is responsible for these atrocities – that history has always been 'just one damned mass murder after another', and our age is no different. However, it would be difficult to deny that the twentieth century has outrun other centuries in atrocities, if only because it has the means to do so; the technical means of destruction at the disposal of Hitler, of the allied leaders who took the decision to bomb Hiroshima, or of the American presidents who devastated Vietnam, were simply not available to Caligula or the Crusaders or the Duke of Wellington.

So if we ask what it is about the nature of technical progress in late capitalism that makes it progress towards barbarism, the answer is: it is the augmentation of dispersed powers. That is to say, the power of those individuals and institutions that possess new, more effective instruments, is increased; but these agents are in competition with each other, which constrains them to use their powers in certain ways – ways that are determined not by their own 'internal' ends, but by the end of surviving and succeeding in the competitive struggle. So one would not expect barbarism to be a unified phenomenon – it is a centrifugal, not a centripetal force.

The exercise of augmented dispersed powers tends to take the form of the destructive utilisation of its objects, rather than their careful tending. Examples are many, and of a diverse nature: modern weaponry, dispersed among nation-states, threatens us with a nuclear holocaust; factory fishing, dispersed among private companies and competing nation-states, threatens species of fish with extinction; the internal combustion engine, dispersed among road-users, kills and maims thousands, vandalises our urban and rural landscapes, and causes mental retardation through lead-poisoning to a substantial proportion of our children; new information technology, in the service of commercial interests or coercive state apparatuses, threatens us with the first truly totalitarian society in history (for neither Hitler nor Stalin had the technical means fully to realise their totalitarian goals) – and the idea that such a society would be any less totalitarian by virtue of the dispersedness of the power rings hollow as soon as one examines it: am I freer if my biography is on the files of six commercial espionage agencies and three nations' security services, rather than on that of one Big Brother? Finally and most obviously, the augmentation of productive powers, dispersed among competing enterprises, causes mass unemployment instead of reduced working hours. It is easy to see, in all these cases, that the danger or damage is caused, not by the augmentation of power as such, but by the dispersedness of that augmentation.

It should also be clear that the prediction on this basis of a 'bad end' for capitalism is not grounded in knowledge of any particular bad end, just as our knowledge that all men are mortal does not rest on there being any particular kind of death that will get you if the others don't.

Of course, the augmentation of dispersed powers is an augmentation of powers, it does enable us to do things we could not do before, and not all of these things are destructive. Humankind has genuinely benefitted from many medical innovations, new ways of raising crops, labour-saving household gadgets. Technical progress has always had certain damaging consequences, and is never likely to be devoid of beneficial ones. But the balance between these goods and harms has changed. For all its horrors, the industrial revolution lengthened the expectation of life in Britain; as much cannot be said of progress in our time. And the enormity of the destructive potential that we now have to reckon with, makes it (does it not?) uncontentious that, on balance, it would have been better if none of the inventions of the post-war era had occurred. But this does not justify a 'Luddite' politics, of opposition to technological innovation. In a competitive market system, a Luddite firm or country is a bankrupt firm or country. The inhibition of technical progress is impossible within capitalism, and it would be unnecessary under socialism – though of course there would be particular applications of technology for which a socialist commonwealth would have no use.

However, the augmentation of dispersed powers in late capitalism does bring certain issues to the forefront of politics which have previously been treated as peripheral in the workers' movement, most importantly, peace and ecology. Neither the peace movement nor the Green movement can achieve their aims so long as the great powers of modern technology are dispersed, that is so long as capitalism and/or the nation-state exist. But this does not mean that these aims can simply be relegated to footnotes to the programme for international socialism, to be seen to one fine day after the mighty have been put down from their seats. For although a lasting solution to these problems must await international socialism, there is a vital role (quite literally, vital) for *defensive* struggles against the cold war and the spoliation of the environment, here and now. Scientific socialists have always recognised the place of defensive struggles – trade union struggles, for instance. Indeed, socialist parliamentary politics can never be more than a defensive struggle. None of these activities can bring about socialism (or disarmament, or care for the earth); but they may slow the advance of barbarism, and more that that may not be possible in the West for some time to come.

Gatheredness and Democracy

We have, then, two parts to the goal of instauration: that which Bacon originally designated by the word, viz. the augmentation of human powers through the scientific knowledge of nature applied in industry; and the subjection of the effects of those powers to human choice and control by means of gathering them under common institutions, rather than dispersing them among competing ones. The question remains, is this 'human control' to be control by all humans, or some at the expense of others. This is the question of liberation – or at least, a great part of it. Oppression in dispersed contexts – raiding, plunder, naked bullying and robbery – is not usually contrasted to liberation, if only because *every* political arrangement, however oppressive, aims to suppress it. The term 'deliverance' might be used, but 'liberation' is usually reserved for the overthrow of oppression in gathered contexts.

In some cases, liberation can actually be achieved by dispersal – for example the liberation of the peasantry in the French and Russian revolutions, by the division of landed estates. Whether or not this is the best solution where it is possible, it is often not possible. Every society must be gathered at the political level, that is to say, the capacity for violence of the members of society must be brought under a unified command, as Hobbes showed. And we have seen that, with the coming of large-scale production, a degree of economic gatheredness becomes inevitable, and a larger one desirable. In all these contexts, gatheredness must either take the form of placing some people's powers at the disposal of others, or of placing all people's powers at the disposal of all (as a group). The former constitutes oppression and, in economic contexts, generates class divisions. The latter is – *democracy*. For the powers of all are not actually at the disposal of all unless there are procedures whereby that 'all' can dispose these powers. Common ownership, for instance, which (as applied to the means of production) is definitive of socialism, makes no sense without democracy. In the absence of procedures by which the sharers in that common ownership decide what to do with their property, it is a legal fiction. Socialism, as understood by the classical Marxists, *just is* economic democracy. The vertical dimension of politics, the dimension of oppression, class struggle and liberation, *just is* the dimension of democracy versus oligarchy.

However, this is all at a very general level. As soon as we get down to the nuts and bolts, it becomes obvious that there are different kinds, as well as different degrees, of democracy. Various distinctions have been made here: direct or representative democracy, bourgeois or proletarian democracy, formal or material democracy, corrective or constitutive democracy. In trying to make clear what these distinctions are and whether they are useful ones, I shall also be trying to exorcise that utopian spectre which haunts both social democrats (or democratic socialists, as they like to call themselves these days, with scant regard for the meaning of words), and many sectarian Marxists: the spectre of transparent democracy, the society in which democracy is a perfect mechanism for translating the will of the majority into action.

That transparent democracy is only a utopian spectre is partly due to the fact that the same is true of direct democracy, that is of democracy without representation. Even Rousseau, who held that *legislative* authority must remain with the whole people, and could not be delegated; recognised that *government* was best carried out by elected representatives. That does not make him an advocate of *parliamentary* democracy; in parliamentary democracies legislation is performed by representatives, government by unelected, or at best indirectly elected, hierarchies (cabinet, civil service, police, army, judges, etc.). In Rousseau's ideal republic, legislation was to be by plebiscite, government by elected representatives. But government by the whole people is not even physically possible outside a tiny village, and anyway undesirable since it leads to the confusion of the making with the application of laws (for example in lynch-law).

The classical Marxists – of whom Colletti correctly says that they added nothing to Rousseau in political theory in the narrow sense[5] – also believed in representative government. Of course Marx – like

Rousseau, and like all who are seriously committed to democracy – advocated the replacement of a professional army by a people's militia. But he did not think that either military or civil or economic organisation could do without officers, ministers, managers. Consider some of his marginal notes to Bakunin's *Statism and Anarchy*:

> *Bakunin*: Will the entire proletariat perhaps stand at the head of the government?
> *Marx*: In a trade union, for example, does the whole union form its executive committee? Will all division of labour in the factory, and the various functions that correspond to this, cease? And in Bakunin's constitution, will all 'from bottom to top' be 'at the top'?
> *Bakunin*: (of worker-representatives) former workers, who however, as soon as they have become representatives or governors of the people, *cease to be workers* ...
> *Marx*: As little as a factory owner today ceases to be a capitalist if he becomes a municipal councillor ...
> *Bakunin*: ... and look down on the whole common workers' world from the height of the state. They will no longer represent the people, but themselves and their pretensions to people's government. Anyone who can doubt this knows nothing of the nature of men.
> *Marx*: If Mr Bakunin only knew something about the position of a manager in a workers' co-operative factory, all his dreams of domination would go to the devil. He should have asked himself what form the administrative function can take on the basis of this workers' state, if he wants to call it that. (*The First International and After*, pp. 335–7)

Lenin was equally committed to representation: 'We cannot imagine democracy, even proletarian democracy, without representative institutions, but we can and *must* imagine democracy without parliamentarism' ('The State and Revolution', *Selected Works*, p. 297). What Marx and Lenin did not perhaps see so clearly as Rousseau was that representative institutions do *also* (as Bakunin stressed in his one-sided way) have their own dynamic, creating a distinct governmental will, general in relation to the members of the state apparatus, particular in relation to the whole community, which is placed in a particularly advantageous position for the usurpation of sovereignty. It would be better to turn from their utopian notion of the withering away of the state to Rousseau's realistic recognition that the tension between popular sovereignty and governmental ambitions is a permanent feature of any state, and to a conception of democracy as a set of devices for forestalling the usurpation of sovereignty by government. But more of this later.

The distinction between bourgeois and proletarian democracy is most clearly drawn by Lenin in *The State and Revolution*, and other writings of 1917. Before examining his views on this, it is necessary to set a few things straight. The usual image of Lenin in the West – in the minds of some admirers as well as detractors – is of a *pragmatist* and a *Blanquist*. He is generally thought to be an unprincipled (or brilliantly flexible) revolutionary tactician, for whom theory, at which he was weak, was never more than a rationalisation for his marvellously (or fiendishly) cunning *Realpolitik*. This is not the place to argue this point,[6] but my own view is that most of his merits were in the realm of theory; that he was in the first rank of political thinkers, and a philosopher of great acumen and sound judgement; his mistakes as a revolutionary tactician and statesman would be easier to excuse as responses to intolerable conditions, were it not that, under his leadership, the first proletarian democracy in history took a road that made it much less likely that there would ever be a second.[7]

The accusation of Blanquism is more serious, since I am discussing Lenin's theory of democracy, and if that accusation is true, he would be a consistent enemy of democracy. However, that is an *ad hominem* argument, and I shall discuss it elsewhere. Here I am concerned only with the theory of democracy set out in *The State and Revolution*.

Lenin's starting point is the central scientific socialist tenet that no state is class-neutral, however democratic. The socialists of the Second International had accepted this in theory, but tended in practice to think that the non-neutrality lay in the party-composition of parliament – so that a socialist majority would give you a workers' state. As against this, Lenin argues that power in the bourgeois state is not in parliament, but in the coercive and administrative machinery of the state, and that it is the specialised and hierarchic character of this machinery which makes the state a state of the exploiting class, unusable by the exploited.

> Engels elucidates the concept of the 'power' which is called the state, a power which arose from society but places itself above it and alienates itself more and more from it. What does this power mainly consist of? If consists of special bodies of armed men having prisons, etc., at their command. (*Selected Works*, p. 269)

The specialisation is not present in primitive communities, and is made necessary, not by the complexity of modern society, but by its class-divided nature. So this specialised apparatus cannot be taken over as a neutral instrument, it must be 'smashed'. What is to replace it?

> The commune, therefore, appears to have replaced the smashed state machine 'only' by fuller democracy: abolition of the standing army; all officials to be elected and subject to recall. But as a matter of fact this 'only' signifies a gigantic replacement of certain institutions by other institutions of a fundamentally different type. This is exactly a case of 'quantity being transformed into quality': democracy, introduced as fully and consistently as is at all conceivable, is transformed from bourgeois into proletarian democracy; from a state (= a special force for the suppression of a particular class) into something which is no longer the state proper. (*ibid.*, p. 293)

Parliamentary democracy is rejected, not because it is democracy, but because it is *only parliamentary* democracy; we should read the phrase 'parliamentary democracy' with the sort of ironic emphasis one might give the phrase 'an Englishman's word is his bond', if one meant 'never trust his written contract'.

> The way out of parliamentarism is not, of course, the abolition of representative institutions and the elective principle, but the conversion of the representative institutions from talking shops into 'working' bodies ... Take any parliamentary country ... in these countries the real business of 'state' is performed behind the scenes and is carried on by the departments, chancelleries and General Staffs. (*ibid.*, p. 296)

This is open to a possible 'soft left' misinterpretation. The point is not to restore to parliament its 'rightful' powers, removing them from these bureaucratic and military agencies that have usurped them; however hard MPs worked, they could not take on all the administrative (let alone military) functions of the state. The point is to abolish these agencies in their specialised and hierarchic form, and substitute democratic ones, that is in some cases replacing a specialised full-time body by part-time participation of the whole people (for example militia in place of standing army, juries in place of judges), and in other cases, having officials elected 'from below' rather than appointed 'from above'. The supreme assembly would be changed in character primarily by the fact that it rested on a pyramid of democratic institutions, rather than on a pyramid of oligarchic ones. The intrinsic difference between these two types of democracy – the type that can only be used as an instrument of bourgeois power, and the type that can only be used as an instrument of proletarian power, is best captured by the contrast between *formal* and *material* democracy. In all societies, power is exercised by a complex of institutions, usually ones that are not even referred to in constitutional laws; the question what sort of institutions these shall be in any given society is not the sort of thing that can be decided by paper constitutions – it is answered by great historical movements which cannot be legislated into existence; formal democracy tops this structure with a democratic constitution, the institutions of which necessarily conform their decisions to the needs of the real bearers of power; material democracy throws up new powerful institutions of society, which are themselves democratic in nature. Clearly material democracy is more democratic than merely formal democracy – it consists in more institutions being democratic in their internal structure; and it is the transition from formal to material democracy that is the qualitative leap referred to by Lenin. That such a leap cannot be taken by a mere decision of the democratic institutions of a formal democracy – since power does not lie in them, and the institutions in which it does lie will not surrender it voluntarily – is Lenin's case against the possibility of a parliamentary road to socialism: a case which every attempt to find such a road has tragically confirmed; a socialist parliamentary majority, unbacked by institutions of material democracy powerful enough to depose their hierarchic opposite numbers, is a recipe, not for peaceful transition to socialism, but for bloody transition to right-wing dictatorship.

In setting up the case for material democracy in which the powers that operate in society at large, and rule through the formally supreme assembly, are themselves internally democratic organisations, we are not talking about what has been called 'constitutive' (as opposed to corrective) democracy – that is a system which would make the electoral process resulting in the supreme authority into the real locus of power. That remains a utopia – the dream of those who see that parliamentary democracy is not what it claims to be, but do not see why it should not be. Just as in a bourgeois democracy real power is not with parliament but with private economic, and hierarchic state, apparatuses, so in a proletarian democracy it is with workers' (and

Liberation and Instauration 99

other popular) institutions, of democratic internal structure – workers' councils,[8] trade unions, co-operatives, political organisations, militias, etc. But these institutions themselves cannot be made transparently democratic, in the sense of 'constitutive democracy', with power existing nowhere but in the people's will.

This, I think, is the point made by Paul Tillich in the section 'Power and Justice in the Structuring of Society', in his book *The Socialist Decision*.

> The experience of bourgeois democracy confirms the point that there is no social structure without a power group. The difference between democracy and the prebourgeois forms of the state is only this: in a democracy, power groups, even though limited in their scope, dominate without being accountable, while in predemocratic circumstances they are accountable, but therefore unlimited. For socialism this implies a demand that socialism's leading groups, as power groups, be made accountable, yet also subject to democratic controls. Accountability and restraint must be combined.
>
> The democratic principle is in the first instance a *corrective*. It cannot be decided in a democratic way which group is called to exercise social power. That is decided behind the scenes by the real significance a group has in society. But it is certainly possible and necessary to put the existing powers under the scrutiny of the demand for justice, not in an abstract way, but in such a way that all groups are given the possibility of asserting their own demand for justice. But this is possible only through democracy. (p. 142)

That is to say: every society is a power-structure; bourgeois democracy does provide a forum for all groups to press their claims, acting as a corrective to the rule of the really powerful agencies, and such a corrective also has its place in socialism; but bourgeois democracy pretends to be what no democracy can be, 'a social structure without authoritative power groups' in which 'Power belongs to all, and is transferred to those chosen by the majority' (p. 141); real power is therefore exercised outside the public sphere – hence unaccountable.

Paul Tillich is rare among socialists in his recognition that socialist democracy cannot supply what bourgeois democracy pays lip service to in this matter, but should openly avow that socialist society, like any society, has a power structure. In this book (like Tillich's others) his wisdom is not always equalled by his lucidity, but the idea of a constitutive democracy, and the case for its impossibility, is easy to reconstruct. In a constitutive democracy, 'the people', considered as an unstructured mass, is the real power in society, without there being, so to speak, any intermediary structures, or any mechanisms for the exercise of power other than voting, for such structures and mechanisms would inevitably become the real depositories and directing channels of power. This is recognisably Rousseau's ideal, but it is also implicit in Popper's claim that political violence is justifiable only to defend or establish democracy: his assumption is that, in a democracy, any possible change can be brought about simply by getting a majority for it; Popper refuses to see what stares any student of history or politics in the face – that 'It cannot be decided in a democratic way which group is called to exercise social power.' The case against constitutive democracy is not at the level of 'value judgements', but of certain facts about all human societies, irrespective of class structure – facts which are not the effects of oppression, though they are the condition of the possibility of various forms of oppression: that all societies have internal structures, they are not simple relations of each to all; that the transmission-belts of power from people's choices to public action are necessarily both constraining channels of that power, and loci of forces other than 'the people's will'; that the different social positions which citizens occupy carry with them different powers; that the relation of representative to represented is such as to place certain powers in the hands of the representative which make it impossible for them to be *nothing but* a deputy or servant; that the degree of gatheredness or dispersedness of different social groups develops unevenly – and therefore so does their power. Scientific socialism substitutes for the spectre of constitutive or transparent democracy the possibility of making the real social agencies which are necessarily the loci of power – workplaces, armed forces, etc. – democratic in their internal structure. Hence Marx's comments on Bakunin:

> Election is a political form present in the smallest Russian commune and artel. The character of the election does not depend on this name but on the economic foundations, the economic situation of the voters ...
> With collective ownership the so-called people's will vanishes, to make way for the real will of the co-operative. (*The First International and After*, p. 336)

The supreme assembly in a socialist commonwealth – however it were elected – could only, like a bourgeois parliament, be a clearing house where many different social agencies, too powerful to be overridden however much a majority might wish to do so, were accommodated and co-ordinated, and an integrated policy arrived at. This would be so, I say, however it were elected. Since the experience of 1917, it has been widely recognised as an important feature of 'material democracy' that the units represented are real social units (for example factories), not arbitrary geographical aggregations of individuals voting in an atomised fashion. At the most basic, 'grass roots' level of democracy, this is of the first importance. Voting should take place among a real community of people, united by the objective gatheredness of their powers. In this situation, they are far more likely to know what, or whom, they are voting for, take responsibility for their decisions, and be immune to deception by mass propaganda or hearsay. Socialists are right to oppose postal ballots, which register nothing but the influence of the makers of 'public opinion', and to support voting at meetings. At this level, 'direct democracy' has an essential place – in the factory, the village, the street, or the local branch of an organisation. But if such local democracy is not linked to wider (necessarily *representative*) democratic institutions, its value is nullified by its dispersedness. And when we are concerned with constituencies of, perhaps, hundreds of thousands, it makes little difference whether they are united by occupation or geography. The essential difference between the summit institution of a material democracy and that of a formal democracy is in the fact that the strings that pull the one are held by democratic institutions, the other by oligarchic ones; and beyond that, by the fact the the electors' opinions in a material democracy are formed in the process of exercising collective control over their conditions of life, rather than consumed ready made in the belief-making factories of Fleet Street or Wapping.

Socialists should have learnt from the experience of internal democracy in existing trade unions, trades councils, co-operatives and political groups that such institutions, which are to be the very texture of socialist society, are beset with tensions between representatives and represented, members and full-timers, leaders and conferences – by no means all of which tensions could be eliminated either by constitutional reform or by the changed context of a socialist commonwealth. Democracy cannot be an unimpeded flow of decisions from bottom to top; it can only be groups of people getting together to place constraints on their governors. *Groups*: democracy cannot exist where people are atomised, for atomised people are powerless; *constraints*: the government can never *express* the will of the people, but only be pushed or held back by it (or rather, by 'the real will of the co-operative' – or co-operatives). The right to de-select one's representatives in periodic elections is one important mechanism of constraint, but not the only one, nor even the most important.

All this means that democracy is a matter of degree, not 'all or nothing'. One cannot have pure democracy but neither can one have pure tyranny (other than in most exceptional circumstances), since even a tyrant rests on a degree of consent, and by the same token is constrained by a degree of potential resistance. The degree of democracy cannot be measured by any single indicator (such as the nature of elections) since it is also determined by such things as freedom of information, and distribution of the power to disseminate it, distribution of economic power and the extent to which it can be used to deflect government policies, distribution and organisation of armaments, and so on. A country with a people's militia, economic equality and popular access to the media might be more democratic even without elections than a country with free elections but lacking these features. An institution may be conducive to democracy at one time and destructive of it at another: nineteenth-century democrats such as Marx and John Stuart Mill were right to regard freedom of the press as essential to democracy, yet it is now one of the main obstacles to democracy, and something like the original Soviet press law (never, alas, to be implemented), introducing a sort of proportional representation into the control of that medium, would be more to the point. The test of democracy can only be: how much can the people push or pull the government, and what happens when they do?

This in turn means that the degree to which the supreme assembly (parliament or whatever) gets its way is not necessarily a positive indicator of democracy. Certainly, parliament is more likely to reflect popular interests than are, say, the multinationals, or the General Staff of the British Army, but that is a feature of the undemocratic nature of those institutions. It is (to say the least) not obvious that the Long Parliament represented popular interests better than Cromwell's army, or Ted Heath's parliament than the trade unions that brought him down, or the Portuguese Constituent Assembly than the Armed Forces Movement, or the *Sejm* than *Solidarnosc* (I am referring to the period up to 1981).

Further, these considerations make it clear that democracy has nothing whatsoever to do with *majority* rule. Majority decisions have a place in all sorts of constitution, from triumvirates to the House of Lords. And rules requiring numerical preponderance of more than 51 per cent (for example the two-thirds majority necessary to override the President's veto in the United States, or the three-quarters of states required to endorse amendments to its constitution), may be good or bad, but would not be called undemocratic. And we would *not* call a country democratic if a permanent substantial minority were effectively excluded from public life by the coherence of a permanently hostile majority (as has happened to Blacks in America, Catholics in Northern Ireland – and perhaps, increasingly, to Welsh, Scottish and Northern English people in the United Kingdom).

With all this in mind, a comparison of bourgeois democracies with some other states that exist or have existed may not be so favourable to the former as many, even socialists, usually think. Of course bourgeois democracies are infinitely better countries to live in than other forms of bourgeois state: fascism and military dictatorship. But even that is not primarily because of free elections. Rather, parliamentary democracy and the relative freedom and humaneness that characterises these countries are effects of a common cause: a workers' movement strong enough to limit capitalist power (though not to oust it). Fascism and military dictatorship are either means to, or effects of, the crushing of the workers' movement. A bourgeois state which managed to crush the workers' movement yet retain the forms of parliamentary democracy might be every bit as nasty. 'Formal democracy' – the free election of the supreme authority – is usually worth defending, but never worth fetishising. Sometimes, other considerations should override it. We would probably be safer from nuclear annihilation if the American President was *not* subjected to a four-yearly check on his *machismo*.

Finally, a recognition that the seats of power are necessarily *outside* supreme representative assemblies (whether those seats are themselves democratic as in material democracy, or oligarchic as in the formal democracies of capitalism) should dispel the naive superstition that when 51 per cent vote for socialism, the capitalists and their state officers will (unless perhaps they are cads) hand over their wealth and power and take early retirement. It should also dispel the levity of Eurocommunists who promise that, should 51 per cent in a socialist democracy vote to restore capitalism, they would behave with the same polite irresponsibility. Can anyone *really* imagine a country with evenly balanced capitalist and socialist parties, in which every five years, on the basis of 2 per cent swing, caused perhaps by a wet summer, all the country's factories would be transferred from workers' committees to shareholders and back again, health care would switch from free to fee-paying and back again, universities for the people would become finishing schools for public school kids and then universities for the people again, people's militias would give way to nuclear weapons and replace them again – and so on? Could one even respect the statesmanship of anyone – on whichever side of the barricade – who sat back and permitted such transitions to occur? These are not things that can be decided like the members of a club might vote whether to paint the clubhouse blue or green. Power, of whichever form, lies deep in the texture of society, not at its pinnacle (that is the supreme assembly). History can no more produce societies in the form of inverted pyramids than nature can produce mountains in the form of inverted pyramids.

Appendix

'Existing Socialism'

The question arises, if socialism is by definition democratic, and if material democracy is the kind that uniquely embodies workers' power, what is to be said of the 'existing socialist' countries, Russia, China and their allies. Clearly, their degree of democracy, both formal and material, is generally low, and in some cases non-existent. A purist adherent of classical Marxism can really only say one of two things: that they are a specific mutation of capitalism, 'state capitalism'; or that they are a new mode of production and exploitation, which some have called 'bureaucratic collectivism'. Either way, they would be analysed as class societies. For if, as Trotsky said, the state owns the industry but the bureaucracy sort of owns the state, then (*pace* Trotsky) the bureaucracy 'sort of' owns industry too, and might be expected to make rich pickings from the exploitation of the workers.

Of these two hypotheses, the state capitalist one (to which I adhered until recently) is the weaker for several reasons:

(i) planning and the market occupy quite different relative roles than in traditional capitalism. Of course there are market mechanisms in 'existing socialist' countries, and there is planning in the West, but the difference is not just more of one here and the other there. This is one of those 'dialectical leaps' where quantitative change passes into change of kind. Furthermore, a healthy workers' state would have, for the foreseeable future, no fewer market mechanisms than the 'existing socialist' countries do.
(ii) All the evidence seems to show that a parliamentary road to 'existing socialism' is as manifestly impossible as a parliamentary road to socialism.
(iii) The 'existing socialist' countries have generally formed a 'camp' – or camps – distinct from traditional capitalist countries, and in antagonism to them in world affairs. Such exceptions as there are to this are of the sort that prove the rule (that is their manifest exceptionality makes it clear what the rule is, like 'man bites

Liberation and Instauration 105

dog'). If they are only another sort of capitalist country, one would expect their alliances to be much more shifting and varied.

But more than this can be said: the 'existing socialist' countries have in most cases been (once the state of siege resulting from post-revolutionary insecurity and hostile encirclement has been lifted) much better than a Marxist purist would expect, in several ways.

(a) Most of them have secured a degree of economic equality, and of equality of opportunity between the sexes, and between manual and non-manual working families, unequalled in class societies.
(b) They have achieved (within the limits of the nation-state) a degree of economic gatheredness, and hence of human control over social forces (even though it is control by some, not by all) unequalled in other times and places.
(c) Their international policy has, with very few exceptions, been both more conducive to peace, and more favourable to progressive movements in the 'Third World', than has that of Western capitalist countries.
(d) The people's freedom (once again: since siege-conditions have ceased) has – whatever its absolute level – tended to increase as time goes on, whereas in the West it tends to decrease in certain important respects.
(e) Even ideologically, despite the state interference (of greatly varied extent in different times and places) in intellectual, artistic, scientific and religious life, and the consequent inhibition of development in these areas, there is a commitment to certain values of the Enlightenment, on which the West has largely reneged: the value of objective knowledge and rationality in theory and practice; of conscious human control of natural and social forces; the idea of the essential unity of humankind, as opposed to its supposedly inevitable dispersion into mutually uncomprehending races, sexes or cultures. In the West even the left – perhaps I should have said particularly the left – has ratted on these ideas.
(f) Finally, although the liberation movements which might have inaugurated a full, socialist democracy have been repeatedly defeated in 'existing socialist' countries – Hungary 1956, Czechoslovakia 1968, Poland 1981 – the striking fact is that they got so far. Perhaps if wiser counsels had prevailed in the Kremlin, or the Soviet Army had been busy elsewhere, they might have succeeded. They have come closer than anywhere in the West since the 1920s – even republican Spain and Chile under Popular Unity. And if such movements did succeed, it would hardly be such a total upheaval for the societies in question as would a socialist takeover in a Western capitalist country – that at least is something that Trotsky got right.

For these reasons, 'existing socialist' countries are, for all their faults, the torchbearers of human progress and civilisation today. Yet the stubborn fact remains that one cannot honestly talk about workers' power or common ownership existing in them: only bureaucratic power and state ownership.

Using the concepts that I have been discussing in this chapter, the 'existing socialist' countries can be described as ones with a high degree of gatheredness (within the limits of the nation-state), but a low degree of democracy. It is therefore not surprising that they have some of the benefits of gatheredness (for example full employment, the non-existence of a lobby of arms-profiteers), or that they lack some of the benefits of democracy (for example freedom for opposition parties, the non-existence of prisoners of conscience). What *is* surprising is that they have some of the benefits that one would expect to flow from democracy rather than from gatheredness (for example economic equalities); and it is noteworthy that the issue of material, as well as formal, democracy tends to get raised whenever there is a popular upsurge – that the idea of material democracy is endemic in the ideology of those countries, even though it is not realised in them.

One explanation, which is no doubt part of the truth, is that these are cases of the economic and political effects of ideology. Just as the bourgeoisie's work-ethic could be used to lend force to demands for a better deal for workers, and its arguments for representative government made it difficult to resist the demand for universal suffrage, so the Communist Party's goal of a classless society makes it difficult for it to justify great inequalities of income, and its invocation against the bourgeois democracies of Marx's praise of the Paris Commune and Lenin's of workers' councils has kept material democracy on the agenda. But while ideology has its own efficacy, it is never self-explanatory. I would suggest that the deeper reason is that the tendency towards greater gatheredness, which is inherent in the structure of the 'existing socialist' countries, itself generates a tendency towards democratisation, since those sections of the people who are excluded from power inevitably resist, with a degree of success, the gathering of *their* powers into the public power. For instance (a point which some Trotskyists have overplayed, but which is real enough), planners who exclude the workers from the planning process forgo the information that only the workers could have provided. The degree of gatheredness desired by the bureaucracy requires the people's confidence and willing service, which in turn requires the people's belief that they, not only the bureaucrats, will benefit – and you can't fool all the people all the time. Some scientific socialists, usually in the Trotskyist tradition, have argued that it is actually *impossible* to have planning without democracy. Scott Meikle, for instance, in his book *Essentialism in the Thought of Karl Marx*, claims that the Soviet economy, since it is not run by the associated producers as a whole, is not planned at all. I think that is too far-fetched. But in order to understand why there are serious moves, even from the top, for openness and democratisation in government, we have to suppose that lack of democracy sets a limit to gatheredness, and hence that a system which tends to maximise gatheredness will generate a tendency to democratisation. And since the primary locus of the tendency towards gatheredness is the economy, such moves can never be made in the political arena without generating at least the demand for, sometimes the actuality of, their extension to the workplace.

At this point, it may look as if I have overstated my case, for if such a tendency to democratisation exists, why has it not triumphed? One might say, of course, that the democratic tendency of representative government was visible as early as the Putney Debates of 1647, yet no fully independent country had universal suffrage until the twentieth century. But a historical parallel is not an explanation.

Rather, we should look at the fact that, while *internally* gathered, the 'existing socialist' countries are dispersed as nation-states, competing with each other and the West; and in particular, that they are (whatever the balance of power in firepower terms) the economically poorer military camp(s) in the cold war. It is the consequent drive to catch up that has generated most of the economic similarities with capitalism which the theorists of state capitalism point out; politically, it has elevated foreign affairs and defence to the status of overriding factors in policy – a situation which is never conducive to democracy, East or West.

These considerations have implications for the attitude of Western socialists to the 'existing socialist' countries. It goes without saying that we deplore the lack of democratic liberties and support every movement for material democracy, such as the workers' councils in Hungary in 1956, the Prague Spring, *Solidarnosc*. But we must also defend these countries against Western imperialism, for several reasons: (i) because Western imperialism is the cold war aggressor, and, with its private arms profiteers, structurally prone to warmongering, while the economic interests of the 'existing socialist' countries are in peace; hence the interest of the 'existing socialist' economies coincides with that of human survival; (ii) because we have a common cause with them in support for liberation movements in the 'Third World'; (iii) because the *potential* for socialist democracy is greater in the 'existing socialist' countries; they are likely to be the first countries to achieve it; and (iv) because the best service we can do for those pressing for democratic liberties in the 'existing socialist' countries is to end the cold war and the threat of Western imperialism.

Notes

1. 'The Great Instauration' is the title of Bacon's projected (and unfinished) *magnum opus*, of which *The New Organon* is a part. The word 'instauration' means 'restoration', that is, of the dominion over nature supposed to be possessed by Adam before the fall:

   > For man by the fall fell at the same time from his state of innocency and from his dominion over creation. Both these losses however can even in this life be in some part repaired; the former by religion and faith, the latter by arts and sciences. (Bacon, 'The New Organon', in *The English Philosphers from Bacon to Mill*, p. 123)

   Since the word 'instauration' is never now used except with reference to Bacon, I introduced it here to emphasise the identity between Bacon's project of the augmentation of our power over nature through the union of science with labour, and the 'horizontal' project of scientific socialism.

2. '... this development of productive forces ... is an absolutely necessary practical premise because without it, *want* is merely made general, and with *destitution* the struggle for necessities would begin again, and all the old filthy business would necessarily be reproduced' (*The German Ideology*, p. 56). 'So long as the total social labour only yields a produce which but slighty exceeds that barely necessary for the

existence of all; so long, therefore, as labour engages all or almost all the time of the great majority of the members of society – so long, of necessity, is this society divided into classes ...

'But if, upon this showing, division into classes has a certain historical justification, it has this only for a given period, only under given social conditions. It was based upon the insufficiency of production. It will be swept away by the complete development of modern productive forces' (*Anti-Dühring*, p. 334).

3. Cf. Marx's preface to the programme of the French Worker's Party:

> Considering,
> That the emancipation of the class of producers involves all mankind, without distinction of sex or race;
> That the producers can only be free when they are in possession of the means of production;
> That there are only two forms in which the means of production can belong to them:
> 1. The individual form, which was never a universal phenomenon and is being ever more superseded by the progress of industry;
> 2. The collective form, the material and mental elements for which are created by the very development of capitalist society; ... (*The First International and After*, p. 376)

4. The higher animals have of course got feelings, and this generates certain responsibilities towards them on the part of human beings. But nature as such cannot be said to feel or intend, without falling into the sort of mythology to which some Nazis were, and some 'deep ecologists' are, prone. Cf. Marcuse on Nazi economics in 'The Struggle Against Liberalism in the Totalitarian View of the State': 'The current crisis is "nature's revenge" on the "intellectual attempt to violate its laws ... But nature always wins in the end" ' (*Negations*, p. 26). (It is not clear from Marcuse's text which Nazi writer is quoted here).

5. '... so far as "political" theory in the strict sense is concerned, Marx and Lenin have added nothing to Rousseau, except for the analysis (which is of course rather important) of the "economic bases" for the withering away of the state' (Colletti, *From Rousseau to Lenin*, p. 185). From my point of view, while the stress on the economic bases of politics in general is Marx's real advance on Rousseau, the notion of the withering away of the state is less helpful than Rousseau's conception of democratic politics as concerned with a series of devices for forestalling the 'usurpation of the sovereignty by government' – a usurpation which has, of course, taken place in every 'existing socialist' country.

6. Neill Harding's excellent book *Lenin's Political Thought* has done something to correct the balance. But Tony Cliff's four-volume *Lenin*

is as guilty as any of treating Lenin as a (brilliantly flexible) pragmatist, though of course on the issue of Blanquism versus revolutionary democracy Cliff is on the side of the angels. Virtually all modern anti-Marxist biographies treat Lenin as a cunning but mindless Blanquist – even those that are well researched on everything except Lenin's ideas.

7. The mistakes I am referring to are (i) Lenin's utopian attitude to private trade (corrected too late, by the New Economic Policy); (ii) his sanctioning of terror as an instrument of policy (and not only, in common with all wartime leaders, as a means of waging the civil war); (iii) the suppression of the Soviet opposition parties (Mensheviks, Socialist Revolutionaries and Anarchists), and of factions within the Communist Party, just when (since the civil war was won) Soviet democracy should have been made more and more open.

8. By 'workers' councils' I am referring to institutions such as the soviets of the Russian revolutionary period (and some other times, for example the *Biennio Rosso* in Italy, and Hungary in 1956). It would have been convenient to retain the Russian word 'soviet' (even though it only means 'council') to distinguish these from other kinds of council. But aside from the fact that the soviets in Russia are no longer what they were, English usage is increasingly calling citizens of the Soviet Union 'soviets' – though etymologically that makes no more sense than calling a citizen of the United Kingdom a united king.

Part II
Meta-Political Ideas

4
How to Talk about Values by Talking about Facts

I hope the last chapters have given some indication how a political theory can be scientific in the sense that it consists of a set of laws accounting for what can and can't happen in the real world – a set of theories about what exists, how it is to be explained, and what makes it possible – and at the same time can be an action-guiding theory. I now want to defend and generalise this claim that practical reasoning can be a work of explanation rather than injunction – or rather, injunction only as an effect of explanation.

It is a curious fact that the defence of this position, 'ethical naturalism', often elicits charges of monstrous wickedness, just as the non-naturalism of Ayer, Sartre and even Hare once did. In fact, neither position is more likely than the other to be associated with Machiavellian politics, Stirnerian indifference to others, or Sadean orgies. Nevertheless there is a connection (though not one of entailment) between the two sorts of rejection of naturalism: the metamoral position (usually associated with Hume), *non-naturalism*, which maintains that, as a matter of logic or even grammar, indicative premises cannot support imperative conclusions, so that naturalism is said to be a fallacy; and the substantive moral position *anti-naturalism* (for example Kant), which claims that the source of morality is transcendent to, not immanent in, the human condition. For the only possible naturalist case against the latter is an explanatory critique which shows the natural, but disreputable, origins of supposedly transcendent moralities; for example, that anti-natural morality is (as Nietzsche says) 'only a value judgement of life – but of what life? of what kind of life? ... of declining, weakened, weary, condemned life' (*Twilight of the Idols*, in *The Portable Nietzsche*, p. 490). Non-naturalism secretes a protective layer around anti-naturalism by saying that it is *a priori* impossible that such biological (or psychological, or social) facts can have any moral relevance.

Why Shouldn't we Talk about Values by Talking about Facts?

The idea that there is a radical difference between scientific and moral discourse has come to be treated as so obvious that it is widely taken for granted that the attempt to put socialist theory on a scientific footing was an abdication of the right to prescribe, and that if for example Marx nevertheless wrote sentences in the imperative ('Workers of all countries unite!') he was forgetting himself – either consciously taking time off from science or surreptitiously smuggling in unscientific utterances. Yet before Hume and Kant, moral thinkers took it for granted that the way to talk about values was to talk about facts. The ancient Greeks never doubted this, whether the facts were about social power and convention (the sophists), or an eternal world of objective values (Plato) or the nature of humanity as a rational social animal (Aristotle). St Augustine's ethic is entirely ontological: creation as a hierarchy of more or less perfect beings, with correspondingly greater or lesser claims on our love. Spinoza's ethics is entirely in the indicative; Hobbes never doubts he can deduce obligation from human nature.

Hume's remarks about the unexplained passage from 'is' to 'ought' therefore calls in question a lot more than the 'vulgar moralists' of his time. Was he right? Well, if all he meant to do was point out that practical reasoning is not like deductive reasoning, yes. But then *evidential* reasoning is not like deductive reasoning either. It is now, I think, generally agreed that Hume ought not to have been worried about the fact that evidential (inductive) reasoning is not deductive like logic or mathematics. Could not reasoning from 'is' to 'ought' be similarly acceptable, though non-deductive? Alasdair MacIntyre suggests[1] that Hume's real aim was to point out that, as non-deductive, reasonings from facts to values were *questionable*. It needed to be explained how a given fact supported a given value-judgement. Granted that mice are higher beings than cheese, ought we really to prefer to have mice rather than cheese in the cupboard? (an issue which troubled St Augustine).[2] And Hume has an *answer* to the question about which facts are morally relevant: they are the facts about which human qualities are pleasant or useful to their bearer or others. So that Hume's formal non-naturalism does not lead him to reject substantive naturalism – that is the doctrine that we can arrive at moral conclusions by finding out what is true about certain aspects of the real world. Indeed, I shall claim that he and Spinoza are the two philosophers from whom ethical naturalism can learn most.

The real break with the naturalist tradition comes with Kant. Yet it never occurred to Kant to suggest anything so absurd as that practical conclusions could not be argued from factual premises. Indeed, his discussion of assertoric imperatives shows how it can be done: by combining technical knowledge that if you want A you must do B, with the 'anthropological' knowledge that everyone wants A. Kant fully recognised the possibility, and the necessity within its own sphere, of naturalistic practical reasoning. But he claims that it is not *moral* reasoning; that moral reasoning is non-naturalistic, and ought to override naturalistic practical reasoning when the two conflict.

It is my view that Kant's anti-naturalist morality ought to be rejected. My reasons will become clear later. But it should be clear now that such rejection does not leave us with no values at all, as is often stated. Kant believed it would leave us with *lower* values. I believe that most modern arguments against naturalism rest on a conflation of the Kantian gap between naturalist practical reasoning and anti-naturalistic morality, with the Humean gap between indicative discourse and imperative discourse of whatever type. The Humean gap need not stop us talking about values by talking about facts, so long as we have an account of how a factual judgement can support an evaluative or prescriptive one. And the Kantian gap need not worry us provided we are happy (morally happy) about a morality without any anti-naturalistic components. There are also reasons other than the influence (and conflation) of Kant and Hume, why people find ethical naturalism implausible. There is the fact, which is particularly salient in modern times, of breakdown in moral argument. When a socialist comrade to whom I wrote defending naturalism replied by asking 'are there no fascists, only ignorant humanitarians?', this was one of the issues he was raising. Arguments with fellow-socialists or even with liberals may turn on factual disputes, but how can one reason with a Nazi?

In the first place, though there are fascists, there are also millions of people who, under certain conditions (such as those prevailing in Germany in the early 1930s) will vote for fascism, who might well be described as ignorant humanitarians. We may assume that the number of hard-core Nazis, immune to humanitarian considerations, was relatively small. I do not think it would be very useful to argue with these hard-core Nazis, by talking about facts, *or at all!* For the most part, they would have agreed with Hitler that reasoning was a Jewish habit which iron-willed Aryans could do without. There may well have been Nazis who would not listen to reason, yet had some values such that, with a different input of factual beliefs, they would be compelled *if rational* to abandon their Nazism. But the idea that a Nazi might listen to reason, come to agree with his humanitarian interlocutor as to the facts, but remain a Nazi, is a non-starter. The values of the hard-core Nazi involve false factual beliefs, and these beliefs differ as vastly from those a reasonable person might hold as Nazi values do from humanitarian values. It is not the evaluative as opposed to factual nature of the difference that makes it unbridgeable, it is its sheer vastness. Confronted with someone who believes that the human race is actually several distinct species, and that the conspiratorial aims of one of those species explain both American capitalism and the Bolshevik Revolution, one is as much at a loss as with a man who thinks he is a leopard.[3]

Granted that such hard-core Nazis are rather rare, anti-Nazi propaganda can indeed be purely factual. Some of the best anti-NF literature I have seen consisted of bald facts about immigration, its relation to the economy, and so on. Much of it was produced by the Socialist Workers Party, who understand very well that, when such facts are not effective, what you need is not to preach values, but to throw bricks.

If we leave the Nazis out, it is very easy to see that what politicians find it most difficult to agree about is not values but facts. Probably every member of parliament believes in a free and prosperous Britain, but not all agree with Margaret Thatcher that the most efficient means to this end is to let factories rust and mines fill with water, inner cities decay, workers lose their skill and their self-respect through unemployment, public assets be sold off cheap, education be decimated, the commonwealth disintegrate, and key industries be bought up by the Americans.

Finally, there are those who hold to the fact/value dichotomy because they think that political discourse is more honest and less confused if they are segregated – if, for instance, a newspaper keeps 'news and views' separate. This view gains some of its credibility from the fact that some of its opponents do repudiate objectivity and flaunt their persuasive definitions, deriving, not values from facts, but 'facts' from values. Of such people, I can only say: show me a journalist who denies that there is such a thing as objective reporting, and I'll show you a hired liar. But objectivity does not gain from the attempt to segregate facts from values. Objectivity is not the same as neutrality. The statements 'in Germany under Hitler millions of Jews died', and 'in Germany under Hitler, millions of Jews were massacred', are both objective, but the latter is more so, since it fills in more information.[4] In some contexts, the former could be used to mislead, by suggesting the falsity of the latter. But the latter, precisely by virtue of giving more information, is not neutral. By and large, words and sentences have the evaluative force that they do by virtue of, not in addition to, their factual meaning.

It may be possible, occasionally, to substitute one word for another, altering the evaluative force of the sentence, while retaining the factual content. But this is very much the exception. Terms of racist abuse sometimes fall into this category. The offensiveness of words like 'kike' or 'nigger' derives not from their etymology or from any factual content, but from the fact that the communities in which these words are used are communities in which prejudice against the groups concerned prevails. The use of such words is obviously to be avoided in honest political discourse. But this hardly gets us started as far as fact/value segregation is concerned, and such cases can certainly not serve (as they have sometimes been used) as a model for fact-value relations in language generally. The short life of euphemism is a witness to that: a euphemism is an attempt to replace a word that carries a negative evaluative charge with one that is a synonym so far as factual content is concerned, but without the negative charge; but since the value-content is generally an effect of the factual it rapidly re-emerges and kills the euphemism.

I want now to give an alternative account of the kind of political reporting that gets non-neutrality a bad name. We need to distinguish two kinds of non-neutral political language: language can (I am arguing) be non-neutral because of its objective content, and any attempt to *neuter* such language distorts its objective content. 'Millions of innocent civilians were massacred' is not a neutral statement, though entirely objective. 'The kulak class was liquidated' or 'the rural base of Vietcong operations was eliminated', though objective, are as misleading by their incompleteness as if they were lies, and their incompleteness serves precisely to neuter the fuller, objective account which would include the former statement. It is hard to see what would count as an *honest* separation of facts and values in such cases. Adding a bare value-judgement, 'and this was a Bad Thing', as a footnote to one of the neutered statements would be worse than useless.

There is however an important requirement on objective reporting, which is sometimes misdescribed as the demand for neutral reporting. There are statements which are ambiguous between two objective contents; one may be true, the other supply the evaluative force. To start with a politically innocent example (though not a perfect one, since it rests on a misuse of English), take the National Trust sticker: 'I'm one in a million'. For its factual justification, this is presumably supposed to be read as 'I'm one *of* a million', i.e. 'there are a million of us, and I'm one'. But the proper meaning of 'I'm one in a million', that is 'I'm unique among a million' is surely also meant to be understood, providing a quite gratuitous sense of self-esteem.

To give two less innocuous kinds of example:

(i) technical terms in the human sciences and in philosophy are only ever justified to eliminate ambiguities which exist in the non-technical language. Where a technical term is homonymous with an expression in non-technical language, it is important to ensure that the ordinary-language meaning does not cling to it. Sometimes, technical terms are actually chosen to function by means of their ordinary-language meaning, while being sheltered behind the screen of supposed technical exactness should anyone object to the ordinary associations of the word. For instance (as I have said elsewhere) if 'rational economic agent' is defined to mean 'person who pursues monetary gain in preference to all other aims', its corresponding term in ordinary English is not its homonym, but 'moneygrubber'.

(ii) In political uses of language, there is very often a habitual discrepancy between sense and reference, such as Voltaire noted in the title of the Holy Roman Empire ('neither holy nor Roman nor an empire' – in fact, a loose confederation of German states). For instance:

(1) 'Free world': the sense unpacks as, roughly, 'countries with elected parliaments, freedom of speech, freedom from arbitrary arrest or torture, etc.'; the reference unpacks as 'Britain, France, USA, South Africa, Saudi Arabia, El Salvador, etc.' – not the same thing at all.

(2) 'Democratic socialist': the sense unpacks as 'one who advocates common ownership of economic resources, under governments freely elected by the people'; the reference unpacks as 'Denis Healey, Roy Hattersley, Neil Kinnock, etc.' – that is people who can only just make their minds up to re-nationalise British Gas, and who support the manifestly undemocratic 'first past the post' electoral system, in

the hope of coming into office should 34 per cent of those who bother to vote think they are the least of three evils.

What is needed here is a higher standard of unambiguous discourse in politics, so that the evaluative content of what is said will be none other than that which flows from its factual content.

Finally, a less reputable reason why some people want facts and values to be segregated in political discourse. When politicians start talking about *values* instead of about *policies*, the response that they want – and very often get – is that they are taking the debate on to a nobler plane, or getting down to real fundamentals. In reality, they are usually being vague and evasive. First, because many political value-words ('freedom', 'justice', 'equality') have no agreed content, apart from the fact that everyone uses them to mean something that they think is good. Secondly, because even if we could agree a definition and a set of examples for each of these concepts, we are talking more generally, less concretely, when we use these words than when we give the examples. Better to give the examples: the arguments for, say, increasing pensions are likely to be much stronger than the arguments for 'justice' or whatever other value might be appealed to as a 'reason' for increasing them – just as Mill's arguments for particular liberties are much stronger than his argument for 'liberty'. The function of value-words in political discourse is often not that of providing such redundant justifications anyway – it is rather that, when a politician who has promised to increase pensions foresees reasons why he or she might break that promise, he or she retreats to promising 'justice' or a 'caring society'.

The truth is, we have no idea what policies will be motivated by a value until that value is replaced in its natural setting among the facts. Strip values of their factual basis, and everyone can agree about them. I understand that a survey of political attitudes in Britain has shown that a majority of supporters of all parties, from Communist to National Front, place 'freedom' at the head of their list of values. But just try to get two politicians – even slightly removed from each other's position in the spectrum – to agree about the causes of inflation or the prospects for full employment. The intractability of political disagreements, which has tempted some misguided philosophers to try to apply emotivism in this area, in fact requires quite a different kind of theory to explain it: a theory of ideological obstacles to objectivity in forming one's factual beliefs.

Why Should we Talk about Values by Talking about Facts?

I want to discuss only one answer to this question in this section; other reasons have, I hope, already emerged, and still more will do so, in the course of other arguments.

In moral reasoning – and practical reasoning generally – one important thing that is going on is that people are being persuaded to do what they would perhaps not otherwise have done. There are several ways one might go about such persuasion. One is by making the person better informed about the facts of the case – including, importantly, how other people will be affected by it. Perhaps also, more trickily, helping them in increasing their self-knowledge. At the other extreme, one might lie to them, threaten them with temporal or eternal punishment, subject them to moral blackmail. As Nietzsche has said, 'Every means that has hitherto been employed for making mankind moral has been absolutely immoral.'[5] Now if there is a paradigm case of a means of persuasion which is *not* immoral – which respects the autonomy (in a certain sense of the word) of the agent – it is persuasion by information and argument, by 'reason' in the Humean sense of matters of fact and relations of ideas, evidence and logic. But a great deal of moral and political persuasion is not of this kind. It works by flattering vanity, by abusing third parties and appealing to chumminess against *them*, by inducing views in someone by attributing them to them already, by the use of ambiguities such as those discussed in the last section, and so on. That this happens in political argument is commonplace; that it happens in moral persuasion too is perhaps hidden by the fact that such persuasion largely takes place in childhood, and is a *fait accompli* by the time mature moral reasoning gets started.

Are there means of moral persuasion which *neither* violate autonomy *nor* resolve into cognitive enlightenment? By example, perhaps? I would suggest that the means whereby example induces moral beliefs would require critical attention. They can in fact be cognitive: 'it is possible to live thus, and here is how it is done.' They can also be *hypnotic*: the projection of the super-ego on to a hero. This is perhaps the worst kind of moral influence. Even if the hero is well chosen (which itself requires cognitive reason in making the selection) – we can no doubt all think of people who combine the qualities of many truly great thinkers: Bacon's venality, Rousseau's touchiness, Hegel's pomposity, Kierkegaard's self-dramatisation, Nietzsche's misogyny,

Marx's abusive polemical style, Wittgenstein's intellectual coyness, and so on.

'Getting someone to see things differently' might be another candidate for non-cognitive moral persuasion; I suspect that any plausible concrete example will turn out to be a case of seeing different things, or of attending to different aspects of what one sees.

It may be asked, if we remove indicative discourse from moral discourse, whether what remains can be called moral *reasoning* at all, as distinct from moral cajoling, seducing, haranguing, etc. If reasoning involves removing contradictions, these must be contradictions between indicative propositions. Values, considered aside from their factual foundation, cannot be said to contradict each other. They can *conflict*, in that it may not be possible, in a given case, to act in accordance both with the value of (for example) truthfulness and that of kindness. But that sort of conflict is not something that should lead us to revise our ethic in order to eliminate it. Such conflicts are inevitable in any sensitive morality. Someone might say that these values only conflict contingently, and that it would be irrational to have two diametrically opposed values as part of one's ethic. Even this seems to me mistaken; one might value both returning good for evil, and fighting evil. There is nothing unreasonable about doing so: they *are* both good, but in different ways. In order to say anything about why they are good, in what ways, and in which cases each should be applied, we would have to start talking about facts – psychology, both inter- and intra-personal, social structures, conflicts and dynamics, and so on.

The naturalism that I am defending can be described as a *critically rational, historical* naturalism. Naturalism can be characterised as theory of ethical imperatives as assertoric imperatives. In Kant's assertoric imperative, the minor premiss, which asserts the antecedent of the conditional major premiss, is anthropological: that is, it makes a general statement about human beings such as that we desire happiness. In its contracted form the assertoric imperative will read 'Since you wish to be happy, do such-and-such!' The naturalism that I wish to defend is historical rather than anthropological in character. Its minor premisses are statements about particular socio-historically situated groups of people. So we may get assertoric imperatives of the form: 'Since you are an exploited worker (with the interests that that entails), strive for socialism.' Of course, a whole body of socio-economic analysis and explanation is presupposed by and summed up in such a judgement; both the proof that being an exploited worker involves having certain interests and unavoidably being engaged in certain struggles; and the proof that socialism is necessary for the success of those struggles and the furtherance of those interests. This is not the place to provide those proofs; the point is that they are clearly not themselves imperatives, but explanatory theories.

Such prescriptions based on objective social position occupy a fundamental place in political reasoning. However there are others, of particular significance for 'moral' reasoning in the narrow sense (that is personal rather than political), though they inevitably spill over into political reasoning too; I am referring to those based on the particular set of ideological and cultural traditions that have, in the nature of things, formed the values of any group or individual; such values are assumed in assertoric imperatives such as: 'since you care that the human race shall have a future, oppose nuclear weapons', or 'since you desire to be loved by an equal, don't stifle your partner's autonomy'. There is a problem about this sort of judgement, in that an ethic that is critically rational cannot simply accept all the deliverances of the formative ideology. To this I shall return. But there is another 'problem' (as it is commonly regarded) here, which does not bother me at all: that *all* these imperatives are less than universal in scope: they can be addressed only to one who *is* an exploited worker, or who *does* care that humanity shall have a future, or who *does* want to be loved by an equal, respectively.

In a certain sense, this can be regarded as a relativist theory: in so far, that is, as it recognises that what might be right at one time and place might be wrong at another, and not only because 'circumstances' change, that is not only for technical reasons. However, unlike most views described as relativist, it allows for objective answers to questions about what is right for a given socio-historical group.

Refutation of Emotivism: Explanatory Critiques in Ethics

The naturalism with a historical dimension which I am defending contrasts with two approaches that might be called opposite extremes (though this naturalism is not a mere mean between them). These extremes are emotivism, and the idea that there is a single, universal, timeless code of morality.

First, emotivism. According to this view, to make a value-judgement is to express (and in some accounts, to seek to evoke in others) an attitude for or against something – and that is all. If this were true, there would not be a great deal to be said about it at the philosophical level. Despite this, some philosophers such as C.L. Stevenson have said quite a lot about it; but a meta-theory is only as interesting as the first order theory it seeks to illuminate. And if emotivism were true, moral discourse would be of little interest. Morality might still be a matter of deep concern to people – only there would be nothing much to be said about it.

However, there would still be another kind of theory which might have quite a lot to say about moral judgements: they could still be the object of psychological and sociological investigation. We could ask what kind of society, or class within a society, or what type of person, makes such and such a moral judgement. Such questions might be asked with no other aim than the description and explanation of an aspect of human affairs – neither philosophy nor moral reasoning itself need be on the agenda. What is philosophically interesting about such investigations is that their results – knowledge *about* the determinants of particular value-judgements – do *not* leave those value-judgements themselves untouched. This is true, in fact, even of the *biology* of value-judgement, if it is actually possible to say anything about this, as, for example, Nietzsche thought that it was:

> 'Peace of soul' can be, for one, the gentle radiation of a rich animality into the moral (or religious) sphere. Or the beginning of weariness, the first shadow of evening, of any kind of evening. Or a sign that the air is humid, that south winds are approaching. Or unrecognised gratitude for a good digestion (sometimes called 'love of man') (*Twilight of the Idols*, in *The Portable Nietzsche*, p. 489)

– and so on in the same vein. Anyone convinced by such explanations will look on such values in a new light. And this indicates that emotive judgements are never nothing but emotive judgements. Possibly this is true even where they do not involve beliefs. If a particular value-judgement stems from a disease, like fear of water from rabies, we don't take it seriously as a value-judgement. But what if it stems from healthy functioning? The case is somewhat, but not entirely different. If we are persuaded that love of humanity is unconscious gratitude for a good digestion, we are likely on the one hand to place a greater value on good digestion, and on the other, to have a rather less elevated view of love of humanity. The former change is self-explanatory, but why the latter? Is it not because we expect emotions of this kind to involve beliefs, and regard them as not quite the genuine article if they don't?

When an emotive attitude does involve beliefs, it immediately becomes possible to ask whether the beliefs are true or false, justified or unjustified, consistent or inconsistent, etc. – and hence to talk about values by talking about facts, to practise naturalistic moral reasoning. Thus, by taking the most deep-dyed anti-naturalist – the emotivist – at their word, and shifting attention from the moral judgements themselves to their explanation, we find ourselves inevitably engaged in the activity which the emotivist claims is impossible: the rational assessment of moral ideas on the basis of objective knowledge.

Paul Ricoeur has described Marx, Nietzsche and Freud as the three masters of suspicion. His point is that they all expose ignoble origins of what we had thought were our highest virtues. They all practised *explanatory critiques* of morality. This is most explicit in the case of Nietzsche. A great part of his work is devoted to the genealogy of morals – not only the book of that name. And in a great many cases, his arguments show (if we grant their factual truth) that the reasons why we have certain moral values are not good reasons for having those values – that is that those values are 'rationalisations' in the Freudian sense. Adherence to such values cannot co-exist with self-awareness with respect to them. To bring the social and psychological origins of them into the light of day is to undermine them, since it shows them to rest on manifest falsehoods and contradictions. This explanatory critique of moral psychology is Nietzsche's claim to greatness; in epistemology and metaphysics he was not even a competent amateur, and his positive views on morality and politics are often just nasty – though not proto-fascist, as is sometimes thought. But Freud was right to regard him as in the front rank for self-knowledge – and this was not just knowledge of Friedrich Nietzsche, but of the entire European moral tradition that had formed him, the primal traumas of which are abreacted in his philosophy.

In Freud himself, explanatory critique is not just applied to morality. The whole practice of psychoanalysis could be described as a sort of explanatory critique: the unconscious causes of our beliefs and desires are shown to be different from their apparent rationale; as contradictory contents of the unconscious are dredged up into the light of consciousness, the contradictions are resolved by reasoning and reality-testing. Freud's explanation of psychoanalysis to his patient the Rat-man illustrates this very clearly.[6]

Nietzsche and Freud do succeed, I think, in exposing certain supposed virtues as pathological symptoms, which cannot be understood and still commended: those virtues which involve valuing – not as sometimes unavoidable means, but as good in themselves – the denial and repression of the intellect, of sensuality, and of the will to power.

In the case of Marx, it is the theory of ideology that gives us explanatory critiques. The ideology of a society is produced by that society, but does not necessarily reflect that society accurately. In class societies, it typically obscures and misrepresents the reality of the society, and does so in ways that are *functional* for class rule in that society. Perhaps a given kind of society cannot exist without ideological illusion of this kind. So an adequate social-scientific account of that society will reveal facts about how it works, including the fact that its members are necessarily unaware of some of those facts – or if they are aware, that that awareness will be a cause of disruption in that society.

Hence, such an account will be an explanatory critique of the society, for in so far as it exposes contradictions between the facts and the received representation of them, it criticises that representation, and in so far as it shows that representation to be necessary to the stable operation of the society, it criticises the society as a whole as one which can't exist without falsehood. The status of such explanatory critiques has been explored by Roy Bhaskar and Roy Edgley. [7]

The three 'masters of suspicion' have sometimes been regarded as purely negative in their critiques of morality, and as tending towards moral nihilism. But it is incorrect to think that an explanatory critique of a moral ideology will simply destroy it and leave nothing behind. In the first place, because a good deal of that ideology will in all probability be quite appropriate to life in the society that gave rise to it. To expose the class function (for example) of particular values is not to discredit the entire value-system of which they form part. During the miners' strike of 1984–5 in Britain, conservative opinion was very indignant about the so-called 'breakdown of law and order', but of course nothing of the kind had occurred. Striking miners broke laws that they believed – correctly – to have been purpose-built to obstruct them and others like them – workers using the only means at their disposal to defend their livelihood. But they did not start burgling neighbours' houses or mugging old ladies. Explanatory critique is *critical* only when it exposes irrationalities, deceptions, rationalisations and the like. Some values ring true when the explanatory hammer strikes them.

Furthermore, while explanatory critiques may debunk old virtues or duties, they may also propound new ones, by debunking elements in the prevailing moral ideology which *restrict* the scope of a particular virtue or duty. One effect of Marxist critiques of moral ideology, for instance, has been to make those influenced by them take negative responsibility much more seriously.[8]

Explanatory critique is a form of naturalistic practical reasoning, but it is not the only form, and presupposes the possibility of another; in exposing cognitive flaws in the reasoning implicit in the consensus that it criticises, it assumes the possibility of unflawed reasoning in that consensus. For explanatory critique to be possible, there must first be possible an ethic which takes people's actually existing values as its premiss, and constructs assertoric imperatives on their basis. This is the mode of practical reasoning outlined earlier; it is a naturalistic and historical ethic, but not a critically rational one. By itself, it is in fact an inherently conservative one. But such a conservative ethic can only maintain itself as such by suppressing questions about its own explanation. Thus, in Britain in the 1980s, such an ethic might include the assertoric imperative: 'since you want to be an independent individual, work during a strike if it suits you.' But an explanatory theory which showed in what ways we are necessarily interdependent, and under what conditions a degree of independence can be acquired by collective struggle, would render this untenable.

To summarise the critically rational, historicised naturalistic ethics for which I have been arguing:

1. It does not *obliterate* the fact/value distinction; it does not, for example, accept arguments from values to facts. But it holds that some statements have evaluative (or prescriptive) force entirely by virtue of – as an effect of – their factual force; and that *purely* evaluative or prescriptive discourse derives whatever rationality it has from such statements.

2. It takes as the raw material of moral reasoning the moral code of the reasoner, and of their society and time; it elaborates that code in the form of assertoric imperatives. The findings of the human sciences about the society of the time will be among the major suppliers of premisses in this reasoning, both by making the existing moral code explicit, and by providing information about the possibilities for

realising its values, the constraints on those possibilities, and ways of overcoming those constraints.

3. Since the human sciences also explain existing moral codes, and since the explanatory accounts will concern (among other sorts of relation) cognitive relations, logical relations, justifying relations, and functional relations, such accounts may be criticisms, in so far as they discover falsehood, contradiction, malfunctions and rationalisations.

Critique of Moral Absolutism

It might now be asked whether we will not arrive at a universal morality by this method. For if the explanatory critique removes inadequate beliefs, etc. from the basis of a moral code, will morality not, in so far as it is so purified, approximate to a single, undistorted value-system, just as cognitive theories (for example in the sciences) tend to converge in so far as they are freed from ideological admixtures? If moral reasoning is ultimately a species of factual reasoning, should it not hold in this matter too, that errors are many but truth one? We would then be directed towards some sort of moral absolutism, whether composed of Kantian categorical imperatives, or of assertoric imperatives of the anthropological variety.

I shall take as an example of this ethical absolutist position, an essay by C.S. Lewis called 'The Poison of Subjectivism'. Although (in a very loose sense) C.S. Lewis can be said to be criticising subjectivism from the right, and I from the left, I take his case much more seriously than that of his main opponents, that is the sort of relativists who deny the objectivity and rationality of value-judgements. I shall quote it at some length:

> If a man will go into a library and spend a few days with the *Encyclopaedia of Religion and Ethics* he will soon discover the massive unanimity of the practical reason in man. From the Babylonian *Hymn to Samos*, from the Laws of Manu, the *Book of the Dead*, the Analects, the Stoics, the Platonists, from Australian aborigines and Redskins, he will collect the same triumphantly monotonous denunciations of oppression, murder, treachery and falsehood, the same injuctions of kindness to the aged, the young, and the weak, of almsgiving and impartiality and honesty ...
>
> The two grand methods of obscuring this agreement are these: First,

you can concentrate on those divergences about sexual morality which most serious moralists regard as belonging to positive rather than to Natural Law, but which rouse strong emotions ... The second method is to treat as differences in the judgement of value what are really differences in belief about fact. Thus human sacrifice, or the persecution of witches, are cited as evidence of a radically different morality. But the real difference lies elsewhere. We do not hunt witches because we disbelieve in their existence. We do not kill men to avert pestilence because we do not think pestilence can thus be averted. We do 'sacrifice' men in war, and we do hunt spies and traitors. (*Christian Reflections*, pp. 104–5)

The first problem about this is that the values listed as invariant are at a level of abstraction such that they can express vastly differing contents in different societies. Granted, all human societies have rules regulating who may kill whom, who may marry or sleep with whom, and who may use which scarce material goods. Breaches of these rules will be condemned as 'murder,' 'adultery,' 'theft', etc.; applications of the rules that are not evenhanded will be condemned as 'unjust'; systematic violations of them by one group at the expense of another will be condemned as 'oppression'. There will be enough in common formally between the definitions of each of these crimes to make translations possible as between cultures; but within limits set by the survival-needs of human communities, there is room for immense variation in what is actually prescribed or proscribed. Thus, no community can allow anyone to kill anyone at will, but there have been opposite evaluations of vendetta, aggressive war, capital punishment, suicide, abortion, cannibalism, tyrannicide, mercy-killing, killing for jealousy, letting die by neglect and so on. These differences may in the last analysis be due to differences of factual beliefs; but not just between true and false beliefs about universal facts; the facts in different societies have been different. And the different facts do not just enter into the argument in the way that they do in technical reasoning. The people of societies confronted by different facts and hence operating by different rules necessarily have quite different ideals of life, emotions, etc. Vendetta may have been the best way of coping with violence within a certain society, and no sane person would want to return to such a society; but that does not mean that the people of such societies accepted vendetta as a cruel necessity until such time as the need for it could be superseded; they would have regarded failure to avenge one's kin as base, forgiveness as a sign of weakness. [9]

Change resulting from changed factual beliefs about the world outside us can be accommodated in C.S. Lewis's theory ('witches'). But changes stemming from the fact that people are different in one society from what they are in another are not considered. Such changes are obscured by the abstractness of the values referred to – value-slots fillable with many different contents. This becomes clear when we descend to the nuts and bolts of morality – and not only sexual morality. Treachery is universally condemned, but to whom do we owe the loyalty of which treachery is a violation? Brutus was the hero of the French revolutionaries, though Dante placed him in the seventh circle of hell. Patriots regard Kim Philby as a traitor, though he never betrayed anything he believed in.

My point is not the shallow relativism which says that our spies are heroes, theirs traitors, or that our guerrillas are freedom fighters, theirs terrorists. It is that loyalty is quite a different sort of virtue in different societies. Loyalty to a friend, loyalty to a collectivity and loyalty to a principle are quite different kinds of character-traits, involving different emotions, values and beliefs, sanctioned by different kinds of conscience and threatened by different kinds of temptation; and while our society accepts a mix of these loyalties in no fixed order or proportion, some societies stress one to the exclusion of the others.

Does this mean that we cannot talk of progress? C.S. Lewis tells us that 'except on the supposition of a changeless standard, progress is impossible' (p. 103). The image seems to be of someone standing outside history, surveying the succession of different moral codes, and evaluating changes as progress or degeneration.[10] Yet on the following page, he says: 'Real moral advances ... are made *from within* the existing moral tradition and can be understood only in the light of that tradition.' So if there are values in terms of which a change can be assessed, these must be immanent in the historical period. Before they can come to be advocated, they must be objectively present already as a problem and a task, though not yet, of course, as the norms of the time. If we judge a change to be progress, it must be because it answers a need of the time. (That a degeneration must also, in a sense, answer a need, is a problem to which I shall return elsewhere. The acceptance of human slaughter as a form of entertainment by the people of late antiquity and of late capitalism are cases in point. My repetition of the term 'late' should give a clue: it is a feature of systems that have outstayed their welcome upon the earth.)

Now I want to consider whether a Marxist account of progress requires some such changeless standard. According to Marx, feudal society is typically at a lower technological level than capitalism, and restrains or precludes technological development beyond a certain point. Hence, human powers *vis-à-vis* nature are less in feudalism than in capitalism. So less of the total available social labour time is required for producing the means of life in capitalism than in feudalism. A wider distribution of free time and therefore of culture and of participation in public affairs is thus *possible* under capitalism than under feudalism. Also, the work-process under capitalism facilitates co-operation, and hence makes it likely that the workers will be able, by joint struggle, to realise this possibility to some extent.

The advocate of a universal standard will say: then capitalism is freer and more just than feudalism. However, it needs to be asked in what circumstance this evaluation could have any prescriptive force. In a feudal society on the brink of capitalist development, certainly. And that is when people *did* start to say something of the sort. But in the Europe of Charlemagne, a modern time-traveller who described capitalism and claimed it was more just could at best be treated as we would treat someone who claimed that everyone ought to be born with equal resistance to disease or equal physical beauty – as an amiable windbag. At worst – if such a time-traveller came to have a political influence – they would be a public menace. A Connecticut Yankee would have been about as much use in the court of King Arthur as Don Quixote in the Europe of nascent capitalism.

I am not arguing that feudal society was as good in its own way as capitalism, but neither am I merely claiming that no one could have understood the time traveller. I am saying that – for all that capitalism was to be a freer and more just system than feudalism – the time-traveller, were they understood, would be inculcating the wrong virtues for the time. The virtues of the warriors who defended Christendom against Nordic barbarism, and the monks who kept literary culture alive were the appropriate virtues of that age. Along, of course, with the virtues of the hardworking and frugal peasant. But it would not have been possible to generalise the latter and do away with the exploiting classes. The feudal exploiter was absolutely necessary, though naturally he could be more or less humane, more or less just. For concepts such as justice, oppression and so on certainly did have application, and were applied. Bede could praise the good order of the realm under Edwin of Northumbria, when a woman could safely take her baby across England unaccompanied, and condemn the ravages of the crowned thugs who succeeded him, without having to call on values unrealisable before the industrial age; and a modern socialist can endorse Bede's judgement (granted that the facts are accurate) without forgetting that Edwin, too, lived on the produce of the peasants' sweat. It is not that there is a single scale from 'very unjust' to 'very just', and Edwin is a little way up it, the Sandinistas a long way up it; within the constraints of his time, maybe Edwin was supremely just. But neither is it quite that there is a sort of two-dimensional scale: more or less justice-within-a-system, and more or less just systems. The justice of a system comes to be inadequate to the time, when it becomes possible for more people to have a better life – but not within that system. Hence the human race 'sets itself only such tasks as it is able to solve, since closer examination will always show that the problem itself arises only when the material conditions for its solution are already present' (Marx). New demands in the name of justice emerge when the shoe begins to pinch a growing foot.

If I am right that the judgement between two systems is made in the light, not of eternity, but of *kairos*,[11] it might be asked whether the relation 'more free than' or 'more just than', applied to systems, is a transitive relation.[12] For the criteria on which capitalism is judged to be a juster and freer society than feudalism are different from the criteria on which socialism is judged to be a juster and freer society than capitalism.

I think there is enough continuity to treat these relations as transitive. In both cases, an increase in the possibilities available to humanity collectively, and a consequent increase in the proportion of people who can participate in possibilities beyond the production of the means of life, are involved. This indicates that there is an underlying standard. But it is an extremely abstract one: the augmentation of human possibilities. Before this can be an applicable standard for judging anything, it has to gain concreteness from particular historical developments.

Furthermore, 'moral progress', when it occurs, is not unidirectional. A new virtue may become necessary, and then later become obsolete. Danton was magnificent in his defiance of the enemies of his country's liberties – but God save us from Dantons in the White House or the Kremlin.

It is not to changeless standards, but to the contradictions of our time, that our moral ears should be attuned.

The Relation of Critically Rational, Historical Naturalism to Humean and Utilitarian Ethics

The conception of ethics that I have arrived at has in common with Hume's, that it takes existing moral opinion as its starting point, and proceeds by explaining it in terms of some sort of social utility. Elsewhere, I have written of a Humean and a Spinozan moment in moral thinking.[13] Let me explain.

Hume's theory can, I think, be summarised as follows:

(i) Our feelings about human qualities, considered apart from our own self-interest in them, tell us which qualities are virtues, which vices;
(ii) a theory of morality will aim to *explain* why this quality is (perceived as) a virtue, that a vice;
(iii) the explanation is as follows: some qualities are useful or pleasant to their possessors or others, some harmful or unpleasant; our natural motive of sympathy, when not overridden by self-love, makes us value the pleasant and useful qualities (virtues) and abhor the unpleasant and harmful ones;
(iv) since we want to be valued by our fellows, we will do well to cultivate our virtues, overcome our vices.

This position needs to be corrected by the following points (which I think can be described as Spinozan in spirit):

(a) Feelings are not blind responses, they involve beliefs. Hence they are not immune to rational criticism: they may involve false or even contradictory beliefs;
(b) moral feelings differ from epoch to epoch, and from group to group. This should not be surprising given the above account, and in particular the recognition that real social changes make different qualities valuable (e.g. military virtues would be useless and dangerous in a securely peaceful world), and that different classes have different interests;
(c) it will therefore always be possible that a particular 'virtue' or 'vice' is such only relative to a particular epoch or class, and *irrational* when present in another. Point (a) makes it possible, and point (b) makes it necessary, to examine critically the processes whereby our moral judgements came to be what they are.

This provides a rational justification for a type of person which appears merely perverse in Hume: the moral reformer or rebel. Not indeed the moral rebel without premisses, who wants to throw out all the old moral beliefs (like Descartes with cognitive beliefs) and start from scratch. If the moral innovator is 'a philosopher with a hammer', as Nietzsche says, it is not a sledge hammer to smash old law-tablets to fragments, but the little hammer with which we tap something gently to test its soundness. They will be sensitive both to the subtleties of the prevailing consensus, and to the function in it of *rationalisation* in the Freudian sense: the concoction of what look like acceptable reasons (justifying sense) for some practice or institution of the existing moral consensus, but are not the real reasons (explaining sense) why they exist, the real ones being hidden because obsolete and/or tied to the interests of the oppressing group. The method of the moral reformer – the explanatory critique that reveals a true explanation for aspects of the consensus which are not good reasons for them – need not look a bit like a full sociology of morals: it may produce such simple reflections as that 'the Sabbath was made for man, not man for the Sabbath.' Nor is it only exceptional individuals who are moral reformers: anyone who critically examines their own moral inheritance may be using explanatory critique in the same way.

It is perhaps necessary here to raise again in a more specific manner the question whether critical rationality does not direct us to a single moral position – specifically: utilitarianism. After all, Hume's consensus theory could be called *explanatory utilitarianism*. Would not a rational critique of this lead us to prescriptive utilitarianism?

It is well known that Mill defended the latter by appealing to the truth of explanatory utilitarianism. This is generally regarded as a piece of fallacious reasoning – a sliding between a Humean sociology of morals and a normative position. Perhaps it is only an incomplete argument: equip Mill with the notion of explanatory critique, and could he not say that the (Humean) principle of utility explains why we have the values that we do, but does not always justify them; hence the explanation of our having those values (the 'genealogy of morals') will be a critique of those values. It will lead us to adjust them until they are simply instances of the (prescriptive) principle of utility.

Consider, however, what Mill says about secondary ends – that is ends which are pursued first as means, but which then become ends in themselves. Mill's aim in this discussion is to accommodate the idea that we may pursue virtue for its own sake. But in doing so, he puts virtue into the same category as miserliness: money and virtue were pursued at first as means to happiness and became ends in themselves – an account which lends credence to Nietzsche's jibe that English moral psychologists made habit and forgetfulness the basis of everything. For surely, the exposure of the means–end inversion in the case of the miser is an explanatory critique of miserly values: the miser is convicted as irrational.

Now it is not in fact my intention to defend the rationality of the pursuit of virtue. Just as there is much truth in the 'hedonistic paradox' that one who pursues happiness will achieve, not happiness, but dissipation and boredom, so there is too in the 'moralistic paradox' that one who pursues moral virtue will achieve, not virtue, but pharisaism and priggishness. This notion, introduced into philosophy, I think, by Max Scheler, has been known to theologians at least since Martin Luther.

Nevertheless I would want to defend the view that there are explanatorily secondary ends which are not debunked by explanatory critique in the way miserliness is. For instance, it may be possible to explain the love of knowledge, the love of beauty, and love or friendship for another person, in terms of hedonistic impulses, yet hedonistic ends may be entirely sacrificed in the names of these loves, and there is nothing irrational about such sacrifice.

To establish this, we should look, not at the means–end relation, which altogether fails to account for the manner in which the 'pleasure-principle' motivates these loves, nor yet at the part/whole relation with which Mill, inconsistently with his Benthamite premisses, wants to supplement it. We need to look at the socio-historically specific complexity which any human need acquires as a condition of its fulfilment. The passage on production and consumption in Marx's 1857 introduction can serve as a model here. Any human need can only be satisfied in a concrete historical situation which provides its form and its 'finish'. Our needs, so complexified and educated, make much greater demands of the world than can be read off from the physiologically given need. Just as 'the hunger that is satisfied by cooked meat eaten with a knife and fork differs from hunger that devours raw meat with the help of hands, nails and teeth', so civilised humanity requires as a habitat, not just shelter, but beauty, public and private space, the possibility of hospitality; not just sexual release, but the affection, fellowship and loyalty of a partner, and so on. This should be obvious enough, but its consequences are far-reaching and not always recognised: that we can disregard any axiology with claims to universality, since, while raw need may be universal, concrete needs are not. Marx – in this matter if no other fortunate in his Hegelian training – took this so much for granted that he made it explicit only in the occasional throw-away remark. For instance, his jibe against Bentham:

> To know what is useful for a dog, one must study dog-nature. This nature itself is not to be deduced from the principle of utility. Applying this to man, he that would criticise all human acts, movements, relations etc., by the principle of utility, must first deal with human nature in general, and then with human nature as modified in each historical epoch. Bentham makes short work of it. With the dryest naiveté he takes the modern shopkeeper, especially the English shopkeeper, as the normal man ... Had I the courage of my friend, Heinrich Heine, I should call Mr Jeremy a genius in the way of bourgeois stupidity. (*Capital* vol. I, p. 610)

Marx is precise even when he is being abusive. The idea that the historical and individual complexity and specificity of human needs can be stripped away and a theory of rational motivation based on the bare bones of utility that remain is not just stupid, it is stupid in a specifically bourgeois way. The stupidest member of a pre- or post-capitalist society could see through it, yet it was present not only in this first philosopher of industrial capitalism, but in Rawls' postulation of the 'veil of ignorance' behind which the dry bones come to life and construct a social order before they even hear the Word or become clothed in flesh.

What the principle of utility represents is not the rationality underlying the historical complexity of values, but a historically specific degradation and levelling down of that complexity, under the sway of the omnipotence of money. The utilitarian model of means and ends is a desiderative atomism in which pleasures are spatio-temporally isolated from their mode of achievement, each other, the pleasures of others, the environment. It is capitalism which tends to isolate pleasures thus, and the more so, the more it develops into its dotage. It gleefully provides us with motorways by which we can travel with ever greater and greater speed and anxiety to parts of the countryside which are no longer worth visiting since they are carved up by motorways; it urgently seeks for more and more parking space to facilitate trips to cities defaced by huge car parks; and in its public transport vehicles, tries to stop you looking out of the window, and make you gawp at videos instead.

But if we reject the notion that there can be a utility independent of historically specific societies, that should not throw us back into the political morality of the absolute idealists, for which society can say to every individual who protests against its norms 'what hast thou that thou has not been given', and so make itself immune from criticism. Human needs are not infinitely malleable, and societies can make better or worse jobs of catering for them.

One could construct a somewhat Hegelian zigzag (no, I am not going to call it a dialectic) to illustrate the place of individual need acting upon society and of society in forming the needs of the individual. This is a process with many levels, the order of which can partly be interpreted diachronically, partly as an order of synchronic dependence.

Need as biologically given through the inherited physiology of the species (abstract need) becomes determinate only through its interpersonally mediated satisfaction (in biographical terms: the baby's cries of hunger become need for the mother's milk); need, having become determinate, and social, in its object, motivates action in relation to other people and in terms of social rules; through such action the individual becomes enmeshed in a network of social relations and is made a 'social individual'. The self-assertion of this social individual is never purely self-referential – reference to the needs of others is always part of it; but such self-assertion is always liable to encounter the resistance of constraints inherent in the society, making the individual discontented; this discontent may motivate struggle to change the society, which can only be collective struggle; and such collective struggle will in turn induce its own virtues in its participants.

Of course, these alternate 'layers' of appetition and socialisation are distinguishable only by abstraction; it is a crude enough piece of analytical butchery, but at least it forestalls that cruder one which constructs, by extrapolating the individual 'moments', the image of a mature, yet asocial, homunculus in each individual, co-existing with a distinct, socialised homunculus, such that the two could confront each other with their conflicting claims and principles of action.

Different elements of a person's morality will reflect different layers of this process of socialisation/individuation: necessary 'moments' of egoism and altruism; of personal loyalties and group loyalties; of at-home-ness in the rules governing the common life of society, and rebellion against its constraints; of the virtues of peace and the duties of strife against the oppressor. The presence of these layers, interweaved but often uncomfortably joined, should not surprise us, nor lead us to think someone's morality inconsistent in any sense that would be an objection to it.

Notes

1. MacIntyre, 'Hume on "Is" and "Ought"', *The Philosophical Review*, vol. LXIII, 1959.
2. '... living things are ranked above inanimate objects ... This is the scale according to the order of nature; but there is another gradation which employs utility as the criterion of value ... would not anyone prefer to have food in his house, rather than mice.' *City of God*, pp. 447–8.
3. The possibility of the cognitively unflawed villain, the person of sound mind and evil will, has haunted non-cognitivist ethics as the solipsist has the philosophy of mind. But whether or not such a person can be found, it is fruitless to seek them among fascists – not because the latter are not villains, but because they are manifestly cognitively flawed.

    I suspect that, at the very least, a great deal more villainy is inextricable from cognitive error than is commonly believed. But if there are cognitively unflawed villains, that does not refute the version of ethical naturalism that I am defending, since (i) I make no claims for *universal* imperatives, and (ii) I do not claim that convincement of the truth of moral principle necessarily leads to practical adherence to it.
4. I take this example (somewhat abridged) from a passage in Roy Bhaskar's *The Possibility of Naturalism*, p. 75, and he takes it from Isaiah Berlin. My point is the same one that Bhaskar makes in that paragraph, though I dissent from what he says he is doing in the section as a whole. He says he is defending both the derivation of values from facts, and of facts from values. This looks like something actually quite alien to Bhaskar's thought, namely the vicious circle characteristic of Nietzsche's account of morals, in which anti-naturalist moralities are subjected to a brilliant explanatory critique in the name of truth – but then truth is dissolved into biological utility, leaving facts and values alike subject to a vulgar pragmatist pick-and-mix. But what Bhaskar actually does is show, not that facts can be derived from values, but only that factual judgements can be explained by value judgements. Hence the other limb of the argument – that factual considerations can sometimes show certain value judgements to be logically untenable – retains its undiminished force.
5. *The Twilight of the Idols*, p. 59 (Penguin, 1968).

6. 'A Case of Obessional Neurosis' in *Collected Papers*, vol. III; see pp. 312–15.
7. See Roy Edgley's 'Science, Social Science and Socialist Science: Reason as Dialectic' in *Radical Philosophy* no. 15, 1976, and Roy Bhaskar's 'Scientific Explanation and Human Emancipation' in *Radical Philosophy* no. 26, 1980.
8. 'Negative responsibility', that is, responsibility for the effects of our inaction as on a par with the effects of our action. Cf. p. 73 above.
9. In a formula: if the assertoric imperatives constituting morality are spelt out as a hypothetical major premiss and a minor premiss asserting its antecedent, which is a statement about people's wants/needs/interests etc., then moral change can involve change in the minor premiss, not only in the major.
10. And this someone is not God: C.S. Lewis is not one of those theologians who sees moral law as simply divine fiat; it is immanent in the human condition.
11. *Kairos* is a word introduced into the socialist lexicon by the Protestant theologian Paul Tillich. It means 'time', in the sense that it has in 'the time is ripe for change', as opposed to that in 'the time is six o'clock' (*chronos*). See Tillich's *The Protestant Era* Chapter Three, and *Systematic Theology*, vol. III, pp. 393–6.
12. To say that 'more just than' is a transitive relation is to say that, for example, if socialism is more just than capitalism, and capitalism is more just than feudalism, then socialism must be more just than feudalism. In general, relations of a 'more x than' type would be transitive. The denial of this in the present case depends on the claim that social systems are only commensurable at the time of transition between them.
13. See my reply to Brenda Cohen in the symposium 'Positive Values,' *Aristotelian Society Supplementary Volume LVII*, 1983.

5
What is Political?

The 'Keep Politics out of X' Syndrome

The question 'what is political?' is itself a politically contentious one. This should be obvious from the common use of slogans of the form 'keep politics out of x', with education, health care, policing, etc. filling the 'x' slot. It is often said – and with justice – that such slogans usually mean keep *left-wing* politics out of x. How does it come about that the right can plausibly present its case as non-political, and that it wants to?

Take the slogan, popular at the time of the British Labour government's introduction of comprehensive schools, 'keep politics out of education'. The structure of secondary education in England was, of course, already the result of various acts of parliament; the division into a high-status private sector, a grammar school sector for the competitively successful, and a secondary modern sector for the majority, neatly reflected the class structure of the country. It was part of the Conservative candidates' electoral programme to retain the tripartite structure of education. Yet this was implicitly defended as non-political (and that in election addresses), in that those who wanted to reform it were accused of introducing politics into education. 'Keep politics out of education' meant 'keep education the way it is', since only the acts of parliament or of local education authorities could change it. This sounds like a cheap electoral trick, and its exposure a trivial matter. In fact it reflects a far-reaching difference between conservative and radical politics.

But there is also another aspect of such slogans. 'Keep politics out of x' can mean 'keep the politicians out – let it be decided by the experts'. In the case of education, this aspect was not the main one, since many educationists favoured the reform and had hitherto been obstructed by conservative politicians. But consider Douglas Hurd's statement that the worst thing about Labour's programme in the 1987 election (after defence) was the proposal for the 'political control of the police'. Etymology itself might suggest that, however the police were controlled, that control could hardly be non-political. What he meant by political control was: control by elected representatives of the people. What he was objecting to was an increase of democracy at the expense of a specialised hierarchy.

Here we are confronted with the deeply anti-democratic side of the ideology of formal democracy – an ideology reflected and perpetuated in the huge market for police and spy and war stories and films, involving the stereotype of politicians – elected representatives – as bumbling fools whose interference stops the experts from catching the villains. The chiefs of police, the secret service and the General Staff (or perhaps even more so, the middle echelons, above the rank and file but further removed than top brass from public accountability) are presented as the natural defenders of democracy, while those few state officials who owe their position to election by the people are seen as democracy's Achilles' heel.

There is even a curious grain of truth in this. In a merely formal democracy, the elected office-holders lack real power, and lack of power (in an office-holder, at least) corrupts. Where power lies in specialised hierarchies (state or commercial), the skills of a politician *are* those of a public relations person, not of one who has to take informed and responsible decisions. But the fault lies, not in democracy, but in its merely formal character.

'Keep politics out of x', then, generally means either 'keep change out of x', or 'keep democracy out of x'. The latter meaning is specific to a particular political system, formal democracy, which consists in banishing democracy to the margins of social power while maintaining the fiction that it is supreme. The greater part of the business of governing the body politic is treated as outside the public sphere, and democratic interventions into it resented. This resentment is made plausible by the poor quality of office-holder that formal democracy itself breeds.

What of the asymmetry between the politics of conservation and the politics of change? This asymmetry is not a mere propaganda trick: radicals want to *transform* social structures, conservatives to reproduce them, that is to transmit the same structure of social power from one generation to the next. But there is a real asymmetry between the reproduction and the transformation of structures; social structures reproduce themselves for the most part through the non-political activities of people, without anyone having to present their reproduction as a political programme. The economic class division between labour and capital, for instance, is reproduced by the buying and selling of labour power, of products and of property, which happens with little, and no significant, political motivation. A good deal of the point of Marx's *Capital* is to explain how the division into propertied bourgeois and propertyless proletarians is transmitted willy nilly from generation to generation, though it is neither a gift of nature nor (with occasional exceptions) artificially maintained. The transformation of such structures, on the other hand, requires a highly conscious and organised political struggle. It is no accident that, subjectively speaking, people on the left are 'more political' than people on the right. Conservatives have sometimes made a virtue of this pre-occupation of their politicians with non-political concerns.[1] But an alternative – rarer – option for the conservative is to regard every activity as political, since *all* human activities make sense only in terms of some tradition specific to the society in which they are performed, and for the most part tend to perpetuate that tradition. This way of looking at it illustrates the curious effects of treating reproduction and transformation as symmetrical. If dancing, singing and hanging up holly for Christmas are political because they perpetuate the customs of a culture, working and shopping are political because they reproduce the capitalist economic structure, marrying is political because it reproduces the nuclear family – and all these things political in a *conservative* way – then most of us are being conservative politicians most of the time when we are not actually at socialist meetings or on the picket line. There is a certain tradition of radicalism that accepts such conclusions, analysing and assessing as political everything that serves to reproduce the social structure – that is practically everything.

The 'X is Political' Syndrome

Radicals have often urged that (for example) artistic and scientific work or personal relationships should be seen as political, but it is not always clear what is meant by this. It *is* clear that all these things are practices whereby societies of, in each case, a definite kind, are reproduced. But if this proves anything it seems to prove too much, that is that such activities are politically *conservative* ones. The radical would then appear to be committed to some sort of nihilism – to non-participation in society-reproducing activities, which all activities are. This 'Great Refusal' has to take the form of *dropping out* of (for example) capitalist society, but since there is nothing to drop into, this could only be consistently carried out by ceasing to exist. So in practice, such nihilism is always selective: the refusers abstain from recreation or procreation or education or wage-labour or ownership of property; but they nevertheless engage in a whole range of system-reproducing activities. Even if they succeed in creating some sort of 'counter-culture', so long as the system is not changed, this counter-culture must take its place in it. Christian monasticism was in part a reaction against the incorporation of the Church into the imperial world order, yet the monasteries became the great pillar of the society that emerged from that incorporation; the Puritan testimony against superfluities at once expressed the contempt of the artisan class for concentrations of wealth, and facilitated the transformation of a part of that class into wealthy capitalists; in a lesser degree, the 'counter-culture' of the 1960s has had a similar relation to the capitalist 'consumer society'.

At this point, it might be objected that the radical who believes that everything is political need not be a nihilist, for the following reason: the activities that reproduce a society never simply hand down a replica of the society they inherited. To a greater or lesser extent, they transform what they reproduce. An artist or scientist necessarily produces something *new*, and hence leaves the reproduced society different from the begetter society. And something similar may be the case with personal relationships. The next generation may have families like the last, but the division of household labour between the sexes may be altered or abolished, and so on.

All this is absolutely true. However, we must be clear about what is reproduced and what is transformed. In saying that a social structure is reproduced, willy nilly, by activities that have some quite different aim (going to work, shopping, raising children, composing songs) it is fully recognised that all these activities are *practices*, which transform the world in some way, do so with conscious purposes in view, and may do so differently as a result of different decisions that we may take. In this sense we 'make our own history', that is, history is nothing but the successive activities of generations of people transforming the world; and it *matters* how we do this – whether we build a bridge that will stand up to use or collapse, whether we preserve the countryside or foul it up, whether we bring up a new generation to be cringeing and servile or free and forthright. But – and this is the crucial 'but', without which there would be no need for scientific socialism – we do not make history in conditions of our own choosing, and the unchosen conditions include structures into which we must enter independently of our will, and which reproduce themselves through our activities, independently of our intentions, unless and until sufficient social power is organised for their transformation, that is until those who are organised around policies that will transform them become the strongest force in society.

This fact that our world-transforming practices are organised in self-reproducing structures, generates a crucial division between two types of world-transforming activity: those which work for the transformation of social structures themselves, and those that don't. Which is of greater importance depends on the time and place; but in the strictest sense of the word, only those that do are *politically* radical. There are of course other ways of being radical. Scientific socialists have sometimes – quite wrongly – disdained non-political reformers. But this mistake is not rectified by pretending that non-political radicalism is political. Participation in activities that structurally reproduce, and non-structurally transform society (the economic, personal and cultural activities that are the substance of most lives) may be radical or conservative in a non-political sense, but is neither radical nor conservative in a political sense. That is to say, they may leave the world more or less different, but they neither leave the structure different, *nor obstruct the work of those practices that might leave the structure different.* Political practice is conservative when it does obstruct such work. Politics is comprised of struggles between those who would transform social structures and those who would prevent such transformation.

I concede that this definition of politics is a narrow one, not only compared with the view that everything is political, but also compared with common usage. For surely, the governing of the state is political, and this only exceptionally consists in inaugurating or warding off structural transformations. It largely consists, in normal periods in civilised societies, in smoothing the path of the *material* (rather than structural) reproduction of society: in maintaining roads, preventing crime, printing money, publishing health information, etc.

It is true that the public power has these functions. But it always *also* has the function of warding off structural transformation (or, exceptionally, facilitating it); and it is overwhelmingly this conflictual function that determines the structure of the public power. In only calling this function political, I am following Marx and Engels, who claim that under mature communism the administration of things would replace the governing of people, and describe such a public power as having lost its political character, since 'Political power, properly so called, is merely the organised power of one class for oppressing another' ('Communist Manifesto', *The Revolutions of 1848*, p. 87). For this oppression is precisely the same as the warding off or facilitation of structural transformation.

Having thus narrowed the definition of politics, it will be necessary and possible to investigate the causal interactions between political and non-political practices. For of course, anything *can* have political effects, and politics can have effects on anything. That something is causally connected to politics does not make it political. Kollontai tells us that Lenin was a broken man after Inessa Armand's death, and never recovered from it. If so, this personal emotion of Lenin's had profound political consequences. But if that makes it political, then the ice on to which Lenin leapt to save himself from drowning in the Gulf of Bothia on 15 December 1907 would be political too. And if anyone suggests that an ideal revolutionary would not be vulnerable to such personal feelings, I would reply that perhaps an ideal revolutionary would not drown in water either.

We cannot trace the pervasive causal interconnections between political and non-political practices unless we first make a clear distinction between them. If we start by saying that art, for instance, is necessarily political since it is one of the ways in which people transform their world, we will never come to understand the many, complex and ambiguous ways in which any given work of art may have political effects. If we treat *And Quiet Flows the Don* and *Dr Zhivago* as in themselves political acts, we will not be able to explain why most Western readers (I take it) find a more sympathetic portrayal of Bolshevism in the latter than in the former.

Probably the most striking example of the 'x is political' syndrome in recent times is the slogan 'the personal is political'. This slogan has been repeated so often that to many it is a truism, yet it ought at the very least to strike us as paradoxical, like Orwell's three slogans on the Ministry of Truth: 'War is Peace: Freedom is Slavery: Ignorance is Strength'. For part of the function of the expression 'the personal' is to distinguish this area of human life from the public sphere to which 'the political' belongs. And in the scientific socialist tradition, this distinction has been very important – far more so than in other political traditions. We do not regard Engels' contribution to scientific socialism as superior to Marx's on the grounds that he was a nicer bloke; we do not disparage Edward Aveling's translation of *Capital* because of his brutal knavishness towards Eleanor Marx – nor excuse the latter because of the former; we do not vote for a sincere Tory against a Labour careerist; we do not support a personally philanthropic boss in his struggle with a corrupt trade union leader. Not all political traditions agree with us. Parnell fell because of his adultery, not his policies for Ireland. I recall my history teacher telling us, in his unforgettable resonant tone, 'Parnell was an Anglican, but most of his followers were Catholics or Presbyterians, and they didn't approve of their leader committing adultery.' On this question of the political irrelevance of personal morality, we scientific socialists are all more Anglican than the Archbishop, and stand aside from the politics of gossip so dear to the British media. As Brecht put it in his poem 'The Abstemious Chancellor':

> They tell me the chancellor doesn't drink
> Eats no meat and never smokes
> And he lives in a modest dwelling
> But they also tell me the poor
> Starve and die in misery.
> How much better it would be to have a state of which men said:
> The chancellor is always drunk at cabinet meetings
> Eyeing the smoke from their pipes, a few
> Uneducated men sit altering the laws
> There are no poor.
>   (*Poems*, p. 276)

This stand for the separation of the political from the personal is not a bare 'value-judgement', but rests on the conception of politics as about the transformation of social structures, which no amount of personal virtue or vice will either transform, or prevent from being transformed.[2] This flows directly from the absolutely foundational propositions of scientific socialism about the existence of self-reproducing structures. It is no exaggeration to say that, if the personal *is* political, the entire tradition of scientific socialism from 1845 is worthless.

So far, my case against 'personal politics' has been that it is not politics. The improvement of personal relationships (for which there used to be a better name than 'personal politics', viz. *morality*) is important in its own right, but it is no substitute for politics. To treat it as such is to *divert* from effective politics, in a manner such as I shall analyse in the following chapter. But the effects of this confusion are the more pernicious in that the principles of good political practice are in sharp tension with those of good moral practice, and attempts to suppress this contradiction are to the detriment of both politics and morality. Since my concern here is only with the political side, I shall discuss these contradictions only briefly.

Politics and Other Practices

Any practice can have political effects, but some only accidentally. If a cricketer hits a six and the ball, quite fortuitously, kills the passing Prime Minister, that does not make the batsman's act political. But there are also practices which, while not themselves political, have an intelligible and sometimes predictable effect on politics. It would in many cases be incorrect, for example, to regard the propagation of a religious conviction as political, yet the distribution of sections of the people between different religions has often had political effects, and intelligible, even predictable ones at that. It was no accident that the propagation of Methodism in the eighteenth century helped to 'save' England from a republican revolution, while the propagation of Puritanism in the seventeenth century had the opposite effect. There are *intelligible*, causal relations between the two theologies and the two political tendencies. Yet the criteria of Wesley's practice which constituted it as the practice that it was were not political. If a sermon of Wesley's had resulted in a drunken, wife-beating republican becoming a drunken, wife-beating royalist, he would have counted it a failure (just as Bunyan would have counted the reverse conversion).

In many important cases, a practice is both political, and an instance of a type of practice which is not inherently political. Even in these cases, it is necessary to distinguish the political aspect from the other aspects. Take for instance the (often sterile) controversies about whether the miners' strike of 1984–5 in Britain was economic or political. It had specific industrial aims, and as such was economic. But it certainly did not escape the attention of either Arthur Scargill or Margaret Thatcher that the relative strength of the classes in British society was also at stake – and that is a political issue. From Thatcher's point of view, the struggle certainly could not have seemed worthwhile in economic terms, but was successful politically, increasing the relative strength of the exploiting class. Such a discrepancy between economic and political success is a feature of many such struggles.

Hence it is necessary to distinguish the two aspects. Furthermore, class politics can only be understood in terms of its function in the economic struggle of the classes. There is an asymmetrical relation of explanation between economic and political struggles, yet in many cases the same struggle is an instance of both. We should (like Trinitarian theologians) neither divide the substance nor confuse the hypostases.

The demarcation-criterion between (for example) economic and political practices or aspects of practices can only be their different criteria of success: the result to be produced. An investment decision by a multi-national firm, for instance, may have both economic and political criteria of success (profits, de-stabilising an anti-capitalist regime), and the two criteria may pull in opposite directions. But the success or failure of an economic practice cannot be politically indifferent, nor that of a political practice economically indifferent.

Now let us take the example of cognitive practices, that is to say, practices whose criterion of success is that they are to yield objective knowledge, that is reliable information about the real world. Obviously, sciences and disciplines approximating to sciences are cognitive practices, but cognitive practices are also an essential part or prerequisite of many other practices. In the first and fourth chapters of this book, I have argued for their essential function in politics and ethics; art also has its cognitive side, and I would argue (though this is not the place to do so) that it can have political effects to precisely the extent that it is cognitive.

There is widespread pressure to 'politicise' cognitive practices. Of course, cognitive practices can have political effects (intelligible and predictable political effects, not accidental ones) by virtue of their success as cognitive practices: the acquisition of accurate information by the agents of a political practice may transform that practice. But in order to have these political effects, the cognitive practice does not have to be 'politicised', it simply has to acquire (and pass on) the knowledge. One obvious way in which a cognitive practice could be 'politicised' is that it could be made to substitute political for cognitive criteria of success, that is to tell politically convenient lies. But the very fact that it can be politically convenient to lie bears witness to the political effectivity of believing something to be true, for a lie does not succeed in its purpose unless it is taken to report the facts accurately. Hence, the common pseudo-philosophical covering move of political liars – the claim that there is no truth or falsehood anyway, only practical utility – is self-refuting.

It is to be expected that when cognitive practices are governed by cognitive, rather than political, criteria, they are more likely to succeed in satisfying those criteria – that is finding the truth. But it is still possible to raise the question: which is better, that they produce true information, or that they produce politically useful information, that is information in which widespread belief would produce politically desirable results?[3] The whole scientific socialist tradition has answered, bluntly and correctly: it is the oppressors who have something to hide – the oppressed have a class interest in objective truth. So that, so far as the politics of liberation is concerned, the cognitive virtues of objectivity, clarity, logical rigour, are also political virtues – even though they may indeed conflict with some short-term political advantage. Good politics itself requires that cognitive practices be conducted according to cognitive criteria, and not 'politicised' in any sense that conflicts with that.[4] The politics of the oppressor, of course, is another matter. Those of their philosophers who, like Plato, frankly claim the right to lie, deserve more respect than those who, by virtue of a pragmatist notion of truth, can lie through their teeth while preserving 'that invention of the devil', a good conscience.

Philosophically, an even more fundamental point can be made. It can always be asked. Who are the oppressed? After all, the Thatcherites believe, some of them no doubt sincerely, that selling off public assets to profiteers is an act of liberation. Are we to count among the oppressed 'the man who waters the workers' beer', in the song of that name, who laments 'The water rates are terribly high/And meths is terribly dear/And there isn't the profit there used to be/In watering workers' beer'? Unless founded on objective knowledge of relations of oppression and the conditions of their abolition, politics can be no more than arbitrary commitment to contending groups – in which case, why workers versus bosses, rather than Spurs versus Arsenal?

My conclusion is that cognitive practices are not, as such, political practices,[5] but they do have political effects, and their results are related to their political effects in such a way that it is *politically* desirable, from the point of view of human emancipation, that cognitive practices be not politicised, but carried out in accordance with their own criteria. Does it follow that the most likely source of liberatory ideas is a non-political community of impartial scholars?

No, it does not. In the first place because politically relevant distortions of scholarship are not only or for the most part the results of conscious political intervention, but of unconscious ideology. But a brief detour into the theory of knowledge will help here. Not the areas of the theory of knowledge which have dominated the academy – that is on the one hand the philosophy of science (which has yielded important results) and on the other the philosophy of perception (which has not). Rather, we need to develop an approach to the theory of knowledge which is more fundamental, more general, and closer to the concerns of political argument, namely the *theory of hearsay and how to see beyond it*.

First of all it is necessary to recognise, as have Spinoza and Heidegger among philosophers, the primacy of hearsay in knowledge. Not only in the sense that the vast majority of what we know is hearsay and nothing but hearsay (which is uncontentious enough), but also in the sense that such knowledge as has surer foundations than hearsay is a secondary development, that could not have emerged without hearsay as its foundation. Attempts to privilege *perception* as the foundation of knowledge, for instance, can be countered with the fact that what we perceive is determined not *only* (though of course it is partly) by what is there; it is also conditioned by what we have learnt through hearsay, and this is not just a set of prejudicing preconceptions, but the condition of our perceiving things at all in the manner we do, that is in a manner potentially more informative than that in which animals perceive. It is when we have learnt through hearsay about different species of birds that we see swallows and oyster-catchers and great tits, not just birds; and (*pace* Hume) we can see cases of causation, and of many other abstract concepts, not just coloured shapes.

This we could hardly do had we not learnt, along with our mother tongue, the language of causality. But this does not mean we can abstract the causal 'judgement' from the act of perception, and get back to what we 'really' saw, viz, coloured shapes. The coloured shape aspect may be less certain than the causal aspect. One may see the dog chase away the cat, without noticing the colour or shape of the dog.

But hearsay is notoriously unreliable. Having been initiated into knowledge through hearsay, how do we get beyond it? We have only three means of doing so, each of which comes in what I shall call a barehanded form and an armed form. They are *reason, practice* and *suspicion*.

By 'barehanded reason' I mean *logic*, the science of exposing ambiguities in, and eliminating inconsistencies between, our ideas. Logic cannot by itself replace hearsay by better founded knowledge, since it does not tell us which of two conflicting beliefs is true, only that they can't both be true. An inconsistent conjunction of beliefs may be better than a consistent but false one, or even than a consistent, true, but relatively uninformative one. But it can't be entirely true. So the discovery of inconsistencies can motivate further questioning to discover by other means which is false. I stress this, since some sceptics about truth nevertheless value consistency, and there can be no case for such a position. (By the same token, 'coherence theories' of truth are only plausible if interpreted as theories about the *criteria* of truth, presupposing that what it is for a judgement to be true is defined by the correspondence theory.)

The elimination of ambiguities can also be considered a logical skill. Ambiguities are a particularly pernicious source of mystification in politics (for instance, the sense/reference ambiguities that I mentioned earlier with respect to 'the free world' and 'democratic socialists'), so unclarity of political language is usually a sign of something to hide, and hence a ground for suspicion of the user as a class enemy.

In addition to barehanded reason, there is armed reason, by which I mean reason which draws on an already established body of well-founded knowledge, in judging particular deliverances of hearsay to be credible or incredible. For instance if someone claimed to have invented a perpetual motion machine, or discovered a case of spontaneous generation, or a human society somewhere in which there was no homosexuality, or a case of a ruling class handing over its wealth and power to the people without violent resistance, we would quite simply dismiss their stories, without bothering to investigate, since they are incompatible with well-verified information that we already have.

By barehanded practice I mean just any activity which achieves some end by acting on things in the world. All such activities induce beliefs in their agents, and these beliefs may contradict and correct the deliverances of hearsay. We should not underestimate the extent to which errors entrenched in hearsay have been corrected in this manner. It *is* often underestimated because it is *also* true that many errors of hearsay are confirmed in this manner. Pomona, the goddess of apple trees, is said to require that when you drink a glass of cider, you should pour out the last drop as a libation to her. In all probability, generations of cider drinkers have verified this – the sacrilegious being punished by headaches, the pious rewarded by the absence of headaches. But the effect of the dregs on the human organism may have more to do with this than the wrath of the goddess. To discover this, armed practice is required – practice which, on the basis of existing knowledge, frames hypotheses, and has as its aim the testing of these claims about the world, guided by existing knowledge in judging what a given outcome would indicate. Scientific experiments are the most developed form of armed practice. 'Practice' in these cognitive contexts is a near-synonym for 'experience', in a certain sense of that word. But I have avoided it because of the empiricist tendency to identify experience with sensation.

Barehanded suspicion is simply the move, in response to a bit of hearsay, of saying 'well, they would say that, wouldn't they?'. A very elementary move, but it plays an enormous role in our judgement – particularly our judgement of politically relevant information. A man whose job in the British civil service required him to read all the newspapers, back in the thirties when there were papers of all political complexions, wanted to find out the truth about Hitler. He found that socialist and liberal papers all said that Hitler was a tyrant and Germany full of concentration camps, while the Tory papers were full of praise for Hitler. To find out which was true, he went to Germany and spoke to some German friends whom he had known since his student days. One, who came from a traditional gentry family and had formerly been sympathetic to the Nazis in the hope that they might restore paternalistic labour-relations, told him there was a concentration camp in the vicinity of his father's estate, and no one locally could be in any doubt about the atrocities that went on there. This told the Englishman what he needed to know. But why was this piece of hearsay convincing, when after all the left of centre papers in Britain had given much the same information? It is entirely a matter of where the suspicion is to be placed.

In various ways, suspicion can be armed with prior knowledge. One may generalise from instances in which one has been able to compare common reports of an event with one's own experience of that event, in judging common reports about distant events, and 'read between the lines' of the latter reports. One may also become aware of a common species of hearsay that is recognisable, and particularly unreliable. For instance, having learnt about the prevalence of 'urban legends', those (usually nasty) tales that travel rapidly round the world as things that happened to a friend of a friend in the town down the road, one might come to recognise a particular report as bearing the marks of that genre. Certain styles of political discourse can also justifiably alert suspicion. As an adolescent, I read the Stalinist *History of the Communist Party of the Soviet Union (Bolsheviks)*, and was easily able to recognise, even without any independent source of information about Soviet history, the mendacity of a text that included chapters with headings such as:

> Degeneration of the Bukharinites Into Political Double-Dealers.
> Degeneration of the Trotskyite Double-Dealers Into a White-guard Gang of Assassins and Spies. Foul Murder of S.M. Kirov.
> Measures of the Party to Heighten Bolshevik Vigilance.

At the most theoretical level of armed suspicion, there are such weapons as Marx's theory of ideology, Freud's of repression and rationalisation – the theories that earned them the title 'masters of suspicion'. These are accounts of the mechanisms by which false beliefs are generated and come to be accepted. If such theories can show that a given belief is exactly what we would have expected to exist, even if false, given the relevant psychic or social structure, then we should exercise suspicion.

Of these means of checking or going beyond hearsay, the following can be said: reason is the most reliable so far as it goes, but it does not go very far. Practice really does have a crucial role as the unique source of positive information, since only here are soundings actually taken of the objective world. But it accounts (directly) only for a tiny portion of our knowledge, and is also itself so permeated by hearsay as to be pretty unreliable in so far as it falls short of scientific experiment – and most of us can only know of most scientific experiments by hearsay. Suspicion, though the least reliable, must inevitably be massively predominant in determining how we assess hearsay and so form our beliefs.

But suspicion, in so far as it passes beyond the barehanded stage, is not politically innocent. The knowledge that arms suspicion is for the most part the same sort of knowledge as that which determines political standpoints. Theories about the class nature of ideologies, for instance, are essential epistemic armour; but they are also theories with implications about which side one should be on in the class struggle. The point is not that these theories are politicised in the bad sense, but that they purport to be, and at best are, *bona fide* bits of objective social scientific knowledge – and that objective knowledge, as we have seen, is not neutral. The facts believed generate the values to be realised.

So it is not always irrational or naive to believe the reports of your own party or politico-theoretical tendency, provided your choice of party is an intelligent one. One may give credence to the reports of one's own tendency, not because of any assumptions of personal trustworthiness or otherwise, but because the theoretical differences that generate different political positions also generate, not only different explanations of events, but different placements of suspicion with regard to the sources of information, and hence different conjectures as to what the events have been. So, to return to the starting point of this detour, if the class analysis of politics is correct, then a journal of a party committed to class politics is likely to be a more reliable source of information about political conjunctures than an academic journal with pretensions to neutrality – and this goes, not just for explanatory hypotheses, but for reports of events.

Now to return to the distinction between political and moral[6] practices, to consider their mutual effects, and the ill effects of failing to keep them distinct. I have distinguished practices (or aspects of practices) by their criteria of success, that is, in a certain sense, by their goals. And it might be said that in the end the goals of morality and politics are the same – that our common life should be a good one. But this is, and must remain, rather vague. The concrete goals of the two kinds of practice cannot be the same, because they are acting in two distinct kinds of structure which work in very different ways: social structures, and structures of personal relations. We have seen that these structures *are* distinct in that the means of transforming one is not the means of transforming the other. Of course, since some of the bearers of social structures are people,[7] many practices will have both moral and political aspects. As with other practices with more than one aspect, the two can conflict. Sometimes, they will just happen to conflict, as in a conflict of personal loyalties with political principle, for example Shakespeare's Brutus. But it is particularly important to distinguish the moral and the political, since the conflicts between them are not always contingent. Political and moral practices actually require different sets of virtues, and mutually contradictory sets. This is obvious in the case of violence, which is not only sometimes politically necessary, but is (as threat if not actuality) written into the nature of politics, yet is always to be deplored morally. There are at least three other areas of such built-in conflict: distrust, which is a vice in personal relations, but a political virtue (not just 'never trust a Tory'; never trust a leader or a representative either); loyalty, which at the moral level can only be to individual people, while in politics it is necessarily general, if not indeed abstract – quite a different kind of character-trait, and one which does not easily co-exist with strong personal loyalties; and what may be called, in the popular rather than the philosophical sense, materialism: in any non-mystified practice of politics, the stake is power over the material world; the pursuit of such power in personal life is destructive and disastrous.

This is not a problem that can be solved: the essential thing here is that the contradictions between morality and politics be recognised and lived with, not suppressed, either by papering them over, or by suppressing either pole of the contradiction. For despite the conflict, the effect of sacrificing either morality or politics to the other one would be disastrous to the practice chosen, as well as to that sacrificed. Political considerations may override moral ones, but if this happens too easily, we lose that sense of proportion between means and ends without which principle becomes fanaticism. And while in one sense, abstention from politics makes it easier to be moral, that morality is inevitably of narrow horizons, and easily degenerates into self-indulgent philistinism. Any attempt to apply a common set of principles across the two practices can only lead to one or other of these forms of corruption.

For the most part, the question of the political effects of personal corruption becomes a serious one precisely when the form that that corruption takes is the hypertrophy of the political virtues and the atrophy of others – that is when it becomes true, as Brecht said, that 'He who fights for Communism has of all virtues only one: that he fights for Communism.'[8]

The point is that a free socialist commonwealth cannot be built by people who have become political machines – or at the very least, such a corruption postpones that task to another generation, just as Solomon had to build the Temple because David was a man of war.

So in this most crucial instance of the effects of 'the personal' on 'the political', a satisfactory outcome can only be secured on condition that 'the personal' is neither mistaken for, nor subordinated to, politics.

Notes

1. For instance, Quintin Hogg's famous remark that 'Conservatives do not believe that political struggle is the most important thing in life ... The simplest among them prefer fox-hunting – the wisest religion' (*The Case for Conservatism*, p. 10). It is easy to laugh at the incongruous disjunction, but he is pointing to a real moral strength of conservatism (genuine conservatism, not the licensed vandalism that passes for conservatism today), as is made clear by the next sentence:

To the great majority of Conservatives, religion, art, study, family, country, friends, music, fun, duty, all the joy and riches of existence of which the poor no less than the rich are the indefeasible freeholders, all these are higher in the scale than their handmaiden, the political struggle.

The scientific socialist (as opposed to the utopian) ought to be able to say something similar, and agree with Hogg's conclusion that 'The man who puts politics first is not fit to be called a civilised being.'

2. To forestall a possible (obvious) objection: granted, structural change could be prevented by sufficiently prevalent cowardice, lack of proletarian discipline, etc. But these vices, though of course they are the qualities of people, are political not personal vices, in the sense that they are vices precisely *because* they prevent the desirable structural changes.

3. I don't mean to imply that the suppression of information is never justified. In the world as it is, it would obviously be desirable to suppress knowledge of new means of warfare, or indeed, knowledge of how to determine the sex of your offspring.

4. It might be asked: leaving aside misinformation (or 'disinformation', as it is now prissily called), what about the politically motivated *selection* of facts for emphasis? There are two distinct issues here; one may select facts for practical reasons (for example some facts about the economy may be useful for business purposes but useless for the purposes of the workers' movement and vice versa), or for polemical purposes (that is to give a onesided picture of the situation); the former is acceptable, the latter not.

5. That is to say, when a cognitive practice is *also* a political practice, the political effect is *by reason of* the cognitive effect, and so not something which could provide an independent criterion.

6. 'Moral' in the sense of the ethics of personal relations, rather than as a synonym of ethics in general.

7. Some, not all. 'Artificial persons' such as limited companies, and perhaps also material objects such as computers, roads, weapons, tools, books, etc. can be considered 'bearers of social positions'.

8. Consider Lenin's denunciation of Stalin's rudeness as disqualifying him for the post of General Secretary, 'although quite tolerable in our midst and in dealings among us Communists' (*Selected Works in One Volume*, p. 683), and Luxemburg's remarks about politics as 'inane Baal-worship, driving people – victims of their own obsession, of mental rabies – to sacrifice their entire existence' (*Comrade and Lover*, p. 153).

6
Political Sublimation

> Now too much of nothing
> Can make a man a liar
> It can cause some men to sleep on nails
> It can cause others to eat fire
> – Bob Dylan

The Concept of Sublimation in Political Contexts

The concept of sublimation is generally associated with the names of Nietzsche and Freud, and since (i) my use of it is closer to the Freudian use than to the Nietzschean, (ii) I shall nevertheless be drawing on some other ideas of Nietzsche's in this chapter, and (iii) Freud left this concept relatively unclarified, a few words about its use in Nietzsche and Freud are in order.

I take it that Nietzsche takes the root meaning 'making more sublime' seriously; for Nietzsche, sublimation makes something worse into something better. Much of Nietzsche's work is the search for the 'evil' origins of 'good' things, and much of this aims to debunk the 'good' things; but in the theory of sublimation, it is rather the 'evil' things that are partly exonerated as pre-conditions of really good ones. Thus, if the ethos of conquest, piracy and vengeance in the Homeric heroes was, in the course of Greek history, sublimated into the Socratic contest in dialectic, and if the latter is much to be admired, then we may be led to admire the same combative energy in the Homeric pirates that we admire in Socratic debate, without in any way wishing to revert to the former. That at any rate is one reading of Nietzsche. Sublimation here does not pre-suppose aim-inhibition. It is not that Socrates would have liked to be looting the Anatolian shore, was prevented from doing so, and so made do with discomfitting Callicles. The combative impulse has been educated and complexified rather than frustrated and diverted.

In Freud, however, sublimation occurs to a wish the aim of which has been inhibited. Thus, if what had been a simple sexual attraction to someone becomes a loving relationship, that is sublimation in Nietzsche's sense, but not in Freud's. Dante's platonic love for Beatrice is sublimation in Freud's sense. Freudian sublimation calls to mind the use of the word 'sublimation' in chemistry: the transformation of a solid directly into a gas. Hence 'sublimation' as it has passed from Freud into common usage has acquired an ironic sense; we do not necessarily think the substitute aim more sublime than the inhibited aim – often, just more gassy.

Certain political phenomena akin to sublimation in the Freudian sense have long been familiar to historians of ideas. In particular, the Hellenistic philosophies and religious cults that arose in the aftermath of the fall of the Greek and Roman republics have been widely seen as unsatisfactory substitutes for participation in civic life. Likewise, it has been suggested (for instance in Christopher Hill's writings) that the changes that occurred in English radical movements after the defeat of the Levellers in 1649 were a retreat from practice to mysticism. These accounts are often Marxist in inspiration, but not always. Some such reading of the culture of late antiquity was a staple of the intellectual climate in which Marx grew up. A similar theme recurs in Isaiah Berlin's essay *Two Concepts of Liberty*, in the section headed 'The retreat to the inner citadel'; freedom, instead of being a goal to be realised in the public world, is presented as something we can all have by training ourselves not to care about the public world. It comes to mean independence of the world outside, not unimpeded action upon it. Berlin is surely right to see this sublimation as a retreat; public liberty requires people who will not be content to change themselves rather than the world. Freud was of the same judgement, regarding 'alloplastic' behaviour (changing the world) as characteristic of psychic health, 'autoplastic' behaviour (changing oneself, 'adaptation') as characteristic of neurosis. Usually, the retreat from alloplastic to autoplastic strategies involves the substitution of a moral goal to be realised by individual action for a political goal to be realised by collective action. This is obviously the case with the retreat from 'outer' to 'inner' liberty, as described by Berlin; another example would be the replacement of the goal of abolishing poverty through common ownership by that of alleviating it by private charity.

When Freud characterised healthy behaviour as alloplastic and neurotic behaviour as autoplastic (in his paper 'The Loss of Reality in Neurosis and Psychosis'), he also characterised psychosis as remoulding the world in fantasy, having retreated from practical remoulding of it. There is a political equivalent of this, too. The state of affairs which it was previously aimed to bring about by political action comes to be seen as already realised in some 'higher' or 'deeper' metaphysical sense, as when Emperor and slave are seen by Cynic and Stoic philosophy as equal, while remaining Emperor and slave. This can be called a metaphysical sublimation of some political sense of equality; the same can happen to the notion of freedom. Philosophies which claim that we are inherently free, whatever our 'external' situation, sap the urgency of political liberation. My ethics tutor, Dr Aurel Kolnai, once quoted Bernard Shaw to the effect that we ought to try to get what we want or we will come to want what we get; he commented that this both affirmed and denied human dignity. It affirmed it by maintaining that it is better to try to get what one wants than to adapt to circumstances, but denies it by exaggerating our capacity for adaptation. Individualistic ('autoplastic') sublimations of the goal of freedom tell us that it is better to adapt, and metaphysical sublimations of it tell us that adaptation is always possible. Hence there is an intelligible as well as a historical connection between exaggerated notions of our 'metaphysical' freedom, and disparagement of political freedom. The occasional partisan of political liberation who has also defended metaphysical freedom (such as Sartre), is an anomaly – and almost exclusively a recent one.

Sublimation is a vicissitude to which any goal can be subjected, if conditions become adverse enough. Socialism is (for reasons discussed in the appendix to this chapter) rather less prone to sublimation than most political movements. Nevertheless, there does exist a 'sublimated socialist' ideology; it comes in 'right' and 'left' versions. The 'right' versions claim that socialism is something 'deeper' than an economic system, it is a 'moral ideal' or whatever – and thus excuse themselves from the task of transforming the economic system. The 'left' versions aim to transform the economic system, but *also* to go deeper, to collectivise, not just factories and farms, but living quarters, eating arrangements, styles of artistic and scientific work, and so on. In terms of practical politics, 'deep socialists' of the right are usually on their way out of left-of-centre politics altogether, while 'deep socialists' of the left serve mainly to drive others away from it – though the switch from left to right 'deep socialism' is also surprisingly easy to make, as witness so many of the generation radicalised in 1968. In either case, people who say that socialism is 'a new religion' or 'more than a religion – a way of life' and such like need to be firmly reminded that socialism is a way of organising the production and distribution of material goods – no more, and no less.

Quite generally, one should be suspicious of tendencies which try to go 'deeper' in this sense than their political comrades (for example 'deep ecology', 'radical feminism'), as tendencies which, at best, lumber their movements with a lot of metaphysical baggage which alienates potential comrades whose feet remain on the ground, or worse, form routes whereby dissent can be diverted from practice to mysticism; worst of all, when by some freak of history 'deep' politics comes to power, its attempts to perform metaphysical miracles by political means generates appalling cruelties, and discredits the politics of which it was a sublimation for a long time.

So far, I have described political sublimation as a historical process whereby a political goal of one period becomes a non-political ideal or a metaphysical claim at another, later period. I now want to consider the ongoing ideological mechanism whereby oppressed groups produce metaphysical and moral displacements of the goal of their self-liberation, which serve to keep them oppressed. On this matter, a great deal can be learnt from that unlikely teacher of the left, Nietzsche. But a word of caution is needed here, for in so far as Nietzsche has been appropriated by the left recently, it is either the weakest part of his philosophy that has been taken over (that is his pragmatist theory of knowledge), or else he has been used to lend credence to a crude identification of the history of ideas with power struggle – crude in that it is assumed simplistically that if group A becomes more powerful than group B, group A's ideas will prevail over group B's, to the advantage of group A and the detriment of group B. What can really be learnt from Nietzsche is why that is not so.

'Slave Rebellion in Morals'; Hyndman's Hat

According to Nietzsche, moral ideas can be classified as master-moralities and slave-moralities. Master-moralities operate with the pair of concepts 'good/bad'; these are naturalistic concepts; strength, health, happiness etc. are good, their lack bad. The slaves see these qualities as those of their oppressors, and dub them 'evil'; since they themselves lack these qualities, they can see themselves as 'good', i.e. not evil. Hence slave morality is the inversion of naturalistic values, and, since good is only the lack of evil, this morality is not only anti-naturalistic, but ultimately nihilistic. But it has been highly successful; Nietzsche saw the European morality of his day as containing a greater 'slave' than 'master' component. By exposing the ignoble origins of this morality in the mentality of 'sour grapes', Nietzsche wanted to revalue the naturalistic values on the 'good/bad' axis, and take us beyond the 'good/evil' axis of slave morality.

Nietzsche refers to the triumph of slave morality as a 'slave rebellion in morals'. A word of caution is necessary here. People on the left naturally sympathise with slave rebellions – Spartacus is one of our heroes. But a slave rebellion in morals is not a slave rebellion. It is an alternative to one, a sublimation of the aim-inhibited desire for liberation. It is because the slaves believe (possibly correctly) that the good things of their masters' lives can never be theirs, that they treat them as 'sour grapes'; and because they idealise their own slavish qualities, they can retain a self-respect that they would have lost if they had seen these things as essential to a worthwhile life. And because they do not see them as essential, they lack the motivation to rebel.

Since nothing is harder than to endure life believing that one is excluded from what is most worthwhile, it is not surprising that all oppressed groups tend (though there are also counter-tendencies) to idealise features of their life that are (in fact) effects of oppression, and to denigrate power, knowledge, beauty, culture, pleasure, etc. I do not know of any pre-capitalist movement of the oppressed which was without this streak of nihilistic asceticism. For even when such movements do project liberation, they conceive it at first in terms, not of the general appropriation of the masters' benefits, but of the destruction of them, and the generalisation of their own deprivation. This is the 'crude communism' described by Marx as the result of universal envy (*Early Writings*, pp. 346–7). Only so far as liberation becomes a real historical possibility on the basis of modern collective labour, and labour-saving technology, can this 'Nietzschean factor' in the ideology of the oppressed be overcome. Even then, the deadweight of tradition of the slave-morality remains an obstacle to the project of liberation. In this sense, unintended by the Hebrew proverb against which the prophets testified, the fathers have eaten sour grapes and the children's teeth have been set on edge.

It is, of course, part of Nietzsche's claim, that the master-morality is closer to the truth than the slave-morality. And surely he is right about this. The things that the masters value are the things which everyone would value if they did not have to reconcile themselves to their chains; the things that people in a classless society would value, and that the slaves do value when they forget themselves, or remember themselves sufficiently to project self-liberation. They are continuous with (though not reducible to) biological values, and they are consistent with self-awareness in a way that slave-values are not. The adherent of slave-morality is necessarily self-divided and self-deceived. Hence the strength of Nietzsche's explanatory critique of slave moralities – an account which has its parallels in scientific socialist literature. Thus Karl Kautsky notes (in connection with medieval movements of the oppressed):

> A class or community which is in process of decline, or hopelessly trodden down by others, will always oppose itself to knowledge of truth. It will not use its intelligence to define clearly that which *is*, but will try to discover arguments by means of which it can pacify, console and – deceive itself. (*Communism in Central Europe at the Time of the Reformation*, p. 19)

and he also attributes to these pre-proletarian communists a 'gloomy Puritanism' which

> brought the communists into opposition, not merely with the ruling classes, but frequently also with the labouring classes of the day, who were still strong in their ancient love of life, and full of cheerful good humour. (*ibid.*, p. 22)

The slave class, of course, did not come to power and impose its values on European (or any other) civilisation. The notion that it did could only be maintained on the basis of a crude identification of Christianity with the slave morality. But from the standpoint of class ideology, the history of Christianity in the Roman Empire has to be divided into three distinct phases, punctuated by radical transformations. The Christianity of the first century was an eschatological religion of the oppressed, heralding their liberation by divine intervention on this earth; that of the following two centuries was an otherworldly religion of the oppressed, promising liberation after death for those oppressed on earth; that which emerged after Constantine was an other-worldly religion of the oppressors, making good use of slave morality, while enlarging its needle's eye for the safe passage of loaded camels, and exiling communists like St John Chrysostom. Nietzsche's picture of Christianity is recognisable only of the second phase, while it is the third, with its specific appropriation of the slave morality for the use of masters, that is of chief interest to the critic of class ideology. For if the masters adopted slave morality, they did so out of class interest.

To view the matter in abstraction from specific historic instances, let us imagine two arbitrary groups, As and Bs. If As acquire power and appropriate the best things for themselves, what ideas will they benefit from spreading among Bs? Precisely the ideas that As have no real benefits from their power, that in the most important respects it is much better to be a B, that Bs are much wiser, have beautiful souls, will be rewarded in Heaven; that Bs should be proud of being uncorrupted by luxury, free of the guilt that power brings, and having heads uncluttered by useless knowledge; that Bs are close to the earth, full of folk wisdom, free from the cares of the world. Everything is made easy for As by the fact that Bs largely convince themselves of these myths. Wise As will be careful not to disturb this faith of the Bs. And it is the way of such useful myths that the As will come to partly believe them themselves. Only partly: the aristocrat may write poetry praising the life of the shepherd, but call for the rack and wheel if his daughter wants to marry one.

If for a moment we set aside all the other factors at work in producing ideologies (of which of course straightforward class interest is certainly one), we can abstract this 'Nietzchean factor', generating among any oppressed group an ideology which gives it its self-respect, and reconciles it to its oppression by portraying its features resulting from its oppression as 'good', the good things withheld from it by oppression as 'evil'; and the more oppressed the group, the more oppressive the ideology. The Nietzschean factor never operates in isolation from other factors, of course, any more than does any other law of nature or history; but in so far as it operates (and I suggest that in all oppressed groups other than the proletariat it has been the dominant factor), the paradoxical conclusion holds that it is actually the ideas of the oppressed that serve the interest of the oppressor; and even (potentially, at least) the ideas of the oppressor that serve the interest of the oppressed. This last phenomenon might be called 'the Hyndman's hat effect', on the basis of the following anecdote told of Hyndman, founder of the first British Marxist organisation, the Social Democratic Federation:

> His squat, formidable figure, with bushy eyebrows and a huge beard, perfectly dressed in top hat, frock-coat and striped trousers,

was regularly to be seen in Hyde Park and Trafalgar Square, handing out leaflets or denouncing the British governing class. To a down-and-out workman who asked him how he dared dress like that, he answered mercilessly: 'Because your class are idiots enough to enable people like me to do so.' (Raymond Postgate, *The Life of George Lansbury*, p. 32)

The Hyndman's hat effect may be illustrated by the example of the relations between the various moral philosophies of ancient Greece; Aristotle's ethics is by far the most realistic and conducive to human emancipation, not least because he recognises the phenomena noted by Engels:

> Only very exceptionally, and in no case to his and other people's profit, can an individual satisfy his urge towards happiness by preoccupation with himself. Rather it requires preoccupation with the outside world, means to satisfy his needs, that is to say, means of subsistence, an individual of the opposite sex, books, conversation, argument, objects for use and working up. (in 'Ludwig Feuerbach and the Outcome of Classical German Philosophy', *Selected Works in Two Volumes*, pp. 447–8)

We may be sure that the poor and the slaves would not have been attracted by Aristotle's ideas, but rather by those which made virtue and happiness independent of 'externals'. And Aristotle did not intend his ethics for such people: he addressed it quite explicitly to well brought up Greek gentlemen.

But suppose, by some historical freak, there had been a serious political movement of the oppressed for liberation, which had been able to elaborate its own ideology. Its principal enemy in the realm of ideas would have been precisely those ideas (for example Cynic and Stoic ethics) which taught that 'external' freedom and well-being was unnecessary; and there would have been no better intellectual armoury for fighting this enemy than the ethics of Aristotle. This 'master-morality' would have served the cause of the oppressed, at the very least as an irritant and a challenge, a 'Hyndman's hat'.

As I have said, the Nietzschean factor never has it all its own way. People always do *also* defend their real class interests, individually or collectively, and the desire to supplant the masters co-exists with the attitude of 'sour grapes'. Sometimes, in a crisis, the oppressed will fight genuine liberation struggles under slogans drawn from the ideology that, in stabler times, kept them oppressed. But it is noteworthy:

1. that the proletariat, more than any other oppressed class, has always struggled to appropriate the benefits of the 'masters' ' civilisation rather than decrying them;
2. that scientific socialism, unlike the great majority of theories that have guided the politics of the oppressed, has been free from the spirit of sour grapes, as witness its positive evaluation of the arts and sciences, and its refusal to subordinate them to politics (compare Rousseau, or the radical Puritans, or the medieval communist heretics). This is to be explained by the exceptional character of the proletariat among oppressed groups, as described in the appendix to this chapter.

I think these two points will be readily conceded so far as the contrast between the workers' movement in capitalism and pre-capitalist popular movements is concerned. But I think it is also true that other oppressed groups within capitalism, *except in so far as they overlap with the proletariat*, are also far more prone to the Nietzschean factor, far more likely than the workers to produce ideologies which, while often seen as political and emancipatory, are actually more regressive than the ideas typical of the ruling class. (The exception-clause is of the first importance since the majority of members of most oppressed groups defined other than by class – for example women and ethnic minorities – are also proletarians, and the majority of proletarians are also members of some such oppressed group). Populist forms of fascism, and religio-political fundamentalisms are uncontentious instances of regressive ideologies on the part of the non-proletarian oppressed, and exhibit many features of 'slave-morality'.

But in so far as the 'New Left' has abandoned the idea of the leading role of the working class, and increasingly adopted the viewpoint that, since all forms of oppression are morally intolerable to socialists, they should be treated as on a par causally and therefore strategically as well,[1] it has laid itself wide open to the infiltration of the repressive ideologies of the oppressed, forms of political sublimation which end by putting flowers on their chains.

In the following section, I shall discuss political sublimation in relation to some modern political ideals and movements – a discussion which can easily be generalised to others.

Contemporary Instances

In the first place, it must be said that, though the Nietzschean factor is not the dominant tendency in proletarian ideology, it is not absent either. The lifestyle that is generally supposed to prevail among workers at any given time and place is often idealised by workers, and even more so by middle-class socialists who would like to be mistaken for workers. Often this class stereotype will include features which are not only effects of exploitation, but means to its perpetuation. For example, aversion to theory is often treated as an unalterable characteristic of the working class, even by socialist activists. The history of the miners' libraries should be sufficient witness to the fact that, when real class consciousness prevails, workers can run rings round other classes in their capacity for theory.

Even scientific socialists sometimes slide into 'workerist' errors, for instance Lenin's praise of the effects of factory discipline in preparing workers for party discipline of which Luxemburg rightly comments:

> We misuse words and we practise self-deception when we apply the same term – discipline – to such dissimilar notions as: (1) the absence of thought and will in a body with a thousand automatically moving hands and legs, and (2) the spontaneous co-ordination of the conscious, political acts of a body of men. What is there in common between the regulated docility of an oppressed class and the self-discipline and organisation of a class struggling for its emancipation? ('Organisational Question of Social Democracy', *Rosa Luxemburg Speaks*, p. 119)

The contrast between workerism in this sense[2] and the proletarian class consciousness is a conflict between the class's interest in its *emancipation* (and hence abolition), and its interest in its *identity* (and hence self-perpetuation). Quite generally, in any group, the politics of identity is the rival of the politics of liberation. Perhaps this is part of what Althusser meant by saying that ideology hails one as a subject and evokes recognition ('that's me!'). Wherever the group concerned is an exploited class, the politics of identity is necessarily adverse to liberation, since it is precisely exploitation that constitutes the identity of the class. There are also other, contingent effects of the politics of identity, since such politics always projects an image of a group, which never corresponds to the reality of all (even if any) of its members. When we hear of 'the British worker', we are more likely to think (so far as we are influenced by workerist ideology) of a white male factory worker with a passion for football and a taste for bitter than of a black female typist with a passion for ballet and a taste for yoghurt. And such onesided images are usually taken for granted in all that talk about the working class disappearing. Often, no more is meant than that less and less workers would look at home in a Lowry painting.

In groups which are oppressed, but which are not constituted as the groups they are entirely by that oppression, the relation between the politics of identity and the politics of liberation is more difficult to unravel. This is particularly so with nationalism which, even when it starts purely as a movement of liberation, almost always ends in a politics of identity.

Undoubtedly the most important non-class based movement of an oppressed group in the West today is feminism. I use the term 'feminism' here to mean any commitment to women's liberation, whether it accounts for the oppression of women by some autonomous structure such as 'patriarchy' or in Marxist fashion, as an effect of class exploitation. I shall not discuss that difference (which is a scientific rather than a philosophical question), but rather the difference between feminism as a political movement for liberation (that is for an equal share in social power), and the metaphysical sublimation of feminism, which in so far as it has political effects, issues in a politics of identity. I refer only to metaphysical, not to moralistic sublimations of feminist politics for the following reason: while most feminists reject the distinction between the personal and the political, if that distinction is retained (as I have argued it should be), some feminist concerns fall on the political side, and some on the personal. And that is perfectly proper: the liberation of women is served by certain projects of moral reform as well as certain projects of political transformation. So while I would argue that the moral and the political aspects of feminism should be kept distinct, I would not argue that the former are all mere sublimations of the latter.

The topic of the sublimation of feminist politics and its effect on the left in general is so large that I shall limit myself to a single example which, though it might seem too exclusively of philosophical interest, is symptomatic enough to suggest how my point could be generalised. It concerns the manner in which a particular sexist notion is criticised, that is, the notion that men are more rational than women.

This example has been used (though in hypothetical language) by Russell Keat, in his article 'Masculinity in Philosophy' (*Radical Philosophy* no. 34, 1983). He sets up a hypothetical philosopher who believes that rationality is the basis of moral worth (that is who is a 'moral rationalist'), and who also holds that men are more rational than women. Of course, this hypothetical philosopher has many real avatars, that is all rationalist and idealist philosophers from the Greeks to Hegel (and some others). Clearly this view is sexist. One way of attacking it is by arguing that it is *false* that men are more rational than women. This line of attack need not involve any very far-reaching rejection of the philosophy in question – that is one could remain a Thomist, a Spinozist or a Kantian on all points except their denigration of women's rationality. Let me say right away that I think this is exactly the right sort of way to attack the sexism of the old philosophers. It is a false assumption shared with the whole culture of their times, and noteworthy only in that, in the context of thought-systems more rigorous than those of most of their contemporaries, this error usually sticks out a mile. Thus Kant, in his *Metaphysical Elements of Justice*, unwittingly commits himself to the proposition that, in a well-constituted state, every woman should have the opportunity of becoming a man![3]

But Keat contrasts this sort of criticism with another: the hypothetical sexist-rationalist may be criticised for what Keat calls *genderism*, that is the view that this quality that is generally regarded as male (rationality) is superior to whatever the supposedly female alternative to it is (he suggests 'emotionality').[4] He points out that attacks on sexism in philosophy are often tacitly genderist, for example in denying the claim that men are more rational than women, one is likely to be accepting the claim that rationality (which is commonly regarded as the male alternative) is superior to its alternative. An attack on genderism in philosophy would of course involve a much more radical re-assessment of the history of philosophy than would an attack on sexism: in the case in point, the value of rationality would have to be questioned, and perhaps the arch-rationalists like Aristotle, Spinoza and Kant removed from the syllabus, to be replaced by anti-rationalist philosophers like Hamann, Keyserling, Wittgenstein and Feyerabend.

But is this radicalism a liberatory one? I think not. After all, anti-rationalism is not new to European culture, it has a long tradition, though for the most part in other disciplines than philosophy. Though it *has* sometimes praised the supposedly feminine alternatives to rationality (Schleiermacher wished he were a woman for this sort of reason), such praise, as is well known, is endemic in sexist ideology. It does no service to women's liberation to link it with the cult of unreason,[5] which has already done enough evil under the sun. If, as is often said by 'metaphysical feminists', rational values prevail over irrational ones in European universities, that is not because of male dominance, but because the Allied powers defeated the Fascist ones in 1945. Keat tells us that 'nearly all actual cases of sexism and genderism do involve the assumption of male dominance and masculine superiority – since, roughly speaking, all or most societies are and have been patriarchal'. So far as sexism is concerned, this is obviously true, but reversed genderism has played a large role as a slave-morality, devaluing the values that are necessary to any free sex or class. This function of reversed genderism becomes obvious if we change the example from rationality to, say autonomy, or better still, the possession of a share in the social power. These have *really* (and not just in conventional stereotype)[6] been monopolised by (some) men (never all men). But if these values are devalued as merely masculine (as sometimes has occurred in anti-political versions of feminism), then the case for women's liberation itself is undermined.

So while it is necessary (and very easy) to identify and reject the sexism of most of the classical philosophers, their 'genderism' is generally innocuous – even liberating, in a Hyndman's-hattish sort of way. For the qualities assigned to women by sexist cultures are precisely either qualities which in fact result from exclusion from power, or qualities of the sort always imputed to those excluded from power.

My broader conclusion is that the left needs to discriminate in its adoption of feminist ideas between two kinds of feminism: that which demands for women the same share in social power that men have, which should be an integral part of every socialist programme. and that which presses the claims of a supposedly specifically feminine contribution to human society and culture, largely corresponding to what traditional European sexism regards as the specifically feminine qualities. The latter should be regarded as just one more slave morality, one more source of opium for the people. Similar discrimination is necessary with regard to all other 'new social movements'.

Appendix

The Historical Uniqueness of the Proletariat

In these days when the word 'dogmatic' means anyone who is not a slavish follower of intellectual fashion, any talk about the special liberatory potential of the working class tends to be dismissed as dogmatism, mysticism, secular messianism, etc. The 'mystery', as so often in such cases, is not in the absence of arguments for this view, but in the ignorance of those arguments on the part of those who make these accusations.

The first part of the argument for the proletariat's historically unique potential – the part that features largest in the works of Marx and Engels – is simply that it is the main exploited class in the first period of human history in which the material pre-requisites for general emancipation have existed. The case for this must by now be clear: if all are to have enough leisure and training for the management and improvement of civilisation, labour-saving technology must have reached a certain level, which was in sight for the first time in the age of Marx and Engels, and has by now long since arrived in the industrially developed world.

But there are other features, which distinguish the proletariat from its contemporary oppressed classes. Bukharin, writing during the Russian Civil War, lists six necessary conditions for a class being able to 'shunt society from the capitalist track to the socialist track' (*Historical Materialism*, p. 288). Among the three oppressed classes of pre-revolutionary Russia, these conditions were only co-instantiated in the proletariat, as set out in the table reproduced below (see Table 1) – though I do not regard all these conditions as generally applicable, or exhaustive; for instance, freedom from the personal bondage to which serfs and slaves were subject is another qualifying feature of the proletariat, as is its familiarity with the workings of technology; while poverty would need to be defined quite carefully before it could be regarded as a necessary condition in all cases.

Table 1

	Class properties	Peasantry	Lumpen-proletariat	Proletariat
1	Economic exploitation	+	−	+
2	Political oppression	+	+	+
3	Poverty	+	+	+
4	Productivity	+	−	+
5	Freedom from private property	−	+	+
6	Condition of union in production, and common labour	−	−	+

I want to draw attention particularly to the last characteristic – the only single property of the six which the proletariat does not share with any other class. For the typical proletarian, work is a co-operative, collective process under the common control of the exploiter. Both the opportunities and the motives for organisation, solidarity, collective resistance to the exploiter are present to a unequalled extent. As a function of this, the working class under capitalism is organised on a larger scale, and in a more democratic form, than any other class hitherto. The trade union movement is the organisation of a whole class as no other class organisation has ever been. And it is more or less spontaneously democratic. Of course, trade unions have had their share of corrupt bureaucrats and, in some countries, even gangsters, in control. But in no other social organisation in history has the tendency towards internal democracy been so great. This is the social foundation of modern democracy – not only proletarian democracy, which has as yet been an exceptional phenomenon, but also bourgeois democracy, in which the working class does not rule, but which exists only where the working class is strong enough to limit the power of capital.

In other exploited classes and oppressed groups (except, of course, in so far as the latter overlap with the proletariat), political organisation has typically taken either a leader/follower form (compare Marx on the way in which Napoleon III 'represented' the atomised French peasantry), or that of conspiratorial sects – whether these have an overtly authoritarian structure, or are 'libertarian' and 'unstructured', that is subject to the unchecked dominance of informal local leaderships.

For these reasons, the proletariat remains the only class capable of instituting material democracy. For other groups, democracy is something that comes from outside their working lives, something they may encounter in the political arena, but not in the texture of everyday life, weekend democracy. And in so far as material democracy is the necessary form of liberation, the proletariat is its necessary agent.

Of course, the proletariat can always benefit from having allies, and if sections of the old or new middle classes can be won over, since they – particularly those subject to oppression by reason of sex or minority status – share objective interests with the proletariat, so much the better. But, with the best will in the world, it can never be an equal partnership, any more than could that between bourgeois and peasant in the French, or worker and peasant in the Russian Revolution, since the material basis of the democratic organisation of the people is present only in the proletariat. The idea that the emancipation of the working class must be the task of the workers themselves is not an instance of some general thesis that all emancipation is self-emancipation. Whyever should that be so? The conditions of life of most oppressed people makes their self-emancipation out of the question, except in so far as they have thrown in their lot with a powerful enough worker's movement. The proletariat is the only exploited class that has ever had the potential for *self*-emancipation.

How has recent history affected this thesis of proletarian exceptionalism (which was after all a commonplace of classical Marxism)? The type of society known as 'existing socialism' has indeed triumphed in many countries under non-proletarian leadership. But democracy has been conspicuously absent from this process, and the chances of supplying it afterwards have everywhere depended on the emergence after the revolution of a working class sufficiently numerous and organised to challenge the bureaucracy.

Large selections of the Western 'left' have become convinced that the working class is on the decline and the torch of liberation has passed elsewhere. On the decline of the working class, much of the case is based on definitions other than those of scientific socialism (I refer the reader to *The Changing Working Class* by Callinicos and Harman, who show that the British working class, in the relevant sense, comprises more than 70 per cent of the population). But on the question of passing the torch elsewhere, no possible 'elsewhere' has yet emerged across the horizon, since the non-proletarian oppressed, in late capitalism as in early, have conditions of life which atomise them, and consequently no mass organisation, a low degree of solidarity, little capacity (either objective or subjective) for resistance to oppression.

If it were true that we had entered a post-proletarian era – and such an eventuality is not inconceivable – we would have to kiss goodbye to rather more than is imagined by the cheerfully anti-workerist leaderships of the British Labour and Communist Parties. Goodbye to material democracy, certainly, and therefore to any chance of socialism in the industrialised West, since a Chinese or Cuban style revolution (even if it were desirable) is as unthinkable here as a parliamentary road to socialism; probably also goodbye even to *formal* democracy, or at least to such benefits as have come with it. If we try to imagine what a really post-proletarian capitalism might be like, such a conclusion is difficult to avoid. For the class scenario would have to be something like this: the replacement of the productive workers by a small class of technicians operating automatic plants, with many privileges, a relatively atomised work situation, and a life-style and career-structure assimilated to that of the new middle class; the relegation of the rest of the proletariat – perhaps a majority of the population – to a sub-proletarian existence, caught between unemployment, insecure labouring work in service industries, and the black economy; a bourgeoisie and new middle class, rich but increasingly prone to a siege mentality, like that of white South Africa, due to the inevitable 'dangerousness' to social order of the sub-proletariat. If one can imagine formal democracy surviving under such conditions, it would have to be in a form that securely excluded the sub-proletariat from influencing policy, and this, together with the decline of any base for mass political organisation, and the inevitable shift of real power to the keepers of 'law and order', would mean that democracy became *so* formal as to approach vanishing point. If this nightmare ever materialised, liberation could only come from without, as in the case of the late Roman Empire.

Notes

1. This is of course a crude synopsis of the various new left views which flatten out the distinctions and interrelations between different forms of oppression. Some new leftists are simply morally outraged by the idea of assigning priority to some forms of oppression over others, missing the point that one form may in fact cause others, and to know the cause is necessary if we are to know the cure; some have alternative theories

about primacy, for example that patriarchy or imperialism are prior to, or equiprimordial with, class exploitation (these views are social scientific hypotheses, and this is not therefore the place to argue against them, though I think they are false); most have simply regressed to an empiricist conception of history as 'one damn thing after another', and treat each form of oppression as separate from the others, rejecting as 'dogmatism' any attempt to explain them as intelligibly related parts of an asymmetrical structure.

I hope it is clear that the primacy of economic class exploitation in scientific socialist theory is in no sense a moral primacy, entirely an explanatory one. Morally speaking, the economic exploitation of the poor countries by the rich ones today massively outweighs both class exploitation in the 'west', and every non-economic form of oppression. But a successful outcome for working-class politics is a necessary condition of resolving this problem.

2. I think my use of the word 'workerism' is the older and more common one, but recently it has been used as a term of abuse for the position I defend in the appendix. These two senses are not related in any way.

3. 'To be fit to vote, a person must be independent and not just a part of the commonwealth, but also a member of it, that is, he must will of his own accord, together with others, to be an active part of the commonwealth ... The following examples (of passive citizens) may serve to clear up this difficulty: an apprentice of a merchant or artisan; a servant (not in the service of the state); a minor ...; *all women*; and generally anyone who must depend for his support (subsistence and protection), not on his own industry, but on arrangements made by others (with the exception of the state) – all such people lack civil personality ...

'From the fact that, as passive parts of the state, they can still demand that they be treated by others in accordance with the laws of natural freedom and equality it does not follow that they have the right as active members to guide the state, to organise, and to work for the introduction of particular laws; it follows only that, whatever might be the kind of laws to which the citizens agree, these laws must not be incompatible with the natural laws of freedom and with the equality that accords with this freedom, *namely, that everyone be able to work up from this passive status to an active status*' (*The Metaphysical Elements of Justice*, pp. 79–80). Emphasis mine – A.C.

4. Since I am myself deeply committed to moral rationalism, let me say that I believe the opposition between reason and emotion to be a mystification. Reason does not supply its own ends and set them against those of the emotions; rather, it is the emotions themselves which may be rational or irrational. A rational person is not one who has weak emotions or controls them by reason, but one whose emotions tend to be rational rather than irrational ones.

5. I do not for one moment suppose that Russell Keat intends to link

feminism with the cult of unreason. He uses rationality merely as an example to introduce the notion of genderism, and he recognises that oppression may distort the values of both oppressor and oppressed.

6. I am taking it for granted that men are *not* in fact more rational than women. I find this particular stereotype (and the corresponding attribution of greater emotionality or imaginativeness or whatever to women) utterly implausible. But even if it were true that, *as an effect of oppression*, women were less rational, my case would not be altered. I mention this because there may be other cases of real differences between the sexes caused by the oppression of women.

Conclusion

A brief summary of my argument may help to bring out its political intent, for I would like this book to be a contribution, not only to political philosophy, but to some current debates on the left.

In the first chapter, I drew a distinction between two styles of politics which the utopian and scientific types of socialism exemplify; I suggested that utopian politics is essentially elitist and laden with totalitarian and terrorist potentialities, and that in so far as socialist movements have been guilty of these things, they have also adopted a utopian style of political thought, even when they professed to be scientific socialists. I proposed the elimination of residual utopian ways of thinking as a measure towards avoiding such errors and crimes in the future. I also claimed that the alternative to utopianism in political philosophy (that is in the philosophical clarification of political arguments) was to refer all kinds of reason for political change back to *contradictions* present in an existing society.

In Chapter 1 I am staking out the ground – making distinctions, propounding theses and so on. It therefore contains more assertion and less argument than the later chapters. I hope that the conception of political thinking that I put forward in it is justified by the work it does in the later chapters.

In Chapter 2 I tried to clarify arguments about *liberty* by demystifying liberal accounts which present it as an unhistorical ideal. These accounts all select from among possible liberties a subset which are privileged as 'Liberty', narrowing the range of available liberties in ways determined by some specific historical interest, while seeming not to narrow it at all. I urge explicit recognition of the historical specificity of any selection of liberties – for some selection is inevitable. I suggest that similar demystification could be done with respect to other political ideals. In Chapter 3 I make my case for socialism in the modern world. Necessarily, this involves overstepping the limits of philosophy and making a few social scientific hypotheses. This chapter should make it clear that I regard the aims of two of the 'new social movements' – the peace and ecology movements

– as central to the case for socialism today. But these aims can only be achieved by workers' power and international socialism; so class politics remains the main site of struggle.

Much moral and political philosophy in the twentieth century has tried to show that arguments from factual premises to practical conclusions (such as any scientific socialist argument must be) are invalid. In Chapter 4 I defend such arguments.

While in Chapters 2 to 4 my arguments are directed for the most part against liberal politics and political philosophy, the last two chapters are mainly aimed at utopian currents on the recent Left. The account of political sublimation in Chapter 6 presupposes that there is a clear answer to the question what is and what is not properly political, broached in Chapter 5.

I hope that my points against political sublimation will not be taken as uncomradely bickering, but as a serious explanatory critique of a widespread phenomenon with some dangerous manifestations (for example the infiltration of that right-wing ideology *irrationalism* into the ranks of the Left), as well as some that are more trivial own-goals, such as the political sublimation practised by some Labour councils which, unable to carry out their programmes for the common good because of underfunding and legal fetters, resort to such petty tampering with the people's traditions and liberties as changing the names of parks, or banning Noddy books from public libraries.

I also hope that my view that political sublimation is most prevalent among the non-proletarian oppressed, will not mislead anyone into thinking that I play down forms of oppression other than the exploitation of the workers. Most of the worst atrocities on earth are instances of those other forms of oppression. Nor do I claim that all forms of oppression are caused by capitalism – though I do think that it constitutes the most powerful enemy of *all* modern liberation movements, and so perpetuates many evils that it did not initiate.

While this book has contained arguments for socialism, my main aim is a 'second order' one: to define the ways in which we should and should not argue for socialism. That is:

(1) *not* by describing socialism as 'a society in which ...', if this goes beyond its being a society in which wealth and power are held in common. The concrete character of any socialist commonwealth can only be worked out by its builders, in the process of building it, and will be a function of the unpredictable episodes of its building. Of course, we all have our dreams – but not all dreams are realisable, or

indeed mutually compatible. My own dream, for instance, definitely excludes private motor traffic, and any mass media (transport being by train, bike and donkey, and communication by 'learned periodicals and gossip', as W. H. Auden puts it). But I hardly expect widespread support for this, and have no wish to foist my dream on others against their will;

(2) we cannot avoid using the Big Words of political philosophy, like 'liberty', 'justice', 'rights' and so on, which other political tendencies also use. It is important that we make it clear which phenomena we are referring to by these words, and set out our *grounds* (which will always be historically specific) for picking out different instances from those that the liberal picks out (though of course there is some overlap between liberal and socialist lists of liberties). The way to do this is to show which contradictions of an existing society are being criticised as contrary to liberty or justice – or sometimes, which contradictions of a past society, now overcome, have led us to stake out a claim to this or that liberty or right, making explicit and preserving the liberation that has been achieved;

(3) the heart of the socialist case must always be 'the concrete analysis of the concrete situation' (Lenin), uncovering whatever contradictions there are in that situation, and showing how they could be resolved with existing resources and by existing groups of people. If the *understanding* of concrete capitalist societies is not *itself* a case for socialism, then socialism becomes either an ahistorical ideal or a subjective preference. In either case, it is quite unclear what a *reasoned* case for socialism could be.

Bibliography

Althusser, Louis. 'Ideology and the State' in *Lenin and Philosophy*, tr. Ben Brewster (London: New Left Books, 1971).
——. *Essays in Self-Criticism*, tr. Graham Lock (London: New Left Books, 1976).
Augustine, St. *City of God* (Harmondsworth: Penguin, 1972).
Bacon, Francis (Lord Verulam). 'New Organon', in *English Philosophers from Bacon to Mill* (New York: Random House, 1939).
Berlin, Sir Isaiah. *Four Essays on Liberty* (Oxford: Oxford University Press, 1969).
Bhaskar, Roy. *The Possibility of Naturalism* (Brighton: The Harvester Press, 1979).
——. 'Scientific Explanation and Human Emancipation' in *Radical Philosophy* no. 26, 1980.
Brecht, Bertolt. *Poems* (London: Eyre Methuen, 1976).
Bukharin, Nicolai. *Historical Materialism* (Michigan: Ann Arbor, 1969).
Callinicos, Alex and Harman, Chris. *The Changing Working Class* (London: Bookmarks, 1987).
Cliff, Tony. *Lenin* (four volumes) (London: Pluto, 1975–9).
Cohen, G.A. *Karl Marx's Theory of History: a Defence* (Oxford: Oxford University Press, 1978).
Cole, G.D.H. *The History of Socialist Thought, vol. II: Marxism and Anarchism* (London: Macmillan, 1954).
Colletti, Lucio. *From Rousseau to Lenin* (London: New Left Books, 1972).
Collier, Andrew. *Scientific Realism and Socialist Thought* (Brighton: The Harvester Press, 1988).
——. 'Positive Values' (reply in symposium with Brenda Cohen) *Aristotelian Society Supplementary Volume LVII*, 1983.
Edgley, Roy. 'Science, Social Science and Socialist Science: Reason as Dialectic' in *Radical Philosophy* no. 15, 1976.
Engels, Frederick (*see also* 'Marx').
——. *Anti-Dühring* (Moscow: Progress Publishers, 1947).
——. *The Peasant War in Germany* (Moscow: Foreign Languages Publishing House, 1956).
Feuer, Lewis. 'Introduction' to *Marx and Engels Basic Works* (London: Fontana, 1969).
Freud, Sigmund. 'The Loss of Reality in Neurosis and Psychosis', in *Collected Papers, vol. II* (London: Hogarth, 1957).

―――. 'A Case of Obsessional Neurosis' in *Collected Papers, vol. III* (London: Hogarth, 1969).
Gregg, Pauline. *Free-Born John* (London: Dent, 1961).
Harding, Neil. *Lenin's Political Thought* (Atlantic Highlands, New Jersey: Humanities Press, 1983).
Hemingway, Ernest. *For Whom the Bell Tolls* (Harmondsworth: Penguin, 1955).
Hogg, Quintin. *The Case for Conservatism* (Harmondsworth: Penguin, 1947).
Honderich, Ted. 'Against Teleological Historical Materialism', in *Inquiry*, no. 25, 1982.
Kant, Immanuel. *The Metaphysical Elements of Justice* (New York: Bobbs-Merrill, 1965).
Kautsky, Karl. *Communism in Central Europe at the Time of the Reformation* (New York: Augustus M. Kelly, 1966).
Keat, Russell. 'Masculinity in Philosophy' in *Radical Philosophy* no. 34, 1983.
Lenin, Vladimir. *The April Theses* (Moscow: Progress Publishers, 1951).
―――. *Selected Works in One Volume* (London: Lawrence and Wishart, 1968).
Lewis, C.S. *Christian Reflections* (London: Fount Paperbacks, 1981).
London, Jack. *The Iron Heel* (London: Journeyman Press, 1974).
Lukes, Steven. *Power: a Radical View* (London: Macmillan, 1974).
―――. *Marxism and Morality* (Oxford: Oxford University Press, 1985).
Luxemburg, Rosa. *Rosa Luxemburg Speaks*, ed. M.-A. Waters (New York: Panther Press, 1970).
―――. *Comrade and Lover* (letters to Jogiches) (Cambridge, Mass.: M.I.T. Press, 1979; London: Pluto Press, 1981).
MacIntyre, Alasdair. 'Hume on "is" and "ought"' in *The Philosophical Review*, vol. LXIII, 1959.
Macpherson, C.B. *Democratic Theory* (London: Oxford University Press, 1973).
Marcuse, Herbert. *Negations* (Harmondsworth: Penguin, 1968).
Marx, Karl. *The Revolutions of 1848* (Harmondsworth: Pelican Marx Library, 1973).
―――. *Grundrisse* (Harmondsworth: Pelican Marx Library, 1973).
―――. *The First International and After* (Harmondsworth: Pelican Marx Library, 1974).
―――. *Early Writings* (Harmondsworth: Pelican Marx Library, 1975).
―――. *Capital, vol. I* (London: Lawrence and Wishart, 1959).
―――. *Capital, vol. III* (London: Lawrence and Wishart, 1962).
(see also 'Selsam and Martel').
Marx, Karl and Engels, Frederick. *The German Ideology* (selections, ed. C.J. Arthur) (London: Lawrence and Wishart, 1970).

———. *Collected Works*, vol. *IV* (London: Lawrence and Wishart, 1975).
———. *Collected Works*, vol. *V* (London: Lawrence and Wishart, 1976).
———. *Selected Works in Two Volumes* (London: Lawrence and Wishart, 1942).
———. *Selected Works in One Volume* (London: Lawrence and Wishart, 1968).
Medvedev, Roy. *The October Revolution* (London: Constable, 1979).
Meikle, Scott. *Essentialism in the Thought of Karl Marx* (London: Duckworth, 1985).
Mill, John Stuart. *Utilitarianism*, ed. Warnock (London: Fontana, 1962).
———. *The Principles of Political Economy* (Harmondsworth: Penguin, 1970).
Nietzsche, Friedrich. *The Portable Nietzsche*, ed. Kaufmann (New York: Viking Press, 1954).
———. *The Twilight of the Idols* (Harmondsworth: Penguin, 1968).
Parker, Geoffrey. *The Dutch Revolt* (Harmondsworth: Penguin, 1979).
Postgate, Raymond. *George Lansbury* (London: Longmans, Green & Co, 1951).
Raphael, D.D. *Justice and Liberty* (London: The Athlone Press, 1980).
Richards, Janet Radcliffe. *The Sceptical Feminist* (London: Routledge and Kegan Paul, 1980).
Rousseau, Jean-Jacques. *The Social Contract and Discourses* (London: Dent, 1966).
Selsam, Howard and Martel, Harry. *Reader in Marxist Philosophy* (New York: International Publishers, 1963).
Serge, Victor. *Memoirs of a Revolutionary* (London: Oxford University Press, 1967).
Steenson, Gary P. *Karl Kautsky* (Pittsburgh: University of Pittsburgh Press, 1978).
Tillich, Paul. *The Protestant Era* (Chicago: University of Chicago Press, 1957).
———. *Systematic Theology*, vol. *III* (Welwyn: James Nisbet, 1964).
———. *The Socialist Decision* (New York: Harper and Row, 1977).
Trotsky, Leon. 'Their Morals and Ours' in *The Basic Writings of Trotsky*, ed. Irving Howe (London: Mercury Books, 1964).
———. *On Literature and Art*, ed. Siegel (New York: Pathfinder Press, 1970).
———. *My Life* (Harmondsworth: Penguin, 1970).
Winstanley, Gerrard. *The Law of Freedom*, ed. Hill (Harmondsworth: Penguin, 1973).

Index

alcoholic beverages 35, 37, 38, 41, 42, 65, 89, 145, 148, 150, 166
alienation 79–80
alloplastic 157–8
Althusser, Louis x, 9, 20, 32, 165, 177
anarchism (*see also* Bakunin, Godwin) 33, 34, 35, 42, 46, 47, 48, 49, 109
Aristotle 54, 114, 163, 167
Armand, Inessa 144
assertoric imperatives 115, 121, 122, 126, 138
Auden, W. H. 176
Augustine, Saint 90, 114, 137, 177
Austen, Jane 32
autoplastic 157–8
Ayer, A. J. 113

Babeuf, Gracchus 78
Bacon, Francis (Lord Verulam) xvi, 74, 76, 78, 93, 107, 120, 177
Bakunin, Mikhail 3, 95, 100
Barebone, Praise-God 9, 78
Bede, the Venerable 130–1
Bellamy, Edward 3
Bentham, Jeremy 134, 135
Berlin, Isaiah 51–8, 61, 73, 137, 157, 177
Bernstein, Eduard 22
Bhaskar, Roy x, 125, 137, 138, 177
Bible 4, 32, 51, 55, 68, 74, 89, 133, 154, 160
Blanquism 96, 108, 109
Böhme, Jakob 11
Bolsheviks 18, 22, 30, 144, 151, 152

bourgeoisie 6, 19, 63, 81, 106, 171
Brecht, Bertolt 145, 154, 177
Bukharin, Nicolai xiii, 19–20, 169, 177
Bunyan, John 146
Burke, Edmund 4, 5, 10

Callinicos, Alex 171, 177
Calvin, John 4, 89
capitalism ix, x, xiv, 3, 6, 9, 11, 12, 16, 21, 22, 23, 26, 27, 28, 32, 34, 36, 42, 61, 62, 63, 64, 67, 68, 75, 76, 79, 80, 81, 82, 83, 85, 86, 87, 88, 91, 92, 103, 104, 105, 130, 131, 138, 142, 164, 170, 171, 175, 176
censorship 42–4, 53
Chrysostom, Saint John 161
classes, class struggle 6, 8, 11, 14, 19, 22, 26, 31, 60, 61, 62, 65, 66, 68, 74, 75, 83, 89, 90, 94, 96, 97, 108, 123, 125, 132, 139, 144, 146, 147, 148, 152, 161, 162, 163, 165, 172
Cliff, Tony 108, 177
Cohen, G. A. 20, 24–8, 177
Cole, G. D. H. 26, 177
Colletti, Lucio 94, 108, 177
Collier, Andrew 177
common ownership (public ownership, nationalisation) 5, 7, 8, 16, 17, 22, 60, 88, 94, 100, 105, 118, 157
communism 15, 18, 23, 30, 34, 73, 106, 109, 119, 143, 151, 154, 155, 160, 161, 164, 171

Index

conservatism xv, 4, 5, 9, 10, 21, 31, 43, 44, 59, 125, 126, 139, 140, 141, 143, 151, 154, 155
contractualism 60, 61, 71, 72
contradictions x, xi, xii, 10–15, 21, 31, 33, 65, 73, 78, 80, 81, 82, 83, 88, 90, 121, 124, 127, 131, 146, 154, 174, 176
Cromwell, Oliver 78, 102
Cynics 158, 163

Darwinism 6, 19, 25, 27, 28
democracy 5, 6, 7, 18, 23, 24, 29, 32, 41, 54, 59, 62, 66, 70, 77, 78, 84, 85, 86, 87, 93–108, 118, 140, 170, 171
Descartes, René 133
dialectic (*see also* contradictions) 10–11, 14–15, 29, 136
dispersedness 62, 79, 83–93, 100, 105, 106
Dylan, Bob 156
Dzerzhinsky, Felix 32

ecology (*see also* environment) 14, 78, 81, 87, 92, 108, 159, 174
Edgley, Roy 125, 138
Engels, Frederick xiii, 5, 9, 10, 11, 15, 16, 21, 25, 31, 32, 48–9, 74, 79, 80, 81, 82, 88, 89, 96, 108, 143, 144, 163, 169, 177
environment 5, 11, 16, 39, 47, 48, 82, 86, 93
equality (or justice) ix, xv, 4, 5, 7, 8, 13, 14, 23, 39, 46, 67, 68, 69, 74, 78, 130, 131, 158, 166, 176
'existing socialism' 15, 44, 72–3, 104–7, 108, 170
explanatory critiques 113, 122, 124, 125, 126, 133, 134, 137, 161, 175
exploitation (or surplus value) 11, 23, 44, 61, 64, 80, 81, 83, 90, 104, 165, 169, 170, 172, 175

fascism xi, 31, 34, 54, 66, 90, 91, 103, 108, 115, 116, 119, 137, 151, 164, 168
feminism 159, 167, 168, 172
feudalism 75, 130, 131, 138
Feuer, Lewis 32, 177
Feuerbach, Ludwig xiii, xiv, 89
Feyerabend, Paul 167
Freud, Sigmund (and Freudianism) xvi, 124, 125, 133, 138, 152, 156, 157, 177

gatheredness 62, 79, 83, 84, 86, 87, 88, 93, 100, 105, 106
Godwin, William 4
Green, Thomas Hill xi, 65
Gregg, Pauline 35, 178

Hamann, Johann Georg 167
Harding, Neil 108, 178
Hare, R. M. 113
Harman, Chris 171, 177
hearsay 149–52
Heath, Edward 102
Hegel, G. W. F. (and Hegelianism) xiii, xiv, 11, 33, 85, 120, 135, 136, 167
Heidegger, Martin x, 149
Hemingway, Ernest 34, 178
Hill, Christopher 32, 157, 179
Hitler, Adolf 91, 115, 117, 151
Hobbes, Thomas xi, 48, 72, 83, 84, 90, 93, 114
Hogg, Quintin 154, 155, 178
Honderich, Ted 26–8, 178
horizontal and vertical axes of history 47, 74, 80, 81, 83, 87, 90, 94, 107
Hume, David 45, 113, 114, 115, 120, 132, 133, 137, 149
Hurd, Douglas 139
Hyndman, Henry Mayers 162–3
Hyndman's hat effect 162, 163, 168

Ibsen, Henrik 61
incomplete abstraction, fallacy of 72

Kamenev, Lev 17
Kant, Immanuel 54, 113, 114, 115, 121, 127, 167, 172, 178
Kautsky, Karl 73, 89, 90, 161, 178
Keat, Russell 167, 168, 172, 178
Keyserling, Hermann 167
Kidron, Michael 73
Kierkegaard, Søren 121
Kollontai, Alexandra 144
Kolnai, Aurel 158

Laplace, Pierre Simon 89
Lenin, Vladimir xiii, 17, 18, 32, 57, 65, 95, 96, 97, 98, 106, 108, 109, 144, 155, 165, 176, 178
Levellers 35, 36, 54, 157
Lewis, C. S. 127, 129, 138, 178
liberalism xv, 10, 25, 33, 34, 37, 41, 46, 47, 48, 50, 54, 58, 60, 61, 63, 70, 71, 74, 76, 115, 151, 174, 175, 176
liberation (or emancipation) xiv, xvi, 7, 28, 29, 30, 31, 74–9, 83, 87, 89, 93, 105, 107, 108, 148, 158, 160, 161, 163, 165, 166, 169, 170, 171, 175
libertarianism 34, 35, 36, 42, 43, 44, 46, 48, 54, 66
liberty (or freedom) xv, xvi, 4, 5, 6, 7, 8, 13, 14, 16, 20, 23, 33–67, 68, 70, 73, 74, 75, 76, 105, 106, 107, 130, 157, 158, 174, 176
licensed vandalism 155
Lilburne, John 35, 36
Locke, John 50, 51, 72
Lockhart, Bruce 30
London, Jack 90, 178
Lukes, Steven 23, 30, 57, 178
Luther, Martin 4, 134
Luxemburg, Rosa xiii, 31, 89, 90, 91, 155, 165, 178

Machiavelli, Niccolo 4, 8
MacIntyre, Alasdair 114, 137, 178
Macpherson, C. B. 53, 178
Marcuse, Herbert 108, 178
market economy 21, 34, 47, 58, 62, 81, 82, 85, 87, 92, 104
Martell, Harry 32, 179
Marx, Karl ix, x, xii, xiii, 3, 5, 6, 7, 8, 10, 11, 12, 15, 16, 19, 20, 22, 23, 25, 28, 32, 48–9, 67, 74, 77, 78, 79, 80, 81, 86, 87, 89, 94, 95, 100, 102, 106, 108, 114, 121, 124, 125, 130, 131, 135, 136, 141, 143, 144, 152, 157, 160, 169, 170, 178–9
Marxism xii, xiii, 3, 19, 20, 23, 30, 48, 51, 68, 73, 83, 94, 105, 130, 157, 162
Medvedev, Roy 32, 179
Meikle, Scott 106, 179
Mill, John Stuart xi, 11, 13, 35, 37, 38, 39, 42, 44, 45, 49, 61, 72, 73, 102, 119, 133, 179
Milton, John 45
morality 6, 23, 24, 28, 35, 36, 53, 54, 55, 65, 113, 114, 115, 121, 123, 124, 125, 128, 129, 131, 132, 133, 136, 138, 145, 146, 153, 154, 155, 157, 159, 160, 166, 167, 172
More, Thomas 4
Morris, William 23, 70
motor traffic 37, 39, 40, 76, 91, 135, 176
Münzer, Thomas 9, 31

nation-state 21, 77, 83, 84, 85, 86, 87, 91, 92, 105, 106
naturalism, ethical xvi, 37, 55, 113, 114, 115, 121, 122, 126, 137, 159, 160
Nazism (*see* fascism)
needs 11, 12, 17, 67, 72, 77, 129, 134, 136, 138, 163
Nietzsche, Friedrich 113, 121, 123, 124, 125, 133, 134, 137, 156, 157, 159, 160, 161, 179

Nietzshean factor 160, 162, 163, 164, 165
Nozick, Robert 72

Oakeshott, Michael 5
oppression, the oppressed 5, 7, 8, 56, 61, 62, 63, 74, 77, 84, 85, 87, 88, 89, 90, 93, 94, 100, 127, 128, 130, 144, 148, 159, 160, 161, 162, 163, 164, 165, 166, 169, 170, 171, 172, 173, 175
Orwell, George 144

Paine, Thomas 4
Parker, Geoffrey 34, 179
peace 8, 22, 92, 105, 107, 175
peasantry 17, 18, 29, 32, 82, 87, 93, 130, 131, 169, 170
personal politics 144, 145, 154, 166
Plato, Platonism xv, 31, 54, 114, 127, 148
Popper, Karl 9, 26, 100
Postgate, Raymond 163, 179
poverty 8, 12, 31, 69, 74, 157, 169, 172
power(s) x, xi, 6, 8, 9, 13, 20, 22, 26, 28, 29, 46, 47, 56, 57, 59, 61, 62, 63, 68, 76, 79, 82, 83, 84, 85, 86, 87, 88, 90, 92, 93, 94, 96, 97, 98, 99, 100, 125, 130, 154, 159, 160, 162, 168
prefigurative politics 17, 18, 31, 67
progress xv, 21, 33, 35, 68, 74, 75, 77, 78, 79, 91, 92, 105, 129, 130, 131
proletariat (or working class) x, 5, 6, 17, 18, 19, 23, 29, 32, 54, 56, 57, 81, 82, 89, 162, 164, 165, 166, 169, 170, 171, 175
puritanism 4, 35, 65, 71, 142, 146, 161, 164

race 37, 69, 70, 105, 108, 117
Raphael, D. D. 46, 179

Rawls, John 72, 135
realism xvi, 9, 10, 57
religion (including particular religions) xii, 35, 37, 39, 42, 55, 60, 65, 70, 71, 73, 89, 142, 146, 154, 155, 161
reverse discrimination 69
revolution 21, 146, 171
    American 50
    French 70, 93
    Russian 15, 17, 18, 22, 87, 93, 116
Richards, Janet Radcliffe 32, 179
Ricoeur, Paul 124
Rousseau, Jean-Jacques xi, 6, 8, 13, 33, 48, 49, 54, 56, 62, 72, 77, 78, 87, 94, 95, 100, 108, 120, 164, 179

Saint-Simon, Henri 3, 15
Sandinistas 66, 131
Sartre, Jean-Paul 113, 158
Scargill, Arthur 146
Scheler, Max 134
Schleiermacher, Friedrich 168
science x, xii, xiii, xiv, 3, 4, 8, 9, 19, 20, 25, 57, 76, 78, 79, 93, 107, 114, 147, 149
scientific socialism ix–xvi, 3, 9, 13, 14, 16, 19, 21, 22, 33, 60, 65, 67, 68, 74, 75, 78, 79, 89, 90, 91, 93, 96, 100, 107, 114, 143, 144, 145, 148, 155, 161, 164, 171, 172, 174, 175
Segal, Ronald 73
Selsam, Howard, 32, 179
Serge, Victor 32, 179
sex 37, 69, 70, 73, 105, 108, 142, 155, 168, 170, 173
sexism 75, 166, 167, 168
Shaw, Bernard 158
Short, Clare 65
social democrats 22, 32, 73, 94, 162
socialism (*see also* common ownership, communism, 'existing socialism', scientific

socialism) ix–xii, 3, 4, 6, 7, 8, 16, 17, 18, 22, 24, 30, 34, 36, 37, 59, 63, 66, 68, 69, 70, 73, 75, 78, 83, 84, 89, 90, 91, 93, 94, 98, 100, 101, 103, 104, 105, 107, 115, 118, 122, 131, 138, 141, 151, 154, 158, 159, 165, 168, 169, 171, 174, 175, 176

Socrates 45, 156

soviets (workers' councils) 17, 18, 29, 99, 106, 107, 109

Spartacus 78, 160

Spinoza, Baruch 8, 45, 54, 114, 115, 132, 149, 167

Stalin, Joseph (and Stalinism) 18, 30, 32, 54, 71, 91, 151, 155

Steenson, Gary P. 90, 179

Stoics 127, 158, 163

structures, social 8, 11, 12, 20, 21, 30, 62, 64, 99, 100, 140, 143, 145, 152, 153, 172

suspicion 124, 125, 149, 151, 152, 153

technology 7, 8, 16, 20, 74–9, 85, 87, 88, 91, 92, 160, 161

teleology 6, 17, 19, 20, 21, 22, 24, 26, 29, 30

Thatcher, M. H. (*see also* licensed vandalism) 32, 50, 116, 146

Tillich, Paul 99, 138, 179

trade unionism xi, 63, 64, 93, 95, 99, 101, 170

Trotsky, Leon (and Trotskyism) xiii, 19, 28, 29, 30, 32, 33, 61, 66, 67, 73, 74, 104, 105, 106, 179

utilitarianism 55, 73, 132–5

utopianism xv, xvi, 3–7, 15–19, 23, 30, 31, 38, 54, 60, 94, 95, 98, 109, 155, 174, 175

values, value-judgements ix, xv, 13, 21, 33, 43, 44, 45, 61, 67, 68, 100, 113–28, 130, 131, 137, 145, 160, 168, 173

vertical axis of history (*see* horizontal)

weapons 76, 84, 87, 91, 104, 106, 122

Wesley, John 146

Winstanley, Gerrard 9, 18, 32, 78, 179

withering away of the state xii, 16, 17, 18, 51, 95, 108

Wittgenstein, Ludwig 121, 167

workers' movement xiv, 3, 8, 10, 16, 22, 78, 90, 92, 164, 172

Zwingli, Huldreich 9